QUALITATIVE RESEARCH IN ACTION
A CANADIAN PRIMER

DEBORAH K. VAN DEN HOONAARD

OXFORD
UNIVERSITY PRESS

OXFORD

UNIVERSITY PRESS

8 Sampson Mews, Suite 204, Don Mills, Ontario M3C 0H5 Canada
www.oupcanada.com

Oxford University Press is a department of the University of Oxford.
It furthers the University's objective of excellence in research, scholarship,
and education by publishing worldwide.

Oxford is a registered trade mark
of Oxford University Press in the UK and in certain other countries.

Published in Canada
by Oxford University Press

Library and Archives Canada Cataloguing in Publication

Van den Hoonaard, Deborah K. (Deborah Kestin), 1951–

Qualitative research in action: a Canadian primer/Deboroah K. van den Hoonaard.

Includes bibliographical references and index.

ISBN 978-0-19-543919-9

1. Qualitative research—Methodology. I. Title.

H62.V33 2011   300.72   C2011-903522-7

Cover image: ©iStockphoto.com/Dmitry Mordvintsev

Oxford University Press is committed to our environment.
The pages of this book have been printed on Forest Stewardship
Council® certified paper.

Printed and bound in Canada.

1 2 3 4 — 15 14 13 12

Contents

List of Boxes

Preface

Qualitative Research in Action is an introduction to qualitative research methods that is geared to undergraduate students who do not have experience with doing qualitative research. The book provides both a discussion of the theoretical underpinnings of qualitative research and practical advice to help students get their feet wet by trying out some qualitative methods.

I have described my own experiences in carrying out qualitative research to make the book more personal and alive. I have used an accessible and conversational style to make the book readable and interesting. My own theoretical approach borrows heavily from symbolic interactionism, and this preference is clear throughout the text. However, the basic skills of interviewing, observation, and analysis are useful regardless of one's theoretical perspective, and students will learn to adapt them to suit their own approaches.

The book is unabashedly Canadian. In fact, one of the most pleasurable aspects of writing it has been discovering and thinking about qualitative work done by Canadian scholars. For years I used excellent American textbooks in my classes, but I never realized how few Canadian studies they cited until I began working on *Qualitative Research in Action*. To correct this omission, I have included many examples from Canadian research not often cited in other methods' texts. In addition, Appendix A provides an extensive list of examples of qualitative research by Canadian scholars.

In my years of teaching, I've found that many students are full of trepidation when they start a research methods course because they fear the class will be difficult or boring. In reality, a qualitative methods class that gives students an opportunity to get their hands dirty by doing a few in-depth interviews, observing participants in a social setting, and/or analyzing documents (say, magazine advertisements) is often very exciting. This book does not pretend that qualitative research is not a lot of work. It does, however, include moments of exciting discovery and euphoria at the moment of new insights, and I try to communicate these high moments throughout the text. Often students, when they complete the class, are eager to carry out their own studies. By the end of the term, it is not unusual for a student to come to my office to ask, 'How do I get to do what you do?' When that happens, I know the student has caught the bug of doing qualitative research. In writing this book, it was my goal to pass on this bug.

Brief Overview of the Book

Qualitative Research in Action begins by introducing the inductive approach that qualitative researches use in their research. Students will discover how qualitative researchers build concepts and theories based on the data they have collected, and they will see how these methods stand in contrast to the deductive approach of testing theories through research. Further, students will learn how the questions researchers ask determine, to some extent, the answers they find.

With the foundations in place, the book moves on to discuss how to develop a research question and various methods of collecting data to address those questions. Throughout these discussions, students will encounter numerous examples of researchers' actual strategies and experiences, including observation, in-depth interviews, and analysis of pre-existing documents.

Later chapters discuss analyzing data and writing up research reports. These chapters also include lively examples and many hints about how to go about these challenging phases of research. The text concludes with a discussion of new directions in qualitative research followed by a consideration of ethical dimensions of doing research.

Acknowledgements

It was with real surprise and pleasure that I received the invitation from Susan McDaniel and Lorne Tepperman to write a textbook on qualitative research methods. Writing this book has been an adventure from start to finish, and I am very grateful for the opportunity.

As I gathered material for *Qualitative Research in Action,* I relied on the experiences I've acquired over years of teaching qualitative methods. Over these years, my students have inspired and challenged me to think of new ways to talk about conducting qualitative research and have, thereby, contributed to this volume in untold ways. In addition, the students who took my class in the winter of 2010 read early drafts of the core chapters and provided comments that surely improved these chapters.

While writing this text, I became very aware of the rich legacy of qualitative research we have in Canada. I enjoyed finding Canadian work to use as examples, and I am thankful for all the qualitative researchers who have long been working 'in the vineyard'. In particular, the collegiality, friendship, and inspiration over the years from participants at the annual (Canadian) Qualitatives have been invaluable.

I would like to thank the many people who helped me bring everything together for this book. Rick Helmes-Hayes and Emily Milne contributed Box 4.2 on the history of ethnography in Canada. They agreed to write the material, which makes a substantial contribution to the chapter, on very short notice. I would also like to thank Jacqueline Anderson, Jean Carrière, Vera Kohler, Elza Y. Passini, Kira Shingareva, Miriam H. Zaar, and photographer Jesus Reyes for sharing their stories and generously giving us permission to include their photo in Chapter 5.

My research assistant, Kristen Gallant, searched for and found many of the websites that deal with qualitative research. She read each chapter as I wrote it and provided helpful comments. Kristen put together the initial list of terms for the glossary. Her enthusiasm for the work has been a real contribution. Gillian Steeves helped with editing the revised manuscript. In particular, she carefully checked the accuracy of each reference.

My assistant, Lehanne Knowlton, helped in too many ways to name. She was always there to proofread and help with formatting issues that I found impossible to remedy. I also knew that I could go into her office at any time to decompress and eat a piece of chocolate from her stash. Who could ask for more than that?

My colleagues at St Thomas University are unfailingly supportive. The members of the Gerontology Department, Gary Irwin-Kenyon, Bill Randall, and Linda Caissie, always celebrate each other's accomplishments, a rare state of affairs that makes me feel very fortunate. Dawne A. Clarke of the Criminology Department gave the manuscript a trial run in her methods class. Rosemary Clews, former assistant vice-president, research, and Gayle MacDonald, acting dean of research, are constant sources of support and friendship.

Mark Thompson, at the Press, provided timely, encouraging feedback. His gentle email reminders helped me to stay on track and get the job done. Peter Chambers was equally encouraging through the revision of the manuscript. Janice Evans copy edited the manuscript with care. She managed to smooth out the rough edges while preserving my writing style. Working with Janice was an unexpected pleasure from start to finish. A number of reviewers—including Susan Cox of the University of British Columbia and Lesley D. Harman of King's University College at the University of Western Ontario, as well as those who wish to remain anonymous—also provided valuable feedback.

I have been fortunate to receive funding for my studies of widows (Health Canada), widowers (SSHRC), and Iranian Bahá'í refugees to Atlantic Canada (Metropolis, New Brunswick and Atlantic Studies Research and Development Centre). I have served as Canada Research Chair for qualitative research and analysis over the last five years, which has provided me the resources and the time to complete *Qualitative Research in Action* in a timely manner.

My family is a continuing source of joy and inspiration. My children, Lisa-Jo, Cheryl, and Jordan, take real pleasure in my work and keep me laughing and learning. Lisa-Jo, a budding sociologist, has read and commented on drafts of most of the chapters in *Qualitative Research in Action*. I do not have a favourite child.

My husband, Will C. van den Hoonaard, is a support and inspiration in everything I do. He readily agreed to write Chapter 10, 'Ethics on the Ground', and has read every word of this text at least once. Will has always believed in my work even more than I have and has been a staunch supporter of qualitative research methods in Canada. It is to him this book is dedicated.

1 Introduction

Learning Objectives

- To get a sense of what qualitative research is and what it can accomplish
- To acquire an overview of the coming chapters
- To look forward to learning how to carry out your own qualitative study

Introduction

What do dog walkers, customers at beauty salons, outlaw bikers, adopted children and their birth mothers, tattoo artists, and widows have in common? They have all inspired qualitative researchers to study their experiences. In fact, almost any type of person or activity you can think of has been or could be the inspiration for an insightful and fascinating qualitative study. *Qualitative Research in Action* will introduce you to many of these studies and provide you with the tools to try out qualitative research on your own.

As you take your first plunge into qualitative research methods, you may fear that the material will be too difficult, or you may worry that it will be boring and that you will lose interest. These feelings are normal. Yet I believe you will find that once you begin to think about your own research interests and to practise collecting your own data, you will become very excited about what you are learning. My hope is that, through reading this text and trying out some of the exercises at the end of each chapter, you will catch the bug of doing qualitative research.

In this introductory chapter, we look at some examples of qualitative research and get an overview of the chapters and how they fit together to provide what I hope is an interesting and useful introduction to doing qualitative research.

Qualitative Research

I go to the Canadian Qualitative Analysis Conference (commonly referred to as the 'Qualitatives') in the spring every year. It is the one academic conference I never miss. I go with the anticipation of meeting colleagues I see only once a year and hearing papers about methodological issues and topics directly related to my research interests. I also look forward to hearing fascinating papers on topics I know little about and that I am quite unlikely to research myself. And I'm never disappointed. In the 20 years that I have been attending the conference, I've heard papers that explore the social worlds of such diverse groups as veterinarians, divorced people, bird watchers, dragon-fly aficionados, mixed-martial-arts participants, exotic dancers, gun owners, and World Wrestling Entertainment (WWE) performers and enthusiasts. Box 1.1 includes a selection of titles from the 2010 Qualitatives that further illustrates the breadth of topics covered at these conferences.

Qualitative research encompasses a variety of approaches through which researchers attempt to understand the everyday lives and social settings of those they study. These scholars use a variety of methods including in-depth interviewing, participant observation, and document analysis to develop a rich understanding of the social processes involved in everyday life.

Qualitative research methods are powerful because, unlike the quantitative research methods you are probably more familiar with, they allow the studied people to define what is central and important in *their* experience. To illustrate some differences between qualitative and quantitative methods, let's examine how each method might approach a study of widowhood, one of my major areas of study.

Quantitative surveys about widowhood tend to be rather dry. They often reduce one of the most challenging and emotionally taxing transitions

---

BOX 1.1 ❖ **SELECTED PAPERS PRESENTED AT THE 2010 QUALITATIVE ANALYSIS CONFERENCE, WILFRID LAURIER UNIVERSITY, BRANTFORD, ONTARIO**

'Christian Rock and the Quest for Authenticity', Zachary Horn

'Ferry Tales: Interaction aboard BC Ferries', Phillip Vannini

'Becoming a Black Belt', Elizabeth Graham

'Dealing Drugs: Striving for Respectability in a Deviant Way of Life', Arthur McLuhan

'Academic Dishonesty among Elite High School Students', Mark Pogrebin

'Professors on Film: Geniuses, Adventurers, and Mad Scientists', Thomas Fleming

'Boundary Maintenance among Hardcore Motorcycle Enthusiasts', Donald Hickerson

'The Lure and Lore of Conducting Research in the Arctic: The Interactional Dynamics of Inuit-Kablunaaq Interviews', Lisa-Jo van den Scott

'Motion Pictures and Moral Panics: Ideological Representations of HIV/AIDS in Film, 1981–2003', Allyson Stokes

'"I Didn't Notice It, Actually": Teenagers and How They Give Meaning to Litter in Public Places', Thaddeus Muller

a woman might endure to a series of correlations that sum up successful adjustment as well-being. For example, a survey designed to determine a widow's well-being might ask her how often she sees her adult children: more than once a week, once a week, several times a month, once a month, or less frequently. To draw meaning from the response, the researcher must assume that the respondent experiences a high level of well-being if she sees her children frequently. He or she must also assume that the relationship is a positive one and that the widow receives support from her children. As you can see, this approach reduces a widow's relationship with her children to a count of how often she sees them. There is no way for the researcher to find out what the frequency of visits means to her or to discover other aspects of the relationship that are important to her.

In contrast, when I employed qualitative methods to explore widows' well-being, I was able to open a discussion through which they could define their experiences in their own terms. For example, when I asked them if they saw or spoke to their children very often, I was able to ascertain that for some women, 'often' means more than once a week; for others, it means once a month or less. By encouraging the women to explain how frequent 'very often' is and what the particular rate of contact meant to them, I was able to discover that widows' subjective expectations of how often their children *should* be in touch is more meaningful than an objective measurement such as once a week. In addition, some widows interpreted frequent contact as an aspect of their children's overprotectiveness, while others associated it with close relationships (D.K. van den Hoonaard 2003).

Qualitative methods can also uncover details that allow the researcher to gain a deeper understanding of the participants than he or she could acquire through quantitative methods. In my study, asking each woman to talk about her situation in her own way made the process of negotiation visible between the widow and her children as they worked to redefine their relationship after the death of the husband/father. To further explore these negotiations, I invited each woman to discuss what was important *to her*: 'How would you say your relationship with your children has changed since your husband died?' This question elicited a variety of responses, and I was inspired by the creativity many of the participants used in this negotiation.

Sarah's[1] strategy, for example, involves a very refined system of maintaining a sense of balance with her children so that she does not feel that she is either giving or receiving too much help. The process is based on a broad, mutual understanding of their not intruding on one another. Sarah recounted a number of arrangements that rest on a firm foundation of reciprocity that she has established with her children. The following arrangement is only one of several that she described.

Sarah spends her winters in Florida, which means that she needs someone to pay her local bills and to keep an eye on her house. Her daughter pays the bills for her, and her son checks on her house. The reciprocity involved is very ingenious:

> Yeah, well, my son is very fond of ice cream, and he can't get cable [TV] . . . and he loves TV. So I fill the freezer downstairs with ice cream, and I know he'll be down to watch TV. And he watches the house. . . . He checks to make sure that everything's all right.

In addition, Sarah's granddaughter, who attends university, occasionally stops by with her friends:

> If she wants to entertain, she brings the kids down, cooks them supper. . . . So there's always some, they never know. . . . They never know whether I'm here or not.

For Sarah, having family members check her house in an unpredictable but reliable fashion is a tremendous benefit.

As you can see, I learned a lot about widows' relationships with their children and grandchildren by providing the opportunity for them to talk about what they thought was important. This participatory approach leads us to use the word *participant* rather than *subject* to describe those we interview or observe.

Qualitative Research in Daily Life

Qualitative researchers often use experiences from everyday life to develop their research ideas. In addition, they use what they have learned as qualitative researchers to go about their daily lives. As Glassner and Hertz (1999: x) comment, 'the job of the scholar is to take the ordinary events and make them extraordinary and to demonstrate how the extraordinary is routine'. For this reason, people sometimes think that what qualitative researchers uncover and describe is only common sense.

However, this so-called common sense is usually invisible to us unless we are paying close, sociologically informed attention. To illustrate this principle to my class, I've often asked them to consider the gendered use of space. I begin by telling them that, generally, men sit in such a way as to take up as much room as they can, while women take up as little space as possible when they sit. Most students do not believe me. So then I ask them to look around the room. They notice that many of the men sit with their legs extended and their arms outstretched along the backs of their chairs, while many of the women have their legs crossed or pushed back under their chairs and their arms close to their bodies. The students are surprised when they see that I am right. I have noticed this pattern *because* my experience as a qualitative researcher has trained me to be very aware of my environment, who is in it, and how they are acting and interacting. Is this pattern obvious? Is it just common sense? Sure, but only once you have noticed it.

Candace West, an American researcher, has written an essay in which she describes how her sociological knowledge and qualitative experience contribute to the way she understands and interprets what is going on around her in her daily life (see West 1999). In one example, she talks about the different routines she has for waking up on school days and weekends. She notes that, even though she can take her time on the weekends, she still thinks about articles she is writing and mulls over her students' concerns as she prepares for her day. In other words, as a professional, her work commitments do not remain at the office as yours might if you work at Tim Hortons to help pay for your university education. While most non-researchers might accept this distinction and move on, West uses the sociological understanding of what it means to be a professional to explain her experience of feeling 'on call' all the time (West 1999: 3, citing Zerubavel 1979).

My favourite part of West's article involves a story of her taking her dog to the leash-free area of her local park. West notices a newcomer and tries to start up a conversation with him about their dogs as one would with any newcomer to the park. She notes that this man does not really act like a dog owner. He does not release his dog to play, and he asks questions about her that seem inappropriate for this social setting. It turns out that the man is an animal control officer who has gone undercover to catch people whose dogs are not appropriately licensed. To explain how qualitative research contributed to her initial discomfort with the animal control officer, she refers to a classic ethnographic article, 'Dogs and Their People' (Robins, Sanders, and Cahill 1991 cited in West 1999: 5), which observes that among dog owners, it is inappropriate for newcomers to ask for personal information until they have become regulars. Rather, newcomers talk and ask about their and others' dogs as they work their way into the social group. (If you have a dog, you are probably familiar with the practice strangers often have of talking to and through each other's dogs rather than directly to each other.) When the animal control officer in West's account asked if she 'lived around here', West knew that something was wrong, that he was not who he seemed to be. In the end, West had to pay a fine for failing to register her dog.

Another sociologist, Shulamit Reinharz, has described how she uses her knowledge as a sociologist and her experience as a researcher to notice and to interpret the preponderance of warnings in her (and our) everyday life:

> As a qualitative sociologist trained in participant observation, I suffer from the occupational hazard of being extremely attentive to the social and built environment . . . to notice patterns in the mundane experiences of everyday life. . . . Everyday life thus becomes a source of rich data for developing hypotheses about social problems, social structure, and social change. (1999: 31)

Reinharz's situation is not unique. Clinton R. Sanders (1999) also notes that he does not succeed in keeping his professional life as a qualitative researcher and his personal life entirely separate. He describes a period in his life when he had too much time on his hands, and he began to watch a lot of television. After viewing one too many horror films, Sanders began to take notes on the films and ended up writing a book chapter, 'The Armadillos in Dracula's Foyer: Conventions and Innovation in Horror Cinema' (1991). He remarks that 'doing sociology offers the unique opportunity of turning casual interests to account', but 'focussing in a more analytic way on these casual interests tend[s] to decrease some of their immediate sensual pleasures' (1999: 43). Like many researchers, he finds social life so fascinating that he cannot resist thinking about the social processes involved in his everyday social environments.

This fascination with everyday routines truly is an occupational hazard of qualitative researchers. In my own life, I find that I simply cannot turn off my analytical thinking—especially when I watch TV. In particular, I'm often troubled by the portrayal of girls and women as submissive and by the preponderance of *blonde* women. When I watch TV with those closest to me, particularly my children, I can't help sharing my opinions. Ultimately, I believe that such observations enrich the experience, and that it is beneficial to be able to identify the patterns behind events. I'm certain that my observations affected my children in a positive way, enriching their process of growing up as they came to understand how social norms, beliefs, and atmospheres impacted their development. (In fact, as my oldest child likes to recount, this type of thinking helped her on her first sociology exam—before answering each question, she asked herself, 'What would Mom say about this?' She got an A.) As you read this book and try out the various exercises that go with each chapter, you may discover that you, too, are beginning to see patterns in your everyday life that you did not notice before. This sort of analytical thinking certainly makes life more interesting.

About This Book

This text is designed to teach you to think like a qualitative researcher. It will introduce you to qualitative methods and provide you with practical advice on how to use them. As you read through the discussions in each chapter, you will encounter many real-life examples. I have drawn extensively on my own research to talk about the actual experience of doing qualitative work, for these are the experiences I know best. I've also included many examples that demonstrate the range of approaches that other researchers take. In addition to a number of significant examples from international sources, you will find many Canadian examples that will give you a sense of the use and importance of qualitative methods in this country. Ultimately, these examples should not only help you understand how qualitative research intersects with the real world but also inspire you to develop your own questions and conduct your own studies in the future.

Content Overview

The chapters in this book take you through the process of carrying out research, from generating ideas for topics and research questions to designing studies and collecting and analyzing data to writing up the research. The text concludes with a discussion of trends in qualitative research followed by a consideration of research ethics.

Chapter 2, 'Asking Questions and Identifying Goals', focusses on the importance of questions in doing research. It explains some basic assumptions associated with both quantitative and qualitative approaches to research and identifies the major differences between these two approaches. In this chapter, you will also find a brief discussion of symbolic interactionism, the theoretical approach I use in my own research.

In Chapter 3, 'Strategies for Designing Research', we talk about the sociological imagination, undermining the hierarchy of credibility, beginning your research from where you, and turning a topic into a question. The chapter also covers the range of origins of particular qualitative studies—including personal experience, serendipity, and casual observation—and illustrates the ways many researchers combine the theoretical with the personal in their studies.

Chapter 4, 'Observing Social Life through Field Research', presents the first substantial method of carrying out a qualitative study: field research, or participant observation. The chapter traces the historical antecedents of contemporary field research and describes classic ethnographies of the Chicago School of Sociology. It then provides a brief overview of the history of ethnography in Canada. The heart of the chapter outlines the steps of a field study, from planning and gaining access to a research setting to entering the field and collecting data. The chapter also contains a detailed discussion on how to make jottings to record your observations in the field and then write good field notes based on your jottings. Throughout the chapter, I've incorporated examples that make field research come alive!

Chapter 5 discusses in-depth interviewing, which has become a prominent method for collecting qualitative data. The chapter begins by distinguishing between standardized interviews and in-depth interviews, demonstrating how in-depth interviews allow research participants to talk about what is important to them rather than limiting the discussion to topics the researcher chose in advance. The chapter explains that interviews are interactive events in which participants use strategies to locate themselves and the researcher in relation to one another. As you will learn, researchers can analyze these strategies in addition to what participants talk about as sources of data. In other words, it is not just *what* people say but also *how* they say it that matters. The chapter provides an overview of how to plan and conduct an in-depth interview study, from identifying participants and developing an interview guide to conducting interviews that encourage participants to give rich, expansive answers. Finally, the chapter gives advice on how to transcribe interviews.

Chapter 6 looks at unobtrusive measures, particularly content analysis. The chapter emphasizes taking an inductive approach to content analysis. This chapter is different from the previous chapters in that, instead of furnishing an in-depth discussion about how to go about conducting a content analysis, it demonstrates through example by describing an array of studies in which researchers used unobtrusive methods to analyze diverse items. The chapter shows you how researchers have found valuable data in such diverse sources as maps, letters, autobiographies, fictional accounts, professional publications, newspapers, advertisements, and even trash! Ultimately, you will discover that the imagination of the researcher is the only limit to the types of data that can be analyzed. I had a great deal of fun finding studies to use as exemplars of content analysis for this chapter, and I think that you will also enjoy reading about them and coming up with ideas of other types of artifacts you might use as data.

Chapter 7, 'Trust the Process: Analyzing Qualitative Data', looks at how researchers go about making sense out the mountains of data that are characteristic of qualitative research. As you will discover, the mantra of 'trust the process' will help you, particularly when you are doing your first study, to avoid being intimidated by the data or worrying that you not find anything of importance in the data. Part of doing your analysis is having faith that your data include important themes and that you will find them. The chapter also introduces you to qualitative coding, which is a somewhat different process than the coding you may have done in quantitative research. You will also learn the importance of using sensitizing concepts to understand your participants' perspectives. Finally, you will discover how generic social processes figure into data analysis. Throughout the chapter, I have included useful examples to demonstrate how researchers have interpreted their data.

While you are analyzing your own data, it is time to start writing, and Chapter 8 outlines ways to go about writing up qualitative research. Once again, I ask you to trust the process, this time the process of writing. Although this chapter is separate from the chapter on data analysis, writing is an integral part of the analysis process. As you write your research report, you will find that you get new ideas about your research and may need to revisit your data.

The chapter familiarizes you with the parts of a qualitative research report, encourages you to start writing early, and explains how to include data in your report. The chapter concludes by offering advice on how to improve your writing skills. I know that many of you write most of your term papers at the last minute and feel that you do not have time to worry about writing well, but I hope that I might entice you to make the time to produce a good report, one of which you can be proud.

Chapter 9, 'New Directions in Qualitative Research', describes some of the newer ways of doing qualitative work. There has been so much experimentation in collecting and analyzing qualitative data in recent years that it is impossible to cover all the new approaches, but the chapter discusses several of the most common methods: discourse analysis, narrative analysis, autoethnography, ethnodrama, visual sociology, and virtual ethnography.

Will C. van den Hoonaard, one of Canada's foremost writers on research ethics and research ethics review, has contributed Chapter10, 'Ethics on the Ground'. In this chapter, van den Hoonaard identifies principles of ethical research, particularly as they are outlined in Canada's *Tri-Council Policy Statement: Ethical Conduct for Research Involving Humans.* He also relates ethical concerns to the various stages of the qualitative research process covered in earlier chapters, offering advice on how you can take an ethical approach in your own qualitative studies.

At the end of each chapter, you will find questions that will make you think critically and exercises that will help you hone your qualitative skills when you try them out. You will also find suggestions for further reading and useful websites. I have tried to identify sources that are both informative and interesting to read. A good qualitative study can be as much a page-turner as any suspense novel. I have chosen these page-turners whenever possible.

You will also find three appendices at the end of this text. Appendix A provides a list of Canadian qualitative studies that you may wish to consult. The appendix focusses on full-length monographs by Canadian scholars, but it also contains a list of international journals that exclusively publish qualitative articles. Appendix B presents sample field notes from a study of wetlands that I conducted in 2002. The notes present examples of the types of details you should include in your qualitative research. Finally, Appendix C contains a checklist for writing your own research reports. This learning tool will help you polish your work in order to produce well-written academic papers.

As you can see, the arena of qualitative research is dynamic and exciting. This textbook provides only a taste of what it is like to do your own study. The best way to learn how to do qualitative work is to be brave and to go out and try it.

Summary

This chapter has provided a brief introduction to qualitative research and a summary of what each chapter of this text covers. Now you should begin to look forward to becoming familiar with some examples of classic qualitative studies and, ultimately, acquiring the tools to implement a qualitative research project of your own.

As you begin your studies, you should note that, while chapters 4 (on field research), 5 (on interviewing), and 6 (on unobtrusive research) each focus separately on only one qualitative method, it is quite common for researchers to combine various methods in their work. For example, when I studied a Florida retirement community, I primarily used field methods, but I also interviewed many residents of the community and analyzed 10 years' worth of the community's monthly newsletter. When I studied widows, my main method of data collection was interviewing, but I also observed meetings of widowhood support groups. When I interviewed widowers, I used unobtrusive methods to analyze the portrayal of widowers in novels and movies.

At this point, I encourage you to look at the list of studies in Appendix A and start reading a book whose topic tickles your fancy. Reading qualitative studies will inspire you in your own work, give you ideas about possible topics, and broaden your understanding of social processes.

Questions for Critical Thought

1. Do you have any misgivings about taking a course on qualitative research methods? How has this chapter addressed your concerns?

2. You've probably noticed someone wandering around your campus who somehow did not seem to belong there. What aspects of the person's behaviour, demeanour, or dress gave you the feeling that he or she just did not fit in?

3. Think about your daily life. What aspects of it might lead you to develop an idea for a research topic?

Exercises

1. Look through an issue of a qualitative research journal. Note the range of topics that the articles report on.

2. The next time you enter one of your classes or go to a coffee shop or pub, notice how much space the women take up compared to the men by virtue of the way they sit. Look carefully around the room and try to find other interesting patterns of behaviour.

3. Look through the list of ethnographies in Appendix A. Note any entries that look particularly interesting or surprising to you. Choose the one that appeals to you the most, find a copy at your library, and skim through the text to gain insight into a real-life qualitative study.

Suggested Readings

Barry Glassner and Rosanna Hertz, eds. 1999. *Qualitative Sociology as Everyday Life*. Thousand Oaks, CA: Sage. In this edited text, various seasoned qualitative researchers talk about how doing qualitative research has affected their everyday lives and how their everyday lives have influenced the research they do.

Douglas M. Robins, Clinton R. Sanders, and Spencer E. Cahill. 1991. 'Dogs and Their People: Pet-Facilitated Interaction in a Public Setting', *Journal of Contemporary Ethnography* 20, 1: 3–25. This article reports on a participant-observation study of dog owners in a public park. It chronicles the social processes through which regulars and newcomers encounter each other and use their dogs to facilitate inclusion or exclusion from the group. The article is very readable and nicely integrates theoretical analyses with descriptions of the social practices.

Related Websites

Atlantic Centre for Qualitative Research and Analysis (ACQRA)
http://w3.stu.ca/stu/sites/acqra/index.html

ACQRA, located at St Thomas University, hosts research workshops and talks, has research associates, and provides links to other qualitative research centres.

International Institute for Qualitative Methodology (IIQM)
www.uofaweb.ualberta.ca/iiqm/index.cfm

IIQM, operating in association with the University of Alberta, hosts research seminars and educational programs. It also produces the *International Journal of Qualitative Methods*, an online open-access journal.

2 Asking Questions and Identifying Goals

Learning Objectives

- ⊛ To understand the importance of questions in social research
- ⊛ To comprehend the differences between qualitative and quantitative research
- ⊛ To understand the underlying assumptions associated with qualitative research
- ⊛ To learn about generic social processes and how scholars use them in their research

Introduction

'Any questions?'

It is the first day of class, and the professor has just walked into the room. She has not handed out the course outline or given any introduction. 'Any questions?', she repeats. After a few minutes of awkward silence, a student asks whether there will be a final exam. Another asks what the assignments for the course will be like. Other questions follow, and the professor responds to each one in turn. By starting the class in this way, the professor has effectively communicated the importance of questions and of having a question in mind at the start of any project. Without questions, there are no answers.

The questions a person asks indicate what is most important to that person. When I ask my students on the first day of class if they have any questions, they typically ask about course requirements and evaluation. I infer two things from their questions. First, many of the students are still shopping around for the classes they want to take. Some, I believe, will withdraw from the class if I include oral presentations as a requirement, while others might decide to stay because they like the fact that my class does not have a final exam. Second, most of the students plan to do only the work that I will evaluate. Some will not do anything that does not receive points. To be fair, however, I need to recognize that my assumptions about my students are not necessarily true, they simply reflect my beliefs. I would need to ask the students themselves how they came up with their questions to find out if I am right. I would have to do research.

Deciding what questions to ask is not always a simple matter. The way we ask questions determines what kinds of answers we get. For example, if you were to design a multiple-choice question, you would limit the potential answers to your question. If I say, 'What is your favourite food: (a) steak, (b) pasta, or (c) fish?', you cannot answer, 'ice cream'. The answers to some questions might, moreover, be hard to interpret. Imagine that I ask you how often you go drinking with your friends: (a) more than once a week, (b) once a week, (c) less than once a week but at least once a month, or (d) less frequently. Those options may provide an exhaustive list, but they will not tell me if you consider going out drinking with your friends once a week enough or too much, very often or not often. I would not find out what the answer means to you.

We also know that if we, as researchers, do not ask people why they have particular opinions or act in certain ways, we will guess—we will, in effect, invent their motives. Often we will be wrong. Herbert Blumer, one of the founders of symbolic interactionism, noted that if we do not ask people why they do things and what those things mean to them, we will nevertheless still talk about their meanings, and, 'of necessity, invent them' (Becker 1996: 58). According to Howard S. Becker, one of the most important qualitative researchers of the twentieth century, the problem is that we are just as likely to guess wrong as to guess right; because our experience and understanding likely differ from the those of the people we study, it is equally likely that 'what looks reasonable to us will not be what looked reasonable to them' (Becker 1996: 58).

For example, a number of years ago, my university took a poll among our students and professors to find out whether they preferred classes that met three times a week for 50 minutes or two times a week for 80 minutes. Not surprisingly, the two groups did not have the same preferences. The students preferred the shorter classes and the professors, the longer. Then it got interesting. Some professors guessed at the students' motivations for preferring shorter classes. They suggested that the students had short attention spans or that they were too lazy to pay attention for a whole 80 minutes. No one actually asked the students why they liked the shorter classes; perhaps it was easier for them to juggle work and school schedules if the classes were shorter. I do not know why the students preferred the shorter classes, and neither did the professors who provided their own explanations. They were, in fact, guessing and then assuming they were right. It is likely that the students also made guesses that assumed particular motives on the part of the faculty.

To illustrate this principle, Becker (1996) tells a story about a student of his who was studying the culture of mail carriers. This student wanted to know what kinds of delivery routes the mail carriers preferred. He guessed that they would prefer routes they perceived to be most safe, such as those in middle-class neighbourhoods or in neighbourhoods where there were few dogs. Perhaps they preferred to deliver mail in areas where people got fewer heavy packages or catalogues. All of these possibilities made sense, but none of them were correct. When the student actually asked the mail carriers what kinds of routes they preferred, they answered that they preferred routes in flat areas where they would not have to walk up and down hills. Becker's student would never have come up with that answer on his own because he did not share the experiences of his **research participants**. By asking for their preferences and the reasons for those preferences, the student did not have to 'invent' the viewpoint of the mail carriers. Rather, he discovered their actual motives. If the professors at my university had asked the students why they liked shorter classes, they might have found that the students, like the mail carriers, had their own good reasons for their preference.

In this chapter, we look at the assumptions associated with quantitative and qualitative approaches in social research and the primary differences between these approaches. You will discover that each approach has its own distinctive ways of asking questions, and that the approach a researcher chooses reflects the way in which he or she understands the social world. You will also learn more about the underlying philosophy of qualitative research and examine examples of how researchers use sociological concepts in their work.

Underlying Assumptions and the Research Process

At this point, you may already be familiar with some of the ways in which qualitative research differs from quantitative research. In general, a researcher's choice between engaging in quantitative research and engaging in qualitative research often comes down to that researcher's theoretical perspective and, by extension, the types of information that he or she wants to find. This section will introduce you to some of the theories and assumptions commonly associated with each approach. In the discussion of qualitative research, you will also encounter several examples of how theoretical assumptions have led researchers to develop specific methods that complement their perspectives. To prepare you for the more in-depth discussions to come, Figure 2.1 provides a brief overview of the basic assumptions that commonly lead researchers to prefer one of the approaches over the other.

Quantitative Approaches

If you have some background experience with quantitative research methods, you may already know that these methods were first developed for the social sciences by Auguste Comte (1798–1857). Impressed by the advances he observed in the natural sciences, Comte argued that researchers could adapt the quantitative methods of science for use in the social sciences. He developed these methods in accordance with his theoretical perspective, which he called **positivism**. Positivism has three principal attributes: adherence to a realist

Qualitative Research	Quantitative Research
• Research should focus on human lived reality	• Research should focus on theory development and testing
• Inductive reasoning (from the specific to the general) leads to understanding	• Deductive reasoning (from general to specific) leads to truth
• Participants' meanings are key	• Researchers' meanings are key
• Researchers must identify the definition of the situation	• Researchers must find 'objective' definitions
• Social settings are highly complex and can affect the outcome of an experiment	• A valid experiment should arrive at the same conclusion no matter where it is performed
• Understanding exists in our agreed-upon experiences	• Truth is an objective reality

FIGURE 2.1 Comparing Qualitative and Quantitative Approaches: Differences in Basic Assumptions

perspective, trust in causal knowledge, and reliance on deductive reasoning. Today, many quantitative researchers still support these principles and the assumptions that they entail. Let us take a look at each of these elements.

A **realist perspective** assumes that reality is out there, waiting to be discovered, or, in the case of psychology, reality is in there waiting to be discovered. For positivists, therefore, the objective of social science is to uncover the 'laws' of human behaviour—what Émile Durkheim (1858–1917) called 'social facts' ([1897] 1951). Because reality is out there, like a planet waiting to be discovered, truth is the criterion social scientists attempt to meet. This approach implies predictability. If we discover the 'truth' about social life, we ought to be able to predict how people will act in particular situations, just as we can predict, based on the 'truth' of gravity, that an object will fall if we drop it. And, just as we can stop an object from falling because we understand why it will fall, we will have the potential to control social situations once we understand why they occur. Therefore, the emphasis in positivism is on both the prediction and the control of what people will do (Prus 2005: 9).

Trust in **causal knowledge** involves a belief that the world is made up of causes and effects that are external to individuals, observable, and measurable. This perspective borrows from the natural sciences and, indeed, has the goal of making social science worthy of the term 'science'. Because they believe that all interactions involve objective causes and effects, positivists hold that objectivity is achievable in social-science research, and they attempt to follow the lead of the natural sciences. They have, therefore, emphasized operationism, the development of research techniques that emphasize quantification and precision. This type of research relies on statistical significance and often uses sophisticated techniques, such as factor analysis and multiple regression, to interpret data.

Deductive reasoning is a form of reasoning that uses a process of inference to derive conclusions from general laws or premises. When researchers use a deductive approach, they develop a theory, **operationalize** the theory (that is, put it into a testable form by developing hypotheses based on the theory), collect data, and then perform an analysis. If the results confirm the hypotheses, the theory is considered plausible, and the researcher writes up the results.

Qualitative Approaches

For nearly 100 years, positivism ruled social science, but in the early 1960s, things began to change. Experimenters began to realize how heavily an individual's behaviour is influenced by her or his social situation and past experiences. This revelation led to an interest in the dynamics of interpersonal exchange. For example, researchers began to question how the gender or cultural background of an interviewer might affect the responses of a research subject and, in turn, how a subject's gender or cultural background might influence how she or he responds to an interviewer.

In addition, the social unrest of the 1960s led to the questioning of the status quo. In 1962, Thomas Kuhn published *The Structure of Scientific Revolution*, in which he showed how traditional methods of observation are 'theory laden' and emphasized that data do not 'speak for themselves'. Soon, other researchers began to understand that even very careful researchers are likely to see what they expect to see and to interpret data in line with their own theoretical assumptions. Later research into the social psychological aspects of psychological experiments (for example, a 1968 study conducted by Cannell, Fisher, and Marquis) confirmed that an experiment involving human participants is an interpersonal event and that the experimenter's perspective can influence the results.

In response to these and similar developments, sociologists began to express a renewed interest in qualitative approaches to research. Since the 1960s, this interest has continued to grow, and qualitative methods are frequently used in sociological research today. Modern researchers adopt qualitative research methods for a variety of reasons, but many do so because they believe in the importance of two concepts developed in the first half of the twentieth century—sympathetic understanding and definition of the situation.

The first of these concepts, sympathetic understanding, was introduced by the social theorist Max Weber (1864–1920). Although he believed in such quantitative ideals as value-free research, Weber (1949) exhorted researchers to seek a level of *verstehen* (a German word that translates as 'sympathetic understanding'). He suggested that we, as researchers, should strive to put ourselves in our research subjects' shoes, to try to see their world through their eyes. For example, in my research I've worked with many older widows and, through interviews, I've developed a sympathetic understanding of the enormity of their loss. This understanding, in turn, has helped me to interpret the information that I gather from the interviews in a way that is appropriate to their experiences. This understanding has helped me on a personal level, as well. When my father passed away, my sympathetic understanding of widows' situations helped me to understand how devastated my mother was. As a result, I arranged to stay with her for a longer period of time than I would have if I had not done my study of women's experiences as widows.

The second of these concepts, **definition of the situation**, was introduced by the American sociologist W.I. Thomas (1863–1947). As Thomas (1937) described it, this concept means that if we define a situation as true, it is true in its consequences. For example, when I started a job as a waitress when I was in university, the person who was training me told me that women were poor tippers and I should, therefore, not worry too much about how well I served them. That was her definition of the situation, and many servers in restaurants share this definition. The consequence? Women often receive poorer service than men do. In response to poor treatment by wait staff, some women will, indeed, give a small tip, thus reinforcing the servers' definition of the situation.

The definition of the situation can have an impact on intercultural relations as well. For example, most people might expect that only Icelanders can understand Icelandic. That certainly was the definition of the situation held by most people in Iceland when Will C. van den Hoonaard (2009b) went there to do research. Van den Hoonaard did, in fact, understand some Icelandic. Nonetheless, when he went to a shop one day, the proprietor of the shop believed that, as a foreigner, he could not understand Icelandic, because that was her definition of the situation. The consequence of this belief was that the woman spoke to him in Icelandic baby talk. Now, if you know baby talk in any language, you know that it can be quite difficult for a non-native speaker to understand, and van den Hoonaard could not follow what the proprietor was saying. She then used even more 'simple' language, which van den Hoonaard still could not comprehend. In the end, the consequence of the woman's definition of the situation that only Icelanders can understand Icelandic was that van den Hoonaard, a non-Icelander, could not understand Icelandic.

Many contemporary qualitative researchers are also influenced by the principles of **symbolic interactionism**. This perspective, first formulated by Herbert Blumer (1900–1987), based on the theoretical approaches of George Herbert Mead (1863–1931), suggests that the meaning of an object evolves through individuals' shared understandings of and interactions with that object. The object, or 'thing', has no intrinsic meaning except for the ones we give it. For example, in the West we take for granted that black is the colour of mourning. However, the colour black, in itself, has no inherent meaning. Hence, in some Asian cultures, black signifies experi-ence or respect, while white is the colour of mourning. Such 'things' also include people. In some cultures, elders represent wisdom, and people seek their advice before making important decisions. In contemporary Western societies, we often see old people through the lens of ageism and, as a result, they occupy marginalized social positions.

Questions of meaning have led researchers to investigate what events and social roles mean to people. As Howard S. Becker has written, 'all terms that describe people are relational'. Hence, a trait, such as being tall, is not sim-ply a 'fact but rather an interpretation of that fact' (Becker 1998: 122, 134). In Canada, at five foot three, I am considered pretty short. In Korea, I would be considered tall. Even though the objective fact of my height remains the same, it is interpreted differently when the average height of the population changes.

Researchers who adopt qualitative methods are often interested in the ways in which the meanings things have for us emerge out of our inter-actions with other individuals, our interactions with groups, and our interactions with institutions. Consequently, many qualitative researchers design studies to achieve the goal of understanding those interactions and the emerging meanings that grow out of such interactions. They are also interested in the ways in which we see ourselves as 'things' and define our-selves through our interactions with others. Charles Horton Cooley (1902) referred to the self we define through this process as 'the **looking-glass self**'. Many later researchers have shared his belief that our sense of self is a result of our perceptions of how others see us.

Similarly, many researchers use qualitative methods to investigate the understanding that we rely on social meanings to define ourselves as mem-bers of certain groups. Let us take the concept of an ethnic group. As Everett C. Hughes ([1971] 1984) pointed out, many people who use the term *ethnic group* would say that one ethnic group is distinguishable from another by some objective criteria—language, physical characteristics, religion, cus-toms, and so forth. He argued that when we take that approach, we have it backwards. An ethnic group is not an ethnic group because of objective, observable differences. Rather, it is an ethnic group because people—both inside and outside the group—recognize it as one. As such, the identification of an ethnic group depends on an established relationship with that group. For example, when I went to China, I, as a foreigner, could not tell that there were any discernable ethic groups. But my Chinese guides could immedi-ately identify the members of ethnic groups within their society because they had learned, through social interactions, the meaningful attributes of local ethnic groups. When Chinese people immigrate to Canada, they come into contact with many individuals who perceive all Chinese people as belong-ing to a single ethnic group. As a result, Chinese immigrants tend to place less importance on the ethnic differences that were meaningful to them in China. It is the social context rather than individual characteristics that makes the difference. This understanding of identity as a social construct has led many sociologists to replace the term *race*, which implies that 'races' are objectively real, with *racialized*, which demonstrates that the concept of 'race' is socially constructed rather than real.

Hughes' solution to the problem of trying to decide who is a member of a particular ethnic group was simply to ask people about how they perceive themselves. They know whether or not they are members of a particular group regardless of any criteria social scientists might come up with. Think of the Québécois in our own country. We know that they are Québécois not because they speak French but because they see themselves as Québécois and because they and non-Québécois Canadians see each other as belonging to different groups.

Researcher Harold Garfinkel (1967) took the question of a socially constructed reality even further and introduced his own approach, **ethnomethodology**. He questioned how people go about everyday life in the absence of visible or formal rules. He sought to discover the unwritten rules by which we communicate. For example, if your friend calls you and asks, 'Do you want to go to the movies?', you do not say 'yes', hang up the phone, and set off to see a movie by yourself. You know that the person is really asking you to go to the movies with him or her and that he or she expects you to understand this intention and to stay on the phone to discuss which movie you will see, when you will go, and where you will meet.

To make these tacit understandings visible, Garfinkel designed **breaching experiments**, qualitative experiments in which the researcher intentionally breaks one of the unspoken laws of interaction. For example, if you were to meet a friend on the street and ask, 'How are you?', you would likely expect the person to say 'fine' and continue walking. If your friend were doing a breaching experiment, she or he might answer, 'How am I in regard to what? Finances? School work? Love life?' When Garfinkel's students tried this out, the people with whom they interacted sometimes lost their temper and shouted that they were not really interested, they were just being polite (Garfinkel 1967). Ultimately, these experiments demonstrate the necessity of the tacit understandings that underlie social life. Our trust that both parties know the unspoken rules—for example, that 'how are you?' is simply a pleasantry rather than a serious question—is what makes everyday interactions possible.

As you can see, there are a number of assumptions that can lead researchers to adopt qualitative methods. In general, most qualitative researchers share an understanding that they must pay attention to how participants perceive and interpret their situation within their social context. To accomplish this task, researchers have developed a variety of methods with which to collect and analyze data: field methods, interviews, document analysis, and photo elicitation, among others. Later chapters of this book will introduce you to some of these methods and provide you with opportunities to try them out.

The Research Process

Qualitative versus Quantitative Methods

As you might expect, the research process in qualitative research is different from the process in quantitative research. The main difference is as follows. In qualitative research, which generally follows an inductive approach, researchers usually start with the social world and then develop a theory that is consistent with what they see. In quantitative research, which generally follows a deductive approach, researchers tend to begin with a theory and then test that theory in the empirical world. Because qualitative researchers begin the process of collecting data before they define their specific research question, qualitative research tends to be more open to the unexpected.

To illustrate some of the fundamental differences between qualitative and quantitative methods, let us use the analogy of planning a vacation.[1] If you were to take a vacation using an inductive method of planning, you would know what guidebooks to take—say, one from Lonely Planet and one from Fodor's—but you would not be sure what parts of each guidebook would end up proving to be most useful. You would have some idea of what you wanted to see and do. However, you would not be locked into a fixed itinerary, so you would have flexibility to explore what you wanted to see along the way. You would be free to change plans as new adventures enticed you. Quantitative research, in contrast, is more like taking a package tour. You do the research of possible tours up front and choose the one that looks most interesting. But, once you have begun, you pretty well have to go where the tour guide leads you, even if things are not quite as interesting as you expected or if something else catches your attention.

I had such an experience when I visited Beijing a few years ago. I was lucky enough to have graduate students from Beijing Normal University act as my guides. For most of my trip, I acted as a qualitative traveller. I often followed the advice of my guides, such as their suggestion that I see the Forbidden City, but I was also free to explore the sites on my own. For example, one day, when I was buying stamps at a post office, I noticed a breathtakingly beautiful garden. I immediately knew I wanted to see it, so I adjusted my itinerary and my guides were happy to take me there. This unplanned excursion turned out to be more worthwhile than some of the outings I had planned in advance. While in China, I also experienced a more 'quantitative' tour that included a trip to the Great Wall. The tour guide took us to several interesting spots, and we learned a lot about the Great Wall. In all, we had a very good day, but we could not explore anything on our own, as we had to keep up with the pace of the tour. We could not spend more time at the Ming Tombs than the package tour had allowed for, and we could not stop to look at the Disney Park that was in the process of construction at that time.

As you can see from the example of my trip, qualitative strategies often lead to unplanned yet highly worthwhile experiences. So, how does qualitative research encourage us to find the unexpected? Qualitative research is, at its most fundamental level, flexible and open to change.

Qualitative research allows you to adjust the design of the research as you go. Thus, the design itself is **emergent**. Often, adjustments are necessary to correct for preliminary assumptions that turn out to be incorrect. For example, I did research in a condominium-type retirement community in Florida to study conformity among its residents. I assumed that members of the Board of the Homeowners' Association, the governing body of the community, would be the most active in the community; therefore, I made these members central to my research design. However, during an early interview, one person mentioned that a particular board member was not active in the community. It turned out that members of the Entertainment Committee, rather than members of the Board, were most active in the community. Because qualitative studies are flexible in their designs, I was able to quickly change my research plan so that it included members of the Entertainment Committee. It makes sense that, in a community whose residents say they 'live like other people vacation', the committee whose mandate is to plan parties would be very important. In hindsight, this became obvious, but if I had not had the flexibility to adapt my research design, I would never have been able to explore the centrality of the Entertainment Committee.

Also, because data collection and analysis go on simultaneously in qualitative research, you can adjust the breadth of your study as you progress. You can start with broad questions and then narrow down your questions as you discover what is important. You can stop when you are no longer learning anything new, a stage called **theoretical saturation**. You can also expand your selection of participants as new questions arise. For example, when I noticed that snowbirds, individuals who spend only the winter in Florida, did not seem to be well-integrated into the retirement community, I made sure that I interviewed a few snowbirds to get their points of view (see D.K. van den Hoonaard 2002). (Chapter 5 will further discuss how the interviewing process works.)

In addition, in a qualitative research project, you can adjust your questions throughout the life of the study. This flexibility allows you to examine new ideas and themes that emerge as you go along. Another example from my retirement-community research illustrates this aspect of qualitative work. One day I was interviewing a widow about how becoming widowed had changed her experience of living in the community. Her house cleaner walked into the room and remarked that the biggest problem for widows was negotiating who pays for dinner when they go out with couples. The

Qualitative Research	Quantitative Research
• Involves little or no advance knowledge of the type(s) of data to be collected	• Involves advance knowledge of the type(s) of data to be collected
• Allows participants to define how the study progresses and what the data mean	• Minimizes participants' input into types of data collected
• Strives for accuracy—researchers do not invent the actor's viewpoint	• Strives for reliability—researchers make sure that the findings can be replicated
• Often involves in-depth interviews	• Often involves questionnaires or surveys
• Relies on subjective observation	• Relies on objective experiments
• Includes a literature review at the end of the study	• Includes a literature review at the outset of the study

Figure 2.2 Comparing Qualitative and Quantitative Approaches: Differences in Typical Methods

woman I was interviewing agreed and commented that deciding who pays is a very contentious issue. I had not known about this topic when I walked into the house for the interview, but it became a standard and very important point of discussion during the rest of the study (see D.K. van den Hoonaard 1994). Had I been carrying out survey research, I would not have been able to add new questions once I had begun collecting data.

Before we move on to discuss how qualitative and quantitative methods can work together, take a moment to review the key aspects of each method. Figure 2.2 presents an overview of the major differences.

Mixed-Methods Research

In recent years, there has been a movement that aims to combine the strengths of qualitative and quantitative approaches to research. It argues for **mixed methods**, an approach through which the researcher uses both quantitative and qualitative methods and integrates the findings in a single study. Those who promote mixed methods argue that it is a 'third approach alongside quantitative and qualitative approaches' (Creswell and Plano Clark 2007: 16). They suggest that a combination of qualitative and quantitative approaches provides more complete understandings of a phenomenon than either one alone. To get a better idea of how researchers have used mixed methods, let us take a look at a few studies that use mixed methods.

John H. Parmelee, Stephynie C. Perkins, and Judith J. Sayre (2007) decided to use a mixed-methods approach to investigate why a high proportion of young people abstain from voting in national elections—a phenomenon that is not uncommon in Canada. In particular, they wanted to find out why so few young people voted in the 2004 US presidential election. They, therefore, decided to examine why the political ads for the election did not engage university students. The researchers designed a mixed-methods study that involved holding focus groups made up of students and conducting a quantitative content analysis of more than 100 ads to see why the members of the focus groups felt alienated. The researchers used a deductive approach in that they chose the theory they would use (framing theory) in advance of collecting quantitative and qualitative data. Focus-group participants believed that the political ads neglected their age group in both style and substance and that the ads showed every demographic except young adults. The way the advertisements framed the issues resulted in a perception that the issues did not matter to young adults. The researchers' content analysis confirmed that the ads ignored the students' concerns. In this case, the quantitative content analysis played a secondary role, as it was the qualitative interviews that revealed a reason for young people's choosing to abstain from voting. Even if the students had been mistaken about the *actual* content of the ads, it would not change the fact that they *believed* that the advertisements neglected them and the issues they cared about.

Although most mixed-methods researchers suggest that it is important to choose a design for integrating the various methods in advance, Thomas W. Christ (2007) provides a case in which it was beneficial to begin without a predetermined design. He carried out a study of disability-support services in post-secondary institutions. His study began with a survey of 1,500 disability-support coordinators; he then repeated the same survey to determine changes over time. His analysis of the surveys resulted in questions that he could not answer using quantitative research. He, therefore, carried out qualitative interviews within three institutions that the survey had identified as 'exemplary'. Christ used 'inductive logic to develop emerging themes and categories . . . to generate overarching theoretical conclusions' (2007: 228). Finally, to gather more information, he carried out additional interviews at a university that had faced budget reductions. In this case, if the research design had been predetermined, the researcher would have had to treat the third phase as a separate study.

In a recent study, Brenda H. Vrkljan (2009) used mixed methods to explore the ways in which older drivers and their 'copilots' (or passengers)[2] use navigational technology. The study involved four steps. The first step was a demographic survey (quantitative) that included questions about how familiar each pair was with technology. The second step involved interviews that explored the driver–copilot relationship (qualitative). The third step was a usability analysis of the navigation systems (quantitative). In this step, Vrkljan analyzed performance measures that included the time it took to finish a route-planning task and the number of errors made per task. The final step allowed participants to talk about their impressions of using the navigation technology (qualitative). Vrkljan notes that 'although the sample size was small, it was large enough to achieve the statistical power necessary to detect differences' between pairs who were used to using technology and those who were not (2009: 376). In reviewing the place of mixed methods in her research, Vrkljan notes that incorporating qualitative methods into her study allowed her to modify the research design as the early findings became clear. She compares the process of determining her approach to taking a road trip: 'The decisions [i.e., to alter the design] may have altered the map [i.e., the design structure] but not the final destination [i.e., the results]' (2009: 376).

These three studies demonstrate the diversity of mixed-methods research. I have served on national committees that adjudicate research-grant applications and have seen a growth in the number, particularly in the area of health services, that involve mixed methods. Many of these studies begin with what Thomas W. Christ has described as an 'exploratory qualitative component' followed by 'confirmatory survey research' with a goal of 'generalization' (2007: 226). One of the biggest challenges for such research is to find ways to truly integrate the findings so that the qualitative components do not disappear in the analysis. In fact, in locating and reviewing mixed-methods studies, Creswell and Plano Clark (2007) report that three out of four studies have a quantitative emphasis, while only one out of four has a qualitative emphasis. As Lynne S. Giddings, a proponent of mixed-methods research, cautions, 'the positivist scientific tradition continues to be privileged as a way to know; its dominance is strengthened, rather than challenged, by mixed-method research' (2006: 202).

Perhaps the best way to ensure that the richness of qualitative research is not marginalized in mixed-methods research is for investigators who have skill and experience in qualitative research to be responsible for the qualitative component. Hence, before attempting a mixed-methods study, it is important to understand and know how to use qualitative research methods.

Identifying Researcher Perspectives and General Assumptions

We create theories all the time, even when we do not realize it. We have ideas about why certain people get paid more than others, why the Atlantic provinces have traditionally been 'have-not' provinces, or why professors act the way they do. Our theories help us to explain what our senses tell us about the empirical world. When our theories are reinforced by enough empirical data, they often become assumptions—theories we hold without question.

Our assumptions about social life and society also influence how we approach topics and interpret data when we do research. When beginning any research project, we need to ask ourselves what we think we know and how we know it. We need to examine our biases and investments in particular issues. Although many social scientists believe that research *ought* to be unbiased, most of us who do qualitative research agree that this goal is unrealistic. Everyone has preconceptions. Of course, our research will be better if we can identify our biases and take them into account. Unfortunately, it is impossible for us to recognize all of them or to eradicate those we do recognize.

In addition, some bias is inherent in any research process. Recall the underlying assumptions associated with quantitative and qualitative research that we discussed earlier. In adopting a research perspective, a researcher will necessarily be influenced by the assumptions associated with that perspective. In turn, those assumptions will influence the types of questions the researcher asks and the ways in which he or she asks those questions. To get a better idea of the kinds of basic assumptions that researchers make, let us take a closer look at the assumptions involved in symbolic interactionism, one of the major research perspectives that qualitative researchers can adopt.

The primary assumption of symbolic-interactionism is that we, as social actors, create, or construct, social reality. In fact, symbolic interactionists believe that it is only as members of a community or society that we come to understand and believe 'what is' and 'what is not' (Prus 2005: 10–13). Contained within this assumption is the belief that humans are social—as opposed to individualistic—beings. Therefore, as a research perspective, symbolic interactionism assumes that we cannot examine the actions of an individual person without also considering the social context in which that person exists.

Symbolic interactionists also assume that language is the essential mechanism for meaningful knowing and acting. Those who object to using a specific word to describe a particular group of people understand the importance of language as a signifier of meaning. They see that naming a group using a particular word affects both the way people see and act towards members of that group and the way members think about and act towards themselves. Hence, members of various social movements have long advocated a move away from the term *handicapped* to refer to individuals with physical disabilities. They believe that the handicaps people experience, rather than residing in the individual, result from the barriers society has constructed. For example, by not building ramps to go into a building, we handicap a person who cannot climb steps. When we put in ramps, we make it easier for all kinds of people to enter the building—for example, a person who is pushing a baby stroller. Hence, buildings without ramps disable new parents and people carrying suitcases just as they do people in wheelchairs. By choosing language that avoids labelling an individual based on his or her physical 'ability', we not only give that individual an identity as an *individual*, but we change the connotation from seeing the individual as the problem to seeing the social context as the problem.[3]

Symbolic interactionists also believe that we give meaning to things by the ways we act towards them and, in turn, we act towards things based on the meanings we have for them. Further, they believe that we create and adapt those meanings by watching how other people act towards and react to those things. Many qualitative researchers identify sensitizing concepts to get at those meanings (see Chapter 7 for a discussion of how researchers identify and use such concepts in their research). For example, in a classic study by Howard S. Becker et al. ([1961] 2009), researchers used a sensitizing concept to understand how medical students define certain patients and then adjust their behaviour towards those patients based on their definitions. Becker (1993) tells the story of how he found out what medical students meant when they referred to a patient as a 'crock'. As a sociologist, he anticipated that the students would hold a shared definition of the concept of a 'crock' and that their definition would reflect their own interests. With this knowledge in mind, Becker asked the students, 'What's a crock?' They responded that a crock was someone who was a hypochondriac, a person with complaints but no pathology. For the students, this concept was implicitly negative, as the crocks wasted what little time the students had to get practical experience in the field. Of course, such patients would not hold the same meaning for others—for example, a doctor whose aim is to make money by seeing as many patients as possible might enjoy treating hypochondriacs. In the end, by attending to the meaning those patients had *for the students*, Becker learned much about the social context of being a student in a medical school.

Another commonly accepted symbolic-interactionist principle holds that social meaning is negotiable. Individuals do not blindly accept norms, values, and behaviours. In fact, many people engage in influencing understandings of normative behaviours. For example, Howard S. Becker, in his pioneering work *Outsiders* (1963), gave the example of **moral entrepreneurs** who engage in campaigning to establish certain social behaviours, such as using marijuana, as deviant and illegal. The persisting debates around abortion also provide examples of the strategies that groups with different understandings use to persuade the community of their particular moral position.

In relation to self-identity, symbolic interactionists believe that we can only know ourselves through our relationships with other people. They hold that these relationships allow us to understand how society works and our place in that society. In addition, a shift in these relationships reflects a changing understanding of the social order. Consider the changing role of students in universities. In the past, most students saw themselves as apprentices who were learning from masters in the academic community. Today, most students see themselves as consumers rather than as apprentices. As such, they expect universities to see them as customers and to serve their needs and wants in that light. By extension, students as consumers see knowledge as a product and judge whether their professors are capable of delivering that product.

Finally, symbolic interactionists understand group life in terms of social processes. They see our lived experience as active and emergent, as we are always engaged in negotiating relationships—we negotiate with others, with ourselves, and with broader social structures.

From this example, you can see the many ways in which theoretical assumptions can influence a researcher's work. When you conduct your own research, remember that all researchers make assumptions, but the *best* researchers avoid making unfounded or careless assumptions.

Generic Social Processes

Unlike quantitative research, qualitative research is not in the business of seeking generalizable findings. At the same time, qualitative researchers do recognize that certain social processes are often consistent across different social settings. Thus, as Canadian sociologist Robert Prus (2005) has noted, they can identify several social processes of a 'general or transcendent nature'. These **'generic social processes'** include (1) acquiring perspectives, (2) achieving identity, (3) doing activity, (4) developing relationships, (5) experiencing emotionality, and (6) achieving linguistic fluency (Prus 2005: 19). These categories reflect researchers' interest in the emergent nature of human life. Researchers do not look simply at perspectives, but at the process of *acquiring* perspectives, not just at identity, but at how people go about *achieving* their identities.

Generally, researchers look for generic social processes within a specific group of individuals. By observing the behaviour of members within this population, researchers can identify common elements of that process that are shared across that population. A good example of a study that examined the social process of acquiring identity comes from the work of Jack Haas and William Shaffir (1994, [1987] 2009). In the study, the researchers examined identity formation within a group of medical students. They wanted to find out how medical students transform their identities from those of lay people to those of professional doctors. They noticed that the students observed doctors' ways of working and the neutral demeanour characteristic of doctors in hospitals. In turn, the students began to imitate the behaviours of those doctors. Using the concept of **impression management**, Haas and Shaffir demonstrated that each student participated in a process of adopting a 'cloak of competence' through which they communicated to themselves and others a confident, professional self.

Identifying a generic social process can also help a researcher to expand the scope of the research project to uncover hidden aspects of the participants' collective experience. For example, when I interviewed widows, my over-arching research question was 'What is the social meaning of being a widow?' As I discussed this topic with my participants, it became clear that the process of identity formation was central to their experiences. This realization led me to explore how becoming a widow had forced the women to form new identities and how this process of identity formation affected their lived experiences. They revealed that, in losing their husband, their identities as wives disappeared (D.K. van den Hoonaard 2001, 1997). They seemed like different people to themselves and to others. As a result, they had to negotiate new relationships with their children and with their closest friends. They also had to integrate the fact of their being widows into their own identity, their self-perceptions.

Another example, from the work of Daniel and Cheryl Albas, demonstrates how researchers can use a generic social process to categorize subsections within a population. In a classic study, Albas and Albas (1988) studied the process of acquiring an identity within a population of university students. First, they noticed that students acquire an identity related to how well they do in their classes. Through observation, the researchers identified three subgroups within the student population: aces, who saw themselves as overachievers and tended to do very well in their classes; bombers, who tended to fail or just scrape by; and moderates, who got decent grades but did not stand out as high achievers. The researchers found that the process of identity formation drew students within each subgroup closer together, as the students were attracted to other students who participated in identity-formation processes similar to their own and therefore had similar identities and perspectives, particularly in relation to study habits.

With these categories in place, the researchers could then expand their analysis to cover the ways in which the students negotiated their relationships with others based on their identities as aces or bombers. Most interesting were the strategies students used when their professors returned exams or assignments. Aces, for example, would not want to give the impression that they were showing off, but they would want others to know that they had gotten a good grade. Some reported that they might 'accidentally' leave their papers on their desk with the grade showing or 'drop' their paper so that the mark would be visible when someone picked it up. Alternatively, they might underplay their grade by a remark, such as 'I did okay', if they wanted to avoid bragging about the grade. Conversely, bombers would hide their grade or say something like, 'not too bad' when asked about their grade. In the end, the categories of students that researchers were able to develop based on the observed generic social process of identity formation allowed the researchers to gather a great amount of information on the social study habits of students. Box 2.1 includes a discussion from the Albases' work on how aces and bombers accomplish study activity.

Box 2.1 ❖ Generic Social Processes: Accomplishing Activity

The accomplishment of the study activity typically comes to a climax in a period of about two weeks before the examination period. A new atmosphere seems to emerge on campus. . . . [T]he nearer to exam time, the more sensitive students become to exam-related stimuli and the more intensely they concentrate on study. . . . [S]tudents are entirely on their own and must rely on their own self-discipline to apply themselves or experience drift—according to their category (Ace or Bomber).

Aces: Keeping 'Noses to the Grindstone'

These diligent students are characterized by an awareness of the necessity to keep their 'noses to the grindstone'. . . . They studiously avoid the distraction of itinerant Bombers who ask irrelevant questions and 'waste their time'.

> As exams approach, those who have not yet begun their preparations always seem to want to start up conversations. Though it might sound impolite, I try to discourage them by answering in monosyllables. I hardly look up from my work. It eventually gets through to them that studying is the most important thing to me at that time . . .

Aces tend to view any frivolity or present pleasure as resulting inevitably in future pain. . . .

> At the beginning of the year I felt guilty if I refused to go out with my friends and instead stayed home to study. . . . At exam time I would feel even more guilty if I did go out with them. . . .

Bombers are students who procrastinate about studying. . . . Perhaps the most typical characteristic of this category of students is their propensity to use fritters [i.e., time wasters] as a rationalization for avoiding study. . . . For example:

> The last day of lectures is when the professor ties everything together and says the most important things. It's a waste of time to start studying before then. . . .

[or]

> When I start to study, I'm particularly sensitive to the smallest speck of dust on my desk. When I dust that off, it seems necessary to get the whole room in order before I can settle down to study.

. . . [**Moderates**] have multiple roles to enact and consequently are the group most likely to experience problems of role competition. . . . Moderates are characterized by a non-calculated effort to achieve sense of balance in their lives.

> If you can have fun and get half decent grades, you're in the best position to have a good university life.

Source: Daniel Albas and Cheryl Albas. 1994. 'Studying Students Studying: Perspectives, Identities, and Activities', in M.L. Dietz, R. Prus, and W. Shaffir, eds, *Doing Everyday Life: Ethnography as Human Lived Experience*, 273–89. Mississauga, ON: Copp Clark Longman.

Research Questions

So far, we've discussed a number of assumptions that researchers can and do make. Now we will consider how our most basic assumptions shape the ways in which we formulate and ask research questions. At the most fundamental level, the questions behind qualitative research are motivated by a researcher's assumption that research should shed light on people's real lived experiences. We want to know what people do and what people say they do in real life. How do people go about their daily lives? What sort of meanings do they attach to what they do and say? We are not interested in what they should or should not do. So, rather than ask *why* people do things, we ask *how* they participate in a particular process or *how* they start, maintain, or break their relationships with other people. For example, if I asked you *why* you are taking a class in research methods, you might tell me that the course is required, or that it falls at the right time of day, or even that your friend is taking it. If I ask you *how* you ended up taking the class, you might talk about how you got interested in sociology or nursing or whatever discipline you are studying. You might talk about how you came to attend your university or about how a professor encouraged you to consider taking courses that would prepare you for graduate school. When I ask you 'how', I usually discover 'why', but I also have the potential to learn much more about your experiences, your relationships, and the process of being in university.

Because we do not know what we will find when we enter a research situation, we must be very detailed in our observations (Prus 2005: 16). Our early observations will then help us to define our central research question. (Chapter 4 will explain and give you an opportunity to try taking initial field notes.)

When I was a graduate student, I learned the importance of taking detailed field notes before developing a research question for qualitative study. In my field methods class, my professor, Howard S. Becker, began by asking everyone to choose a research setting or topic. Then, he instructed us to go to our settings and take detailed field notes. It was only after about a month of note taking, and thinking about those notes, that we each developed our own actual research question. With a research question in mind, we were ready to do more observation and to carry out interviews with research participants that would help us to understand our observations. This method is characteristic of the Chicago School of Sociology, where researchers are told 'to go out among the people whose cultures' they are studying (Shaffir, Dietz, and Stebbins 1994: 30).

In Becker's class, one of my classmates was interested in the panhandlers who approached people in a particular park. After a few weeks, the student had noticed that the panhandlers approached some people but not others. The student could not figure out why they chose certain people. After much discussion, the class came up with a more fruitful research question about the process involved: *How* do the panhandlers know whom to ask for money? *How* do they decide who is more likely to respond positively rather than just walk away? At this point, it became necessary for the student to initiate direct contact with the panhandlers in order to ask them what kinds of people they approached, how they had learned to identify the most approachable people, and how they decided who would be most likely to respond to them positively.

Summary

And so we have come full circle. We looked at the way questions affect research, and we discussed basic differences in the ways that qualitative and quantitative researchers design and carry out research. We examined some common underlying assumptions that researchers make, and we saw examples of how researchers go about discovering generic social processes. Along the way, we noticed that both social life and qualitative research are emergent. Finally, we returned to talking about the importance of questions in the research process. In the next chapter, we will continue to explore this topic as we go through the step-by-step process of developing a research question.

Key Terms

breaching experiment
causal knowledge
deductive reasoning
definition of the situation
emergent design
ethnomethodology

generic social processes
impression management
looking-glass self
mixed methods research
moral entrepreneurs

operationalization
positivism
realist perspective
research participants
symbolic interactionism
theoretical saturation
verstehen

Questions for Critical Thought

1. Think of an example of how a particular definition of the situation had consequences in your life. How might a different definition have led to different results?

2. What are the fundamental differences between qualitative and quantitative research?

3. How well do the identities of 'aces', 'bombers', and 'moderates' fit your experience? If you do not recognize students who fit these descriptions, what identities have you noticed?

Exercises

1. With a partner, go to a public place on campus where people are gathered. Observe for about 20 minutes and take careful notes of everything you think is important. Then, meet with another pair from your class and compare your notes.

2. To practise becoming sensitive to your environment, count and record how many security cameras you see during one full day. Are there more than you expected? Were there any in places that surprised you?

3. Make a list of differences between being a consumer and being an apprentice. Focus on the assumptions you associate with each role. Which of these roles more closely relates to how you see yourself as a student? How has your perception affected how you think about and what you expect from your university?

Suggested Readings

Daniel Albas and Cheryl Albas. 1988. 'Aces and Bombers: The Post-Exam Impression Management Strategies of Students', *Symbolic Interaction* 11, 2: 289–302. The topic of this very readable article should seem familiar to you.

J. Haas and W. Shaffir. 1987. *Becoming Doctors: The Adoption of a Cloak of Competence*. Greenwich, CT: JAI Press. This book, based on a participant-observation study, documents how medical students acquire the identity of professional doctors.

Related Websites

Research Methods Knowledge Base, Qualitative Measures
www.socialresearchmethods.net/kb/qual.php

This website includes a nice discussion of the differences between qualitative and quantitative research and an overview of the methods qualitative researchers use.

Society for the Study of Symbolic Interaction
www.espach.salford.ac.uk/sssi/index.php

This is the website for the academic association of those who use symbolic interactionism in their work. It includes links to interactionist resources as well as its journal, *Symbolic Interaction*.

3 Strategies for Designing Research

Learning Objectives

- ⊛ To understand the role of the sociological imagination in identifying research topics
- ⊛ To discover common sources of inspiration for research topics
- ⊛ To learn to develop researchable questions based on a topic

Introduction

Because social life is pervasive, almost any aspect of experience can be the basis of qualitative research. This principle was first illustrated to me when I took a graduate course in field methods. My instructor suggested that we could look at anything and come up with important sociological questions. The example he used was a vending machine that sold soft drinks outside the door of our classroom. By thinking about how that machine came to be there, we could learn about student culture, about the relationship between universities and private industry, or about how we had come to depend on machines for our drinks. In other words, any aspect of collective life can tell us something interesting and theoretically important, but the research questions we choose to explore will depend on our perspective.

For example, I was passing by a bulletin board at my university the other day and I noticed a poster that was advertising for someone to donate her eggs to a couple who were unable to have a baby. At the bottom of the poster there were tear-off tabs with an email address. Several of the tabs had already been pulled off by the time I came across the poster. As soon as I saw that poster, my mind began to swirl with potential research questions. As a sociologist, my first questions were on the social meaning of being an egg donor. If I were a psychologist, I might have questioned how donating eggs affects the emotional compass of the donor. If I were a social worker, I might have wondered about what kinds of programs might be available to assist both the donor and the recipient throughout the process. And, if I were involved in religious studies, I might have been interested in the spiritual connection between the egg donor and the recipient or between the biological mother and the baby. As you can see, the perspective we bring to our work partially dictates the kinds of questions we will ask.

In this chapter, we will look at how you can move from the kernel of an idea or from a basic question—a question about something you have noticed going on among your friends or family, or even in the media—to a *research-able* question. At this point, you may be wondering exactly where to begin looking for an idea for a study. Researchers are often interested in a topic because of a personal experience or because they feel strongly about an issue. Sometimes, a researcher's professional experience may lead to a study. In other cases, a topic may be the result of serendipity—a researcher may, through chance, find him or herself in a situation that inspires a study. A researcher may also develop an interest in a topic by hanging around in a certain setting or because it is convenient. Finally, the idea for a topic might come from a researcher's interest in a theoretical challenge. But before we look at examples of where researchers find inspiration, let us consider what drives researchers to conduct studies in the first place.

Origins of Qualitative Studies

The Sociological Imagination

In identifying potential topics for a sociological study, researchers manifest what C. Wright Mills ([1959] 1976) famously called 'the **sociological imagination**'—the capacity to recognize the connection between individuals and their social context. Mills referred to the sociological imagination as 'the promise of sociology' because it allows us to identify social issues and determine the questions that need to be asked in order to understand those issues. So how can you use the sociological imagination to develop your own research questions? Let's consider a few examples that stem from Mills' work.

Mills believed that the sociological imagination could lead us to understand the connections between biography and history. In other words, he thought that we could use the sociological imagination to explain why particular types of people are tied to particular periods in history. For example, 'the greatest generation', the generation of young adults who were willing to sacrifice and remain steadfast during World War II, was defined by the experiences through which they lived. Thus, we can identify social influences that contributed to shaping that generation. We can apply this concept to our own society as well. In recent years, we have seen the growth of a new celebrity culture. Everywhere we look, we see celebrities' faces on magazines, television, and the Internet. Many people look at celebrities and their fans as individuals and associate them with 'unflattering personality traits' (Ferris 2004: 375). However, if we see the ubiquitous obsession with celebrity as a characteristic of this period in history, we can use a sociological lens to explore this situation. We can then ask questions that will help us to explain the sociological factors behind the situation: What is it about today's society that encourages a focus on celebrities? How does one become a celebrity? How does the pervasiveness of celebrity culture affect non-celebrities?

Mills also believed that the sociological imagination could help us differentiate between private problems, which exist 'within the character of the individual', and public issues, which have to do 'with matters that transcend [the] local environment of the individual and . . . his inner life' [1959] 1976: 8–10; see Box 3.1). The classic example Mills used to illustrate the distinction between private problems and public issues has to do with unemployment. If one person is unemployed in a large city, it is likely a result of his or her private problems. In such a case, the solution to the problem is individual: Perhaps he or she needs to take some job-training courses or learn how to identify job opportunities. However, if a significant segment of the population is unemployed, then this is a public issue, and it is the sociologist's task to investigate the situation: Why are there not enough jobs? How did we arrive at a situation in which so many people are jobless? How has the situation affected the morale of unemployed adults and their families?

BOX 3.1 ❖ **THE SOCIOLOGICAL IMAGINATION**

Perhaps the most fruitful distinction with which the sociological imagination works is between 'the personal troubles of milieu' and 'the public issues of social structure'. This distinction is an essential tool of the sociological imagination and a feature of all classic work in social science.

Troubles occur within the character of the individual and within the range of his immediate relations with others; they have to do with his self and with those limited areas of social life of which he is directly and personally aware. Accordingly, the statement and resolution of troubles properly lie within the individual as a biographical entity and within the scope of his immediate milieu—the social setting that is directly open to his personal experience and to some extent his willful activity. A trouble is a private matter: values cherished by an individual are felt by him to be threatened.

Issues have to do with matters that transcend these local environments of the individual and range of his inner life. They have to do with the organization of many such milieux into the institutions of an historical society as a whole, with the ways in which various milieux overlap and interpenetrate to form the large structure of historical and social life. An issue is a public matter: some value cherished by publics is felt to be threatened. Often there is debate about what that value really is and about what it is that really threatens it. . . . An issue, in fact, often involves a crisis in institutional arrangements. . . .

Source: C. Wright Mills. 1959. *The Sociological Imagination*. New York: Grove Press, 8–9. By permission of Oxford University Press, Inc.

The sociological imagination allows us to develop an understanding of how the social context shapes many phenomena that we often treat as individual problems. This approach has the potential to avoid blaming the victims of structural challenges for difficulties that are beyond their control. Framing a question in terms of a public issue has the potential to lead to very rich qualitative research as well as to transcend an individualistic, psychologistic approach.

Undermining the Hierarchy of Credibility

In any group, people tend to take it for granted that those with the highest social status have the right to define the situation. We often believe that they have the full story or are less biased and, therefore, have the right to explain the way things are. In contrast, we generally assume that those at the bottom of the social hierarchy function with incomplete information or without the skill or background to interpret things correctly. These usually tacit assumptions lead us to take more seriously, or consider more legitimate, the definition of reality advanced by the superordinate group. Sociologists refer to this tendency as the **hierarchy of credibility** (Becker 1967: 241).

In conducting qualitative research, sociologists often seek to give a voice to members of groups whose opinions are frequently ignored or unknown—those at the bottom of the traditional hierarchy of credibility. Thus, researchers seek to undermine the hierarchy of credibility by giving individuals in less influential positions the opportunity to explain, in their own terms, how they experience and understand their everyday lives.

When designing a qualitative study, you must never assume that you can get the 'best' information from the experts. For example, if you wanted to study new mothers and their experiences with childbirth, you wouldn't rely on delivery-room doctors to describe the experiences of their patients. Yes, these doctors are well-educated and understand the technical side of childbirth, but they would not fully understand the *situation* of giving birth unless they have had a baby themselves.

In my own research on old women's experiences of everyday life, I've had to navigate through many levels of the hierarchy of credibility. Think about how we know what we know about old women, in general. The information usually comes from 'the experts'. Who are these people? Well, at the top are the doctors. After them come other health-care and social-care professionals—psychologists, social workers, nurses, occupational therapists, and so on. Then come family members—often a daughter, followed by a spouse who may be considered too emotionally involved (and, in many cases, too old!) to see things 'objectively'. Finally, when there is no one else left, we are left with the woman. She is at the bottom of the hierarchy, even though she is the only person who truly knows what she feels and thinks about her own situation. In designing my studies, I've rejected this commonly accepted hierarchy by choosing to interview the women them-selves, thus giving a voice to a marginalized segment of the population.

Because qualitative researchers often seek to discover the point of view of people at the bottom of the hierarchy of credibility, they 'provoke the sus-picion that [they] are biased in favour of the subordinate parties' (Becker 1967: 241). Yet, as we discussed in Chapter 2, it is impossible to do research that is 'objective'; we always have a point of view. So we must ask ourselves, as Howard S. Becker (1967) asked in a classic article, 'Whose side are we on?' Many sociologists would answer that they intentionally take the side of the subordinate members of society, those who are at the bottom of the hierarchy of credibility, those whose voices or points of view are generally absent from any discussion. As we will discuss below, some researchers take a further step of involving participants in the design of the research, in an attempt to more fully address issues of social justice and oppression.

Participatory Action Research (PAR)

Participatory action research (PAR), a form of **community-based research**, attempts to democratize the research process by taking a criti-cal approach and working 'with (as opposed to on). . . marginalized and oppressed groups to improve and empower their position within society' (Jordan 2008: 603). This approach includes participants in all stages of the research, from planning to data collection to action, to create a situation that involves 'genuinely equal participation' (Esterberg 2002: 138). Hence, the researcher gives some control over the process to the participants. Often, these collaborations are highly effective in identifying the needs and priori-ties of the group, and a common goal of PAR is to use research findings to influence social policy or to develop interventions that improve the situation of the group. Box 3.2 lists the characteristics of PAR.

BOX 3.2 ❖ CHARACTERISTICS OF PARTICIPATORY ACTION RESEARCH (PAR)

- Involves collaboration between researchers and participants in all phases of research
- Progresses through active involvement
- Reflects and mobilizes participants' desires and needs
- Emphasizes co-construction of knowledge
- Promotes self- and critical awareness leading to individual, collective, and/or social change
- Addresses issues of oppression

Sources: Adapted from A. McIntyre. 2008. *Participatory Action Research*. Los Angeles: Sage, p. 5; and O. Fals-Borda. 1987. 'The Application of Participatory Action Research in Latin America', *International Sociology* 2 (4): 329–47.

As an example of what PAR can accomplish, let us consider Geraldine Dickson's (2000) project involving older Aboriginal women—'grandmothers'—in a mid-size Canadian city. Dickson describes her approach to PAR as 'inquiry by ordinary people acting as researchers to explore questions in their daily lives, recognize their own resources, and produce knowledge and take action to overcome inequities' (2000: 189). Because the 'grandmothers' were partners in the research and did not want the research to focus on their problems (as more traditional research might), the interviews were designed to elucidate their strengths. Dickson documents a number of actions the women took as a result of their participation in the project. She comments that these 'demonstrations of assertiveness and advocacy' reflect the grandmothers' 'growing self-confidence and improved self-esteem' (2000: 201).

Now that we have considered several of the motivations behind conducting a qualitative study, let us examine some of the more practical considerations involved in designing a research project.

Where to Find Ideas for Research Topics

Personal Experience as a Source of Research Ideas

The topics of many studies come from a researcher's personal experience. This experience may originate in childhood or be something that happened when the researcher was an adult; it may be tied to the researcher's personal life or to his or her occupation.

Norman K. Denzin, who spent thirty years studying alcoholism and its treatment, traces his interest in the topic to his early life experiences. At the time that he was beginning his study, most researchers who studied alcoholism focussed on trying to identify a specific personality type associated with presumed character flaws of alcoholics. In other words, the common perception was that the problems of alcoholics rested on some objective, innate weakness (Denzin 2009: 154). As a sociologist, Denzin was more interested in identifying treatments that might help alcoholics than in developing a so-called objective definition. As he notes, his interest in this topic was highly personal:

> The topic of alcoholism is biographically meaningful to me since I have alcoholics in my family. I wanted to make sense out of what it means to live in an alcoholic family. I wanted to know how alcoholics experienced treatment and how they came to terms with their own problems with alcohol. (2009: 158)

While there are many significant sociological reasons for studying alcoholism, Denzin's decision to study the topic was rooted in his personal connections with alcoholics.

Difficult or unexpected personal experiences can also provide the source for qualitative research. Claudia Malacrida did the research for *Mourning the Dreams: How Parents Create Meaning from Miscarriage, Stillbirth and Early Infant Death* partly to understand her own experience of losing a baby:

> My experience was not abnormal. In undertaking this project, I felt a compelling need to find something outside myself that might account for the devastation I experienced. (1998: 1)

In an equally personal example, researcher Jennifer Dunn, who had been a victim of stalking, developed a study to reveal the 'workings of patriarchal culture' that dismissed the impact of stalking or even condoned such practices (2009: 277).

Other researchers have developed an interest in an area on the basis of their professional experiences. For example, Deena Mandell, who wrote *Deadbeat Dads* (2002), worked as a clinician with families who had experienced divorce. She struggled with the challenges of working with non-supporting fathers who presented themselves as 'hostile, self-interested, and provocative' (2002: 3). She knew that she had to understand the point of view of these fathers if she was to work with them successfully, and a study was born.

Donileen R. Loseke found aspects of the women's shelter in which she worked in the 1970s difficult. As she puts it, she wore 'many hats' and had 'divided loyalties' as a PhD student, evaluator, and volunteer at the shelter (2009: 265). Like many researchers who work with abused or marginalized individuals, Loseke ran into beliefs that victims, in this case battered women, were at least partly to blame for their situation. When Loseke was working in the shelter, several situations puzzled her. First was the distinction workers made between 'battered' and 'not-battered' women. Second was the unequal treatment the women received from the workers. Loseke's research grew out of her desire to understand these two phenomena.

Sociologists have even found their experiences as professors to be good sources of research ideas. Daniel and Cheryl Albas, whose research we discussed in Chapter 2, found that their encounters with students led to a research topic that has spanned their careers. As they see it, their study was 'forced upon [them] by students from the first day of class'. They observed that their students' obsession with their marks manifested itself in questions about exams starting in the very first class. As young academics, the Albases wanted to learn as much as they could about their students' ways of life. They hoped to use this knowledge to draw out the students' 'own best academic efforts' as well as to do their jobs as educators effectively (Albas and Albas 2009: 105).

Lesley D. Harman, who carried out the first Canadian ethnography of homeless women, also drew inspiration for her study from her experiences as a professor. She writes:

> I was giving a lecture in the sociology of deviance at York University, and one student asked, 'What's all this about "bag ladies"? I've never seen one and I don't think we have any in Toronto.' I suggested that the fact that she lived, worked, shopped, and studied in North York might have something to do with her perceptions, and that she might have a change of heart if she ventured downtown. The next week she could hardly wait to announce to the class that she had 'seen one' . . . and that 'there really are such things as "bag ladies"'. My interest in the cultural production of homeless women grew, and came to encompass a concern for the experience of homelessness among the increasingly visible category of women. (Harman 1989: 9)

For Harman, her student's offhand comment led her to identify a topic that interested her and that had not been adequately explored from a sociological perspective at the time.

Often, a research topic develops out of a combination of personal and professional experiences. Kathy Charmaz, for example, author of *Good Days, Bad Days: The Self in Chronic Illness and Time* (1991a), a wonderful study about individuals' experiences of chronic illness, locates the origin of her study in a combination of the personal, both in childhood and as an adult, and the professional. In looking back, she has written, 'I grew up in the shadow of disability and illness' (Charmaz 2009: 48). Perhaps because of her history, Charmaz practised as an occupational therapist before becoming a sociologist. In that role, she noticed things that troubled her:

> I observed instances of staff blaming patients for their lack of progress, inadequate motivation, denial of their disabilities, and I attended several patient–staff conferences that dissolved into degradation ceremonies. . . I saw first-hand the powerful consequences of professionals' derogatory definitions of patients whose view of their situations clashed with staff's. And I realized that staff and patients lived in separate worlds. (2009: 49)

The final inspiration for her study came from an experience she had with a friend who had spent much of her life in a wheelchair. One day, she was with her friend when a branch from a nearby tree fell and knocked into the arm of the woman's wheelchair. The woman exclaimed in surprise, 'It *hit* me!' At this moment, Charmaz realized that the wheelchair 'had become part of the woman's self-concept' (2009: 49). All these observations came together in the form of a research question focussing on how chronic illness affects an individual's sense of self and of time. In addition, Charmaz's example suggests an element of serendipity in the chance occurrence of witnessing a branch strike her friend's wheelchair.

Serendipity as a Source of Research Ideas

Among the most fascinating and theoretically rich studies are those that originate with **serendipity**. In relation to qualitative research, *serendipity* refers to accidental discovery and spontaneous invention (Stebbins 2008). When we talk about serendipity in the development of a research question, we are referring to situations in which the scholar accidentally discovers a social setting or research area when not specifically looking for one.

Clinton Sanders, author of *Customizing the Body: The Art and Culture of Tattooing* (1989), states that his interest in tattooing was the result of 'simple chance'. He explains that he was in San Francisco for several days without any commitments. He decided to browse through the Yellow Pages to find an interesting museum to visit, and he happened upon a listing for the Tattoo Art Museum. He decided to visit the museum, even though he knew nothing about tattooing and had never even been in a tattoo shop. By the time he left the museum, he had visited the 'adjacent tattoo shop [and] impulsively chose[n] a small tattoo' (2009: 63). Thus was born his research interest.

Serendipity can also take the form of a fortuitous personal meeting. Such was the case for Robert Prus, who describes a chance encounter with a student named Styllianoss Irini. At the time, Irini was working as a desk clerk in a hotel that 'served as "home base" for people involved in a . . . variety of disreputable and illegal activities' (Prus 2009: 238). In time, that first meeting led to collaboration on an ethnography of such activity and their co-authored book, *Hookers, Rounders, and Desk Clerks*.

Another example of a serendipitous meeting that led to a study comes from Timothy Diamond's *Making Gray Gold: Narratives of Nursing Home Care* (1992). In his introduction to the text, Diamond reveals that he first became interested in nursing-home culture when he happened to encounter two nursing assistants in his local coffee shop. Over the course of several months, Diamond developed a friendship with the women, and he enjoyed hearing about their work. Then, suddenly, the two women stopped coming to the café. This second unexpected event left Diamond with many unanswered questions and increased his curiosity, leading him to develop his important research project on life inside a nursing home (Diamond 1992: 1–3). Thus, in Diamond's case, two instances of serendipity—his initial meeting with the nursing assistants and the sudden interruption of their friendship—led him to develop his study.

A final example comes from my own experience as a researcher. I had studied with Helena Z. Lopata, who carried out the first major studies of women's experiences as widows, but I had never thought about doing a full-fledged study myself. Then a student lent me a short book by M.T. Dohaney, *When Things Get Back to Normal* (1989), in which the author records her experiences during her first year as a widow. By the end of the book, I was so deeply moved that I cried along with the author and felt that, for the first time, I was beginning to understand the huge emotional impact that becoming a widow has on a woman's life. This book made such a strong impression on me that I found myself collecting and analyzing all the published first-hand accounts of widowhood I could find. That initial study eventually led to my larger interview study of widows and my first book, *The Widowed Self: The Older Woman's Journey through Widowhood* (2001), and then to my study of older men's experiences as widowers and my second book, *By Himself: The Older Man's Experience of Widowhood* (2010). Hence, I have spent the last 14 years studying widowhood all because a student unexpectedly lent me that first short book.

'Hanging Around' to Find a Research Topic

Related to serendipity is what we sometimes call 'hanging around' or 'mucking around'. In this approach, the potential researcher spends time in a setting that looks as though it might be a fruitful site of research. Frida Furman describes such a situation as the genesis of her study of beauty-shop culture:

> The very first time I went to Julie's International Salon to get my hair cut, some eight years ago, I could sense that there was something compelling about it, though I could not quite put my finger on what exactly was going on there. But it had to do with older women congregated together in an all-female salon, manifestly for the purpose of hair and nail care, who seemed to be part of a lively and affirming community. For the next three years, I toyed with the idea of doing a study of this beauty salon. . . . Finally, in 1991, I could resist the place no longer. (1997: 1)

For Furman, the simple act of going to a salon to get her hair cut inspired her to develop a research project. The setting was so engaging that it simply pulled her in and wouldn't let go.

In other cases, a researcher might be inspired to design new research while hanging around a setting for professional reasons. Jaber F. Gubrium (2009) narrates a situation in which he visited a nursing home, Murray Manor, with the intention of gathering preliminary information to help him design a survey on the impact of environmental living designs on quality of life in nursing homes. While he was 'mucking about', he spoke with the residents and staff informally, to 'get a feel of nursing-home life' (2009: 123). In the end, these conversations led him to carry out an ethnographic study of Murray Manor.

Selecting a Topic because It Is Convenient

Some sociologists end up picking topics because they are convenient. This was the case for Patricia and Peter Adler, whose studies have involved their own children. They write:

Our children's social worlds enticed us as an object of study, not only because they were fresh, challenging, important, and unbelievably complex, but because studying them offered us the ancillary benefit of spending more time with our children during their important and formative years. (2009: 226)

In the end, they conducted research on children's experiences and wrote their book *Peer Power: Preadolescent Culture and Identity* (1998), not only because they found their own children's daily experiences fascinating, but also because it was convenient for them to involve their children in their study.

I had a similar beginning to my research on retirement communities, *The Aging of a Florida Retirement Community* (1992). My parents had moved to a condominium-type retirement community in Florida, where I found the social world intriguing. By doing my master's and doctoral research on their community, I was able to study something fascinating while giving my children and myself more time with my parents.

Combining Personal with Theoretical Questions in Research

Although the above studies were inspired by the researchers' experiences, they succeeded because the authors had good theoretical reasons to conduct them. In some cases, researchers work the other way around, starting with a theoretical challenge and then locating their particular study in personal experience.

A good example of this approach comes from Leslie Bella's *The Christmas Imperative: Leisure, Family and Women's Work* (1992). In designing her study, Bella began with a desire to critique what she calls 'the androcentric bias in leisure theory'. She believed that men had developed the concept of leisure to explain the part of their lives when they were not at work. Women, she felt, did not experience leisure because they were always working around the home. As Bella notes, after establishing the theoretical foundation of her work, she turned to observations from her family life to support her perspective:

I narrowed my empirical study to family celebrations of Christmas for reasons that initially had more to do with my personal pain around the season than with the theoretical justification. . . . I coined the phrase 'the Christmas imperative' to capture this compulsion to reproduce Christmas and began the research needed to explain its origins, describe its impact, and promote its transformation. (1992: 11–12)

In other cases, a researcher may arrive at a topic through an equal combination of personal and theoretical interests. This was the case for Andrea Doucet in her study *Do Men Mother?*:

Three particular instances sparked my interest in the 'do men mother?' question. One was an observation at home, the second was a decade of academic inquiry, and the third was an inquisitiveness about embodied gender differences and parenting. (2007: 10–11)

Many researchers also find themselves returning to a single theoretical interest, even if their studies address seemingly disparate topics. For example, I have studied widows, widowers, old women, and Iranian Bahá'í refugees who have settled in the Atlantic provinces of Canada. These topics are united by my overriding interest in the experience and social meaning of being a member of a marginalized social group.

How to Begin Your Own Study

What can we learn from the experiences of the researchers we have talked about? First, the topic you decide to study should be one that 'grabs you' (Pawluch 2009), one about which you have 'a powerful compelling curiosity' (Heilman 2009: 198). As we shall see, qualitative research takes a lot of work, but that work will be very exciting if you are really interested in your topic. Second, you can find your research ideas anywhere. As Bruce Berg (2009: 21) has written, 'the world is a research laboratory . . . you merely need to open your eyes and ears to find numerous ideas'.

Start Where You Are and Acknowledge Your Limitations

To begin, you should choose a topic or setting with which you have some familiarity, something you are interested in or care about. Lofland and Lofland (1995) call this 'starting where you are' and suggest that you find something you care about independent of your interest in social science.

You must also recognize that not all topics are appropriate for all researchers. For example, if you are too emotionally involved in a topic, you may be unable to be 'meet the standards of good, scientific work' and, therefore, '[your] unavoidable sympathies [might] render [your] work invalid' (Becker 1967: 246). In addition, if you find a topic too difficult to talk about, you should acknowledge that you might not be in the best position to study that topic. For example, I recognize that I would not be comfortable interviewing women who had lost their children, as I would find it too emotionally overwhelming. As such, I have never conducted a study on the topic of losing a child, yet many researchers who feel more comfortable with the topic have conducted in-depth studies on this type of loss. Similarly, while I do not find it unbearably difficult to hear about the emotional impact of becoming widowed, many others would not feel the same way. Once, a student in one of my qualitative research methods classes decided to interview a widow to complete an assignment. Whenever the woman became emotional, the student steered the interview onto another topic because she found it uncomfortable and embarrassing when the widow began to cry. Obviously, this student could not do a thorough study on women's experiences of widowhood.

Although you will not always be able to identify how you will react to interpersonal discussions in a research setting before you begin, you should try to be honest with yourself about whether you can tackle a particular topic. Joseph Alex Maxwell (2005: 27) suggests that someone considering a particular topic write a 'researcher identity memo' that includes his or her 'goals, experiences, assumptions, feelings, and values'. This memo will allow you to see if there are any concerns about the viability of your taking on a particular topic as well as to identify your own particular strengths and resources.

Starting where you are will also help you to avoid topics that are not feasible for you to address. For example, you may be unable to gain access to some settings. In many cases, you will be limited by personal factors such as your age, experience, background, and even gender. Social settings that involve social elites—politicians, corporate executives, 'A-list' celebrities, and so on—are notoriously difficult for 'outsiders' to penetrate.

At the same time, your personal characteristics or experience may give you a way of approaching a group that other researchers would find impossible to access. This was the case for Daniel Wolf, author of *The Rebels*, a study of an outlaw motorcycle gang. Wolf grew up in a lower-class neighbourhood and witnessed his friends being sent to prison for crimes such as grand theft auto. He managed to get work in a factory to pay for his university education, but he also participated in the motorcycle culture and shared some of the bikers' views. As he admits, it was this background that gave him the wherewithal to carry out his study:

> I bought myself a . . . motorcycle [and] . . . rode with lean women. . . .
> But it was more than that. I rode my motorcycle in anger; for me it became
> a show of contempt and a way of defying the middle class that had put me
> down. . . . In retrospect, I believe that it was this aspect of my non-academic
> background—the fact that I had learned to ride and beat the streets—that
> made it possible for me to contemplate such a study, and eventually to ride
> with the Rebels. (1991: 10)

In other words, it was Wolf's class background and experience that allowed him to find a way into this challenging social setting. At the same time, I, coming from a middle-class background, to say nothing of my gender, could never dream of studying a group like the Rebels.

Another potentially limiting factor to take into account is the amount of time and money you might need to study a topic. Particularly, as a student, you might have very tight time constraints. Thus, whenever you are designing a study, always consider whether the project is doable in the time allotted.

Finally, remember that, while you want to start where you are when you choose a topic, you do not want to end in the same place as you began. Your topic should take you beyond the point of view you had when you started.

Lynn Davidman, for example, studied the topic of secular Jewish women turning to the very conservative, traditional denomination of Orthodox Judaism for *Tradition in a Rootless World* (1991). This topic arose partly from Davidman's background. She was following the dictum, start where you are. Her initial research question was 'Why in the world would anyone do this?'—notice the strong bias implicit in the question. But Davidman did not end where she started. She was open enough to develop more 'suitable questions', such as 'What is the meaning of this experience for the people who choose it?' and 'How can I better understand . . . their attraction to Orthodox Judaism?' (1999: 82).

In recent years, it has become very common for students to want to study the same topic, related to a strong experience they have had, in every class they take. For example, if a student's parents are divorced, she or he may want to write papers only on the topic of what it means to be the child of divorced parents. Such a narrow focus can lead to 'me-search' rather than research. If you find yourself in this situation, try to branch out and explore other topics. This approach will help you to develop as a researcher and to end up in a place that is different from where you started.

Developing Research Questions

Once you have chosen a research topic, you need to develop research questions that will allow you to create a plan for collecting and analyzing data. In developing questions for a qualitative study, remember that your aim is to produce results that are descriptive and analytical rather than **prescriptive**. You might decide to collect data about what people believe about climate change, how they learned about climate change, or how they have altered their behaviour in response to learning about climate change. You cannot, however, answer questions about whether it is right or wrong for people to change their behaviour in light of what they know about climate change.

A first step in choosing research questions for your study is to brainstorm a list of questions. As you develop this list, keep in mind that these questions are preliminary—you will likely need to adjust your questions as time goes on in response to what you learn. Also, focus on developing questions that you find interesting and that will hold your attention for the duration of the study.

A good way to begin brainstorming is to think about how generic social processes, which we discussed in Chapter 2, relate to your topic. As an example, let us look at how we might use these processes to develop research questions to address the topic of first-year students' transition to university.

First, consider the process of 'acquiring perspectives'. This process refers to how we learn to define objects in certain ways or to have particular attitudes towards objects or individuals. When we think about students who are entering university for the first time, we might develop a number of questions related to this generic social process: How do first-year students learn the attributes of a 'good prof' compared to a 'bad prof'? How do they learn to believe that the only things that count are grades, and, as a consequence, worry more about how they will be graded than what they actually learn in class?

Next, consider the process of 'achieving identity'. This process relates to how one becomes an object to oneself. It includes the 'associations and negotiations' that people have with others (Prus 1987: 275). As you might expect, this process is particularly salient when one undergoes a transition. In the case of transitioning from high school to university, most individuals look forward to leaving behind their old identity; they associate being a university student with social prestige, and they often make efforts to display their new status. Knowing this, we might ask questions about how students display their new status: How do students convey to themselves and to others that they are now *university* students? Do they trade in their high school jacket for a sweatshirt with their university's name emblazoned on it? If so, how does changing the paraphernalia—that is, jackets, bags, notebooks, and so on—from that of the student's high school to that of her or his university contribute to the student acquiring the identity of a university student?

Once you have settled on several questions that will guide your research, you will ascertain whether your questions are suitable to be addressed using qualitative research methods. If you ask questions related to generic social processes, and you are looking for results that are *descriptive* and *analytical*, then qualitative methods are for you. If you want to address a puzzling issue or one that we know little about, and you want to allow participants to explain their points of view, then qualitative methods are for you.

Determining a Theoretical Stance

As we noted in Chapter 2, one of the strengths of qualitative research is its flexibility. You, therefore, do not need to be wedded to a particular theoretical perspective throughout the life of your study. Often, you will adapt your perspective based on your findings. But you do have to have an initial standpoint when you are developing your research questions. Hence, someone with a feminist stance would likely develop questions related to issues of gender. Someone whose standpoint tends towards a Marxist approach might develop questions that focus on the accomplishments of labour. In many cases, a researcher will combine elements from multiple perspectives to establish his or her own approach. For example, Meg Luxton, in her classic book *More than a Labour of Love* (1980), combined a feminist and a Marxist approach to conceptualize the work women do in the home as labour to emphasize her idea that this type of work is not valued as highly as work in the paid labour force.

Michael Atkinson (2003) had an interest in the sociology of the body that influenced his approach to and interpretation of the phenomenon of tattooing. He, therefore, approached his topic as one particular 'body project' in an era when being 'fit' and staying 'young' have created multi-billion-dollar industries. In contrast, Clinton Sanders, who was interested in the sociology of deviance (1989), focussed more on acquiring the identity of a tattooed person and how that person managed his or her impression as a 'normal' person.

Think of your theoretical stance as a jumping-off point for your research. Your findings may lead you to query unexpected theoretical issues. Your ability to remain open to this possibility will add richness to your work. As an example, although I approach much of my work through a gender lens, I had not expected to focus on masculinity when I began my study of widowers. Because I was open to new approaches as the data demanded them, I incorporated issues around masculinity into my analysis.

Choosing a Method

Once you have chosen your topic and identified your research interests, you will need to start thinking about what method or methods you will use. We will discuss several methods in greater depth in future chapters, but for now you should consider how your choice of a method relates to the questions you want to explore.

If you are interested in an activity that is connected with a specific geographical location, you will likely want to conduct an observational study. For example, if you want to learn about the culture of your favourite pub, you will need to spend time in that location. You will have to muck around. (In Chapter 4, we will talk in more depth about how to conduct an observational study.)

In contrast, if you are interested in 'amorphous social experiences—those facets of everyday life that are unique to individuals and not to specific kinds of settings' (Kotarba 1980, quoted in Lofland and Lofland 1995: 20), then you will be more likely to use qualitative interviews to collect your data. In that case, you will have to consider what kinds of people are likely to have the answers to the questions you want to address. As you are deciding whom to interview, avoid relying on the hierarchy of credibility—whenever possible, interview the individuals closest to the lived experience you want to study. (Chapter 5 discusses the processes involved in conducting in-depth interviews.)

In some cases, you may not need to interact directly with research participants at all. For example, if you are interested in how the media contribute to our social definitions, you could gather your data through unobtrusive measures such as reading newspaper articles or watching television programs. (We shall examine various methods of unobtrusive research in Chapter 6.)

Of course, many studies use a combination of methods to collect data. For example, when I was interviewing Bahá'í refugees from Iran about their experiences in Atlantic Canada, I found it useful to attend Baha'i meetings to observe how these immigrants fit into the wider Baha'i community. Observing these individuals in this setting helped me to understand the definition of the situation in that culture. Currently, I am involved in a study that is looking into how the publishers of *Zoomer Magazine* are attempting to create a new identity for baby boomers as they approach the end of middle age. I have begun my research by doing an unobtrusive study of the magazine itself, but at some point I will likely interview some members of the target demographic to find out what they think of the magazine and if it has had any impact on them.

Consulting the Literature

Most qualitative researchers do at least some reading about their research topic and setting before they begin their research. Literature reviews in qualitative research, however, serve a different purpose from literature reviews in most quantitative studies.

In quantitative studies, the researcher usually reads literature related to his or her topic to develop hypotheses that she or he will test in the process of research. The researcher then collects data to see if they confirm the hypotheses. So, for example, I might read literature that suggests that people who have more education display lower levels of prejudice. I would then design my study by developing **indicators** of prejudice—for example, being unwilling to live on the same street as a person from this or that group and not wanting my daughter to marry a person who is a member of a particular group. I would then design a questionnaire that collects information about the level of education my respondents have and where they would fall on my scale of prejudice. Finally, I would analyze my data to see if there were, indeed, a correlation between education and prejudice.

In a qualitative study, the literature serves quite a different purpose. Qualitative researchers read broadly in the area they are interested in and about similar social settings to help sensitize themselves to the issue they plan to study. Qualitative researchers must read very broadly because diverse social settings may involve similar social processes. Thus, if you were studying how divorced people acquire an identity, you might read Helen R. Ebaugh's book *Becoming an Ex: The Process of Role Exit* (1988), which looks at people who have left the clergy, ceased practising as medical doctors, and gone through other types of identity transitions.

As is the case in quantitative studies, having a good idea of what has been published on your topic will help you to situate your study within the greater body of research. It will also give you an idea of what has already been done, and it may even inspire you to create a new study to fill a gap in the existing literature.

Summary

In this chapter, we have looked at how researchers come up with topics for their studies. We talked about how the sociological imagination drives researchers to study the social factors that shape individuals' daily lives. We also discussed the qualitative researcher's goal of undermining the hierarchy of credibility. Thus, Denzin wanted to understand the experience of being an alcoholic from the point of view of the alcoholic, while Charmaz sought to uncover what chronic illness is like for those who suffer with it. In addition, we looked at where you can find ideas for research topics. We observed that many studies originate in the personal experiences of the investigators, but we also noted that researchers must have strong theoretical reasons to carry out a study. Most importantly, we learned that it is often a good idea to start where you are, but you do not want to end up where you began.

The questions you want to answer will determine the research methods you will use to collect and analyze your data. The next three chapters deal with how to implement specific data-collection techniques. The fun is just beginning!

Key Terms

community-based research	indicators	serendipity
hierarchy of credibility	participatory action research	sociological imagination
	prescriptive	

Questions for Critical Thought

1. What is the difference between a private problem and a public issue? Is there a problem on your campus that might be solvable if people understood that it was a public issue?

2. Have you observed any social issues that you would like to address in a qualitative study? How might you approach this topic to give voice to those at the bottom of the traditional hierarchy of credibility?

3. Is there an aspect of your life that you would like to conduct research on? If you were to design a study based on your experience, do you think that you could be open enough to 'start where you are' without ending where you started?

4. How do the different assumptions underlying qualitative and quantitative research affect the ways in which researchers use literature reviews in each of these approaches?

Exercises

1. Spend 15 minutes studying the posters on a bulletin board in a popular location. Think of what these posters tell you about the social setting. Develop several researchable questions based on one of the posters.

2. Think about doing a study on the topic of student life. Identify any social processes involved in this topic, then write down all the questions you can think of that might lead to a qualitative research project on this topic.

3. Imagine that you had to conduct a study about what life is like for prisoners in a jail. Make a list of the participants in prison life, indicating which ones would be at the top of the hierarchy of credibility and which ones would be at the bottom. Decide how you would go about undermining the hierarchy of credibility in your study.

Suggested Readings

Howard S. Becker. 1998. *Tricks of the Trade: How to Think about Your Research while You're Doing It.* Chicago: University of Chicago Press. In this practical book, Howard S. Becker shares techniques he has learned that help us to think about our research projects. You will find this book useful at all stages of your research process, from the inception of an idea through collecting data to finally writing up the results.

Joseph A. Maxwell. 2005. *Qualitative Research Design: An Interactive Approach,* 2nd edn. Thousand Oaks, CA: Sage. This practical book, part of Sage's research methods series, provides a good step-by-step guide to designing qualitative research.

Antony J. Puddlephatt, William Shaffir, and Steven W. Kleinknecht. 2009. *Ethnographies Revisited: Constructing Theory in the Field.* New York: Routledge. In this eminently readable book, authors of classic qualitative studies write about their experiences carrying out research. Topics include the genesis of a researcher's interest in a particular topic and how to transform general interests into studies.

Related Websites

Howie's Home Page
http://home.earthlink.net/~hsbecker/

This is the website of Howard S. Becker. Here, you will find information on Becker, copies of his articles, and links to many interesting and useful sites.

The Sociological Imagination Group
www.sociological-imagination.org/

This website for the Sociological Imagination Group provides information and resources in support of the group's goal to correct 'the failure of sociology to live up to what C. Wright Mills called "the promise of sociology"'.

4 Observing Social Life through Field Research

Learning Objectives

⊛ To learn about the development of ethnography in North America
⊛ To learn how to prepare for and implement a field work study
⊛ To understand how to write good field notes

Introduction

So far, we've discussed the basics of qualitative research, we've noted how qualitative research differs from quantitative work, and we've looked at how to go about designing a study. Now we have come to the point of actually carrying out research—it's time to get our hands dirty. In this chapter, we will learn about the history of **ethnographic** field research and the stages involved in carrying out a field study. As you will learn, there are many ways to go about conducting field research. A field study might tackle a setting as broad as a neighbourhood (see Gans 1967) or as small as a hairdressing salon (see Furman 1997), and the studies themselves are as varied as the social settings they examine. Therefore, you must be flexible and creative with your approach when carrying out your own field studies.

Before we begin, we must understand the purpose of field research. In conducting a field study, a researcher attempts to understand everyday community life from the perspective of the participants. The researcher therefore strives for 'intimate familiarity' (Prus 1993) with the group he or she is studying. Thus, field work requires the researcher to immerse him or herself in a social setting. It involves 'observing people *in situ*, finding them where they are, [and] staying with them in some social role', which allows the investigator to observe their behaviour, analyze it, and report on it in ways 'useful to social science but not harmful to those observed' (Hughes [1960] 2002: 139).

The most common method of field work is participant observation. This technique involves becoming a participant in the setting while retaining some distance as an observer. We will examine the levels of participation from which a researcher can choose later in this chapter.

For now, let's take a brief look at some of the important stages of the evolution of ethnographic field work across history.

Historical Antecedents of Contemporary Field Work

Ethnographic field work has a long history that dates back to the fifth century BCE, when the ancient Greek Herodotus, generally regarded as the first Western historian, recorded descriptions of the Persians and the Scythians. Herodotus travelled widely and gathered 'legends and anecdotes' about the peoples he visited (Lateiner 2004: xvi). He was fascinated by the influence that the natural environment had on cultural forms. For example, as he observed, the Scythians used animal bones and fat as cooking fuel because there were few trees in their environment (Waterfield 1998: xxxviii).

Before the latter half of the nineteenth century, most ethnographic reports were made by travellers—explorers, missionaries, merchants, and colonialists—who recorded their observations of the foreign peoples they met on their voyages. Often, these reports offered the people back home voyeuristic accounts of life in culturally and geographically distant societies. For example, when Marco Polo (1254–1324) returned from his time in the Mongol empire, many of his fellow Europeans were enthralled by his accounts; in fact, Polo's descriptions were so unprecedented at the time that many people did not believe his stories because they could not picture a life so different from their own (Silk Road Foundation 2000). While many early travellers' accounts were highly insightful and informative, others were very provincial, **ethnocentric**, or biased. For example, much research that took place at the height of the colonialist period presented indigenous peoples as 'primitive' and 'other'. In some ways, these accounts tell us more about the writers and their social backgrounds than the cultures about which they were writing.

In the nineteenth century, there was an increased interest in domestic ethnographies, as investigators wrote about conditions in their own societies to promote social change. John Howard, for example, wrote about the conditions of prisons in eighteenth-century Britain. He penned *The State of Prisons in England and Wales* (1777), which included 'the meticulous recording and reporting of what he saw, in order that the general public might be made aware' of the terrible conditions (Hay 2010). In 1883, Beatrice Potter, a social reformer, did participant observation among the underprivileged. She disguised herself as 'Miss Jones, a farmer's daughter,' to bring attention to the plight of the poor in Britain at that time (Berg 2009). The same motive inspired English businessman Charles Booth to undertake a massive 'survey' (door-to-door visits, interviews, neighbourhood observation, etc.) of the living and working conditions of the inhabitants of late nineteenth-century London. Booth published his account, *Life and Labour of the People in London*, in multiple editions and ultimately 17 volumes between 1889 and 1903. Today, these volumes are counted among the founding works of British sociology, and they have had a substantial impact in North America.

Ethnographic reports became more scientific during the late nineteenth and early twentieth centuries as anthropological ethnographers began entering the field. These researchers went to 'exotic' places to document the cultural practices of what were then thought of as primitive peoples. Most influential was Franz Boas (1858–1942), the father of modern cultural anthropology (Prus 1993), who studied the Kwakiutl (Kwakwaka'wakw) peoples on Canada's west coast.

Field work in sociology, although contemporaneous with the development of cultural anthropology, developed 'somewhat independently' (Prus 1993: 6). Though a handful of studies were carried out around the turn of the century, ethnographic research in sociology first became truly prominent at the University of Chicago, beginning in the 1920s.

The Chicago School of Sociology

The early ethnographies from the **Chicago School of Sociology** focussed on social processes and problems that sociologists associated with urban life. Chicago sociologists regarded the city as a 'laboratory' for social research (Faris 1967: 52) and concentrated on two, often interrelated, sets of phenomena—race and ethnic relations and crime and deviance—by doing careful studies of institutions, neighbourhoods, and zones of the city. The early twentieth century was a period of massive immigration to the United States and to large urban centres, such as Chicago, in particular. Chicago sociologists took advantage of the opportunity to study first-hand the social processes by which culturally diverse newcomers adjusted not only to one another but also to the more established social groups and cultural practices they encountered on coming to America. Many of these immigrants, as well as many members of more established groups, had trouble adjusting to big city life and fell into poverty and/or a life of crime. At the time, the common perception was that poverty, crime, and suicide among slum dwellers reflected innate biological qualities of the population. The early studies of the Chicago School demonstrated that the problems of poor people were not a result of individuals' innate weaknesses but rather a 'consequence of the experience of social disorganization' (Faris 1967: 62–3). In other words, the issues associated with poverty grew from the social context, not from individual deficiencies or problems.

Ethnographies from this period include *The Hobo* (Anderson 1923), discussed in detail in Box 4.1; *The Jack Roller* (Shaw 1930), which deals with the experiences of young offenders; and *The Taxi-Dance Hall* (Cressey 1932), which explores taxi-dance halls where 'male patrons would dance with the woman of their choice for a "dime a dance"' (Prus 1993: 12). These books were

Box 4.1 ⊛ *THE HOBO*

One of the earliest and most important studies to develop out of the Chicago School was Nels Anderson's *The Hobo* (1923). Anderson had been a 'hobo' himself and had intimate familiarity with the way of life. The study provided insight into the 'lived experience of homeless men' as well as the urban environment in which they lived (Prus 1993: 11). In particular, it was the first study to identify the concept of 'killing time' as a problem for the homeless.

> 'Killing time' is a problem with the homeless man. . . . For the vast majority, there is no pastime save the passing show of the crowded thorough fare. . . . The homeless man, as he meanders along the street, is looking for something to break the monotony. He will stand on the curb for hours, watching people pass. He notices every conspicuous person and follows with interest, perhaps sometimes with envy the wavering movements of every passing drunk. If a policeman stops anyone on the street, he also stops and listens in. If he notices a man running down the alley, his curiosity is aroused. Wherever he sees a group gathered, he lingers. He will stop and listen if two men are arguing. He will spend hours sitting on the curb talking to a congenial companion. (Anderson 1923: 215)

The concept of 'killing time' continues to have resonance today, as Leslie D. Harman (1989) discovered in her study of homeless women.

---

groundbreaking in that they depicted the social worlds of members of so-called deviant groups. For example, Shaw discovered that, in every case, boys were led into delinquency by experienced delinquents and, therefore, were conforming to the expectations of a **primary group**. This finding moved the understanding of deviance from an individualistic understanding of youth problems to one that acknowledged the social circumstances of the boys' lives (Faris 1967: 76).

During the twentieth century, the ethnographic tradition made popular in sociology by the Chicago School developed through a series of American field studies, including *Street Corner Society* (Whyte 1955), *Boys in White* (Becker et al. 1961), *Asylums* (Goffman 1961), *Outsiders* (Becker 1963), *Passing On* (Sudnow 1967), *Talley's Corner* (Liebow 1967), *The Levittowners* (Gans 1967), and *Making the Grade* (Becker et al. 1968).

Ethnography in Canada

As you might expect, the development of ethnography in Canada has been heavily influenced by the Chicago School sociologists of the early twentieth century (see Box 4.2).[1] Yet even before the Chicago movement had arisen,

BOX 4.2 ❊ THE CHICAGO SCHOOL AND McGILL: CARL DAWSON AND EVERETT C. HUGHES

Without a doubt, it was the efforts of sociologists Carl Dawson and Everett C. Hughes at McGill University in Montreal that did the most to establish the practice of ethnographic sociological research in Canada in the first half of the twentieth century. Dawson, a Canadian from Prince Edward Island, and Hughes, an American born in Ohio, had earned their PhDs in sociology at the University of Chicago. Both were deeply influenced by Robert Park, one of the principal founders of the Chicago School, and are widely regarded as having established an 'outpost' of Chicago sociology at McGill (see, for example, Wilcox-Magill 1983: 1–10).

Dawson was appointed to the McGill University faculty in 1922 and, in 1925, founded an independent sociology department there, the first in Canada. While at Chicago, he had adopted the human ecology approach, and it was this orientation that contoured the research program that he and Hughes developed at McGill during the 1920s, '30s, and '40s (Wilcox-Magill 1983: 1–10). Indeed, with Warner E. Gettys, Dawson wrote *An Introduction to Sociology*, a textbook modelled directly on Robert Park and Ernest W. Burgess' 'green bible' of Chicago sociology, *An Introduction to the Science of Sociology* (1922). Dawson and Gettys' text, which came out in three versions between 1929 and 1948, not only played a legitimating role for the sociology program at McGill (Helmes-Hayes 1994: 474) but was fundamental in supplementing the interactionist elements that characterized the classical human ecology framework (467). In particular, later editions of the *Introduction* incorporated 'a generic interactionist social psychology' that stressed concepts of interaction and process rather than structure (470). As well, during his long career at McGill, Dawson did some research that employed field work techniques (see Dawson 1934, 1936; Dawson and Younge 1940) and, more importantly, supervised the thesis work of several students who undertook field work–based studies of various occupational, religious, and ethnic groups and communities in Montreal and on the Canadian prairies (for example, Brown 1927; Davidson 1933; Bayley 1939).

Hughes was regarded by many prominent ethnographers as a—if not *the*—master field worker in the Chicago tradition (see, for example, Riesman and Becker 1984; Riesman 1983; Chapoulie 1987, 1996; Helmes-Hayes 2010). Recruited to McGill in 1927, Hughes played a central role as a champion, teacher, and practitioner of ethnographic research. He had a background in both anthropology and sociology and was deeply familiar with the field work traditions in both disciplines. During the 1940s and '50s, he taught the field work course at the University of Chicago and helped put together two versions of a field work guide and source book (Hughes et al. 1952; Junker 1960) that were used by generations of students at Chicago, McGill, and elsewhere. As well, during his time at Chicago, he taught and/or worked with some of American sociology's most prominent field work researchers—Anselm Strauss, Blanche Geer, David Riesman, Howard S. Becker, and Erving Goffman, to name a few (Helmes-Hayes and Santoro 2010). Since his death in 1983, his influence has spread from North America to Europe, France and Italy in particular (see Chapoulie 1996; Helmes-Hayes and Santoro 2010).

Hughes helped to carry out a number of important American ethnographies, including *Boys in White* (Becker et al. 1961) and *Making the Grade* (Becker et al. 1968), but his most important and influential Canadian ethnography was *French Canada in Transition* (1943), a detailed analysis of the process of industrialization as it took place under the control of British and American capital in a small Quebec town during the 1930s. Though Hughes left McGill to return to Chicago in 1938, he continued to have a major impact on Canadian sociology. He maintained direct links with McGill's sociology department and, through Jean-Charles Falardeau, a key figure in Québécois sociology of the period, forged a strong and long-lasting connection with Laval University (see, for example, Falardeau 1953). Indeed, throughout the forties, fifties, sixties, and seventies, dozens of Canadian students made the trek south to do graduate work in Chicago (and later at Boston College and Brandeis) with Hughes. A number of the early ones, Aileen Ross and Jean Burnet among them, returned to Canada to become faculty members at McGill, Toronto, Laval, and elsewhere. This group published important field work–based research (see, for example, Ross 1952, 1953, 1954; Burnet 1951) and stewarded the field work culture until the sixties and seventies, when it finally became a part of mainstream sociological practice.[2]

As Chicago-style ethnographic research became more common in Canada, McGill began to lose its stature as the epicentre of interactionist sociology and ethnographic research. By the late seventies, most of the faculty employing Chicago-style research methods had retired or moved on. Since then, McMaster University has emerged as the primary ethnographic research and training centre in Canada (Milne and Helmes-Hayes 2010).

Source: The text for this box was carefully researched and written by Canadian sociologist Rick Helmes-Hayes (University of Waterloo) and Emily Milne (McMaster University).

Canadian researchers had already shown an interest in sociological ethnography and begun to engage in field work to study—and in many cases to try to assist—underprivileged social groups. For example, in the late nineteenth century, businessman and social reformer Herbert Brown Ames carried out a thorough study of the living and working conditions of 38,000 people who inhabited a working-class neighbourhood with deep pockets of poverty in Montreal. As a follower of the Social Gospel, a progressive version of Protestantism popular at the time (Allen 1971), Ames believed that he had a moral obligation to press for social change that would help alleviate the social problems—slums, poverty, crime, etc.—that had developed in the wake of massive immigration, rapid urbanization, and unregulated industrialization. Ames' published account of his study, *The City below the Hill* (1897), has come to be viewed as one of the most important early sociological ethnographies in Canada.

There is also a long tradition of ethnographic research among French-language researchers in Canada. Key early researchers include Charles-Henri-Philippe Gauldrée-Boileau, who wrote *Paysan de Saint-Irénée* (1875), which was published in Quebec in 1968; Léon Gérin, who published *L'habitant de Saint-Justin* (1948); and Horace Miner, who produced *Saint-Denis: A French Canadian Parish* (1930). Everett C. Hughes (see Box 4.2) was also influential. His book *French Canada in Transition* was translated into French as *Rencontre de deux mondes: La crise d'industrialisation du Canada français* (1972).[3]

Ethnographic research developed later in Atlantic Canada. With the growing interest in anthropological field work, Memorial University of Newfoundland established the Institute for Social and Economic Research in 1961 to foster research into the many social and economic questions arising from the particular historic, geographic, and economic circumstances of Newfoundland and Labrador (ISER 2010). Many of the resulting ethnographic studies required social researchers to move to local communities and spend considerable time doing participant observation. A few researchers even 'married into' the community. Some of these studies have become enduring classics in ethnographic research, and their titles express the engagement of the researcher with the vital concerns of the community: *Fisherman, Logger, Merchant, Miner* (Philbrook 1966), *Brothers and Rivals* (Firestone 1967), and *Marginal Adaptations and Modernization in Newfoundland* (Wadel 1969).

Now that we have briefly explored the historical influences that have led to contemporary practices, let's consider how you might go about conducting your own field work.

Conducting a Field Study

The first steps in your field study will begin when you are at the research-design phase (discussed in Chapter 3), as you develop your research questions, identify your participants, and assess the nature of the setting. When designing a field study, you will need to choose your setting carefully. Recall that some settings are easier to get into than others. If the setting is a public place like a zoo or a park, then getting in should not be a problem. You simply have to show up. If the setting is restricted or exclusive—for example, a prison, the offices of a corporation, or the meeting place of a secret society—you may find it more difficult to gain access. In addition, some settings may be dangerous, and you may need to take specific precautions to protect your own safety. This was the case for Patricia Adler (1985) when she chose to study a community of drug dealers and smugglers. If you are considering conducting a study in a closed or dangerous setting, you may need to engage in covert research. There are ethical issues to consider if you plan to do covert research, as we will discuss in Chapter 10.

As soon as you decide on a topic and a setting, you should begin taking notes. If you do not write your ideas down, you will likely forget them. To start, you should keep a notebook or a computer file where you can record your initial musings, observations, and encounters. I always keep a notebook with me when I am preparing for a study. Recently, I started planning a study of the Red Hat Society,[4] and I have started a notebook where I record any articles or other media coverage of the group I come across. The other day, someone mentioned to me that he knew a woman who had been a Red Hatter but had left the club. You can bet that I have that information in my notebook. When I start my study, I will try to contact the woman to get her story.

Preparing to Enter the Field

Before you enter the field, you must plan how you will approach your intended research setting and the participants in that setting. For some studies, this preparation begins with reading. If there is literature about the setting or if members of the organization have published pamphlets, articles, or books about it, you would be wise to read these documents. This background research will give you information about who the participants are and the nature of the setting (Berg 2009). For example, in preparing for my study of the Red Hat Society, I have read books by the founder of the organization, Sue Ellen Cooper, and I have subscribed to the organization's weekly email newsletter. I have also read articles other researchers have written about the Red Hat Society, even though these articles reflect research interests that differ from my own.

In addition to reading, you should spend some time hanging out at the setting until you develop a firm research plan (Rossman and Rallis 1998: 95). You will want to 'case the joint' (Schatzman and Strauss 1972: 9), if possible, to familiarize yourself with the 'routines, realities of factionalism, and the social structure' of the setting (Shaffir et al. 1980: 23). This preparation will help you decide if the setting you have chosen is an appropriate place to study your topic.

This is a good time to define the boundaries of your field setting and think about who you are in relation to the site. You should also think about any connections to the setting that you might already have, in preparation for deciding on your level of participation and developing your story line.

Levels of Participation

Once you have gotten a lay of the land, you must decide how you want to participate in your setting, what role you will take. In 1952, Buford Junker suggested a typology of roles from which the field researcher can choose: **complete participant, participant as observer, observer as participant,** and **complete observer** (Junker 1952, cited in Gold 1958).

When taking the role of the complete participant, the researcher attempts to become a full-fledged member of the group he or she is studying. The researcher, in this case, conceals his or her intent to study the group. An example of a complete participant is Timothy Diamond, who studied life in nursing homes for *Making Gray Gold* (1992). He went to vocational school to become certified as a nursing assistant and took jobs in several nursing homes. He, thus, became a full participant in the workforce.[5] Similarly, Daniel R. Wolf (1991) discovered right away that he would not be able to study outlaw bikers if he explained his goal at the outset. So, before he asked the group's leaders for permission to conduct his study, he 'establish[ed] contact with the Rebels as a biker who also happened to be a university—anthropology—student' (13–14). As it turned out, Wolf rode with the Rebels for three years before telling them that he was doing a study.[6]

The participant as observer makes her or his presence as a researcher known to the group and attempts to form relationships with the members of the group. This is the most common strategy that researchers use in field research, and it is most appropriate when the researcher has something in common with the members of the group. For example, Claudia Malacrida (1998), who lost a child to stillbirth, was both participant and researcher in the support groups she attended as part of her research on how parents cope with the loss of a baby.

The observer as participant also informs the members of the research setting that he or she is doing research but carries out a less involved role. If the investigator is visibly different from the participants in meaningful ways, this may be the only participatory role available. For example, when I was doing my research on retirement communities, I was in my thirties. Even though I participated in many social activities, I was too young to be accepted as a member of the community.

In the role of the complete observer, the researcher does not interact with the members of the setting and might not tell anyone that she or he is doing a study. The researcher simply tries to be accepted or 'tolerated as an unobtrusive observer' (Marshall and Rossman 2006: 98). I took this role when I observed a wetland preserve in South Florida. As I walked around and made observations, I blended in with the many people who took walks on the boardwalk there on a regular basis. In general, the role of the complete observer is most useful in research involving public places or public sites on the Internet.

Keep in mind that these four roles are not mutually exclusive—they are **ideal types**, and researchers often straddle the line between two roles. The line between observer as participant and participant as observer is particularly fuzzy. As well, researchers often move from one role to another as they carry out their research. Wolf, for example, continued to ride with the Rebels after he told them about his study, but he was no longer a full participant. In his new role as participant as observer, he experienced what Shaffir, Dietz, and Stebbins (1994) have referred to as the 'marginality' that all known researchers experience.

All four roles have advantages and disadvantages. Complete participation offers an unobstructed view into participants' lives, but there are obvious ethical issues associated with this approach. In addition, the complete participant risks identifying so strongly with the group members that she or he loses the ability to look at the situation analytically. In some settings—particularly, those involving cults, gangs, and radical political groups—the members may even 'actively seek to convert the researcher' (Warren and Karner 2010: 98). In the role of participant as observer or observer as participant, the investigator has the advantage of being a 'known incompetent'; as a result, insiders will 'teach him [or her] things [and] tell him [or her] things they would never tell one another' (Schwartz and Jacobs 1979: 55). The disadvantage of these roles is that the very marginality that allows the researcher to appear as incompetent prevents her or him from gaining an insider's understanding of the group. Finally, because the complete observer has to rely on what she or he notices and overhears in the setting, she or he may misinterpret the meanings that behaviour and interactions have for the participants.

Once you have decided what level of participation you will start with, you need to prepare to interact with your setting. If you are doing overt research, as is most likely, you will need to develop a story line.

Story Lines

Your story line is the explanation you provide to individuals in the setting about the purpose of your research and how you would like to participate. As you are preparing to enter the field, take the time to develop a standard story line that you can give to everyone. If you try to tailor your explanation to the interests of each person you encounter, you will likely lose track of what you have told each person, and you may undermine your own credibility. Unless you have a compelling reason to do otherwise, you should be truthful about your work. Always answer questions about the research as honestly as possible, and avoid being condescending.

Keep your explanation simple. The story should not be too detailed, or it can commit you to a focus that is too narrow (Schatzman and Strauss 1972: 24). As Lofland and Lofland (1995: 39) recommend, your explanation should be 'brief, relatively straightforward, and appropriate to the audience'. Most people are only interested in a broad overview of your study rather than a long, technical explanation. Often, just telling people that you are interested in them or their organization is sufficient. When I studied a Florida retirement community, I simply told participants that I was interested in learning about the way of life in their community. This explanation was truthful and it satisfied the curiosity of my participants.

Gaining Access

As Adler and Adler (1987: 12) note, the Chicago School researchers, whose early activities entailed 'hanging out' and building up to asking 'what's going on?', had little difficulty in gaining access to their research settings. Based on this precedent, Adler and Adler suggest that field researchers should simply 'enter their settings, announce their intentions, and begin to interact with the people they encounter' (1987: 12). In recent years, partly in response to ethical concerns (see Chapter 10), this approach has waned, but it has not disappeared and, in many cases, it can be quite successful.

William Shaffir and Samuel Heilman, who conducted separate studies of religious Jews, both describe an entry process that includes hanging around, getting to know some people, and frequenting synagogues. Shaffir (2009: 214) struck up conversations with young Hassidic men who were as curious about his world as he was about theirs. Heilman (2009: 203) explains that his approach was 'deceptively simple': he began to go to synagogues, spend time in yeshivas, and wander along the streets of ultra-orthodox neighbourhoods.

Many groups will appreciate the interest of the researcher, particularly if the study deals with an issue that the members feel does not get the attention it deserves. In such cases, the group will likely welcome the researcher into its community. Karen March, who attended self-help groups of adoptees who were seeking information about their birth parents to gather research for *The Stranger Who Bore Me*, recounts such an experience:

> Entering the field . . . I found little difficulty. . . . The two self-help groups . . . were members of [a] larger Canadian self-help search organization [and had] monthly meetings which were open to the public. Non-members attend meetings frequently. . . . Thus, when I contacted both groups . . . I was told to 'just come, mingle with the members, and see what happens.' . . . When I arrived at my first meeting, I found that most group members accepted my presence. (1995: 88)

Claudia Malacrida relates a similar experience:

> At the beginning of the [support-group] meetings, I made known my dual role as participant and researcher by outlining my personal interest in the topic, the purpose of my research, my commitment to the anonymity of the group, my willingness to leave at any time if participants felt uncomfortable with my dual role. . . . No one objected to me either privately or in the group setting; in

fact, many people made a point of expressing their support that this particular topic was being given much-needed attention. (1998: 139)

Establishing Relationships with Gatekeepers

Often, you will need to obtain permission to conduct your study from a gate-keeper, a leader within the group. **Gatekeepers** are individuals who have the power to deny or grant access to a social setting (Berg 2009). In many cases, they have formal authority, and their position as a recognized leader is clear. In other cases, their power may be informal, and their position may not be immediately obvious. In such cases, you may need to hang around to discover who has the status to influence other members in accepting or rejecting your presence within the community.

The way you present your story line to a gatekeeper is very important. If gatekeepers believe that the research will make their organization or them-selves appear in a positive light, they will be more likely to give you access. If they suspect that you are a muckraker or plan to evaluate their organization or threaten their position, they may turn you down. In some cases, it might be useful to build on pre-existing relations of trust to remove barriers (Lofland and Lofland 1995: 38), but a gatekeeper will not always grant you access simply because you have a pre-existing relationship. In fact, some gatekeep-ers might even be hostile to your efforts *because* of a past relationship.

I approached such a gatekeeper when I was doing my research on widows. I wanted to observe a support group that was facilitated by a former student. However, when I phoned to ask for her permission, she was immediately wary of my coming. Eventually, she gave me permission to attend one meeting, with the stipulation that I could continue to attend if the group approved. When she invited me to attend this first meeting, she gave me an incorrect time. So, when I showed up at what I thought was the correct time, I was actually half an hour late. Thus, I began with the group on the wrong foot. After the meeting, the gatekeeper told me that the members were uncomfortable with my presence at the meeting because I was not a widow, but she suggested that I could help them with a tea they put on monthly for 'seniors'. After a few months, the gatekeeper told me I was no longer welcome to help with the teas because the women were uncomfortable with my presence. Later, when I ran into a member of the group at a social event, she told me that the members of the group missed me.

In retrospect, my guess is that this gatekeeper saw me as a potential threat to her status as leader of the group because of my former position as her pro-fessor. Had I been clearer that I was not a threat, that I just wanted to sit in and listen, things might have turned out differently. Or, they might not have. I will never know. The moral of the story is to be very thoughtful in your approach to any gatekeeper. If you do find yourself in a situation in which the gatekeeper shuts the door to the setting, you should be flexible enough to figure out another way to conduct your research. In my case, I organized a six-week workshop for widows that was facilitated by other widows. Both the participants and I benefitted greatly.

In contrast to my experience, a gatekeeper who already trusts you may let you in with the briefest of explanations. For example, Frida Furman (1997: 9) describes what happened when she presented her idea for studying beauty-shop culture to the owner of the beauty salon:

> I asked [Julie] permission to conduct an ethnographic study of her salon. She happily agreed, suggesting that she herself had more than once thought her customers' stories would make a good read. While Julie may not have known exactly what an ethnographic study entails, she seemed flattered by my interest in her work and her world. She was a fine advocate of this project from the start. (1997: 9)

As you may recall from Chapter 3, Furman had been a regular customer of the salon for several years, and her relationship with Julie made it easy for her to ask for permission.

You may also need to consider making a **bargain** with the gatekeeper. This bargain often entails a promise of confidentiality. As with any study, you must also protect the confidentiality of your participants. In making a bargain with a gatekeeper, you must avoid promising to report back to the gatekeeper or to disclose information that could have a negative impact on any participants, especially if they are subordinate to the gatekeeper. The gatekeeper might also insist on hearing about your eventual findings. Occasionally, a gatekeeper will want to approve your analysis before you publish it. Most researchers would avoid agreeing to such a condition. However, it is possible that the researcher would agree in rare situations, particularly if the gatekeeper had commissioned the study. There are alternatives. For example, Elliot Liebow, in *Tell Them Who I Am* (1993), a field study of women's homeless shelters, shared his analysis with one of the women as well as a manager of one of the shelters he studied. He included their response to his analysis in notes his book, but he did not change his analysis.

Gaining Support from Sponsors

Sponsors are individuals who have deep ties to the community and can provide access to certain settings and populations in informal ways.[7] For example, Elliot Liebow (1967), in *Talley's Corner*, explains that after hanging around with young African-American men in a poor neighbourhood, he developed a friendship with Talley, who 'vouchsafed' for him, introducing him to a circle of friends and acquaintances.

Often, a sponsor will be more willing to facilitate your entry into a group if you show a genuine interest in his or her social world. Michael Atkinson (2003) found this to be the case when he was looking for a sponsor to help him access the tattoo scene in Calgary. Box 4.3 provides his description of how he got support from a local tattoo artist. You will notice that Atkinson

Box 4.3 ❊ Connecting with a Sponsor to Gain Access

Before attempting to access the wider world of Calgary's tattoo scene, Michael Atkinson decided to find a sponsor who could help ease him into the setting. Atkinson notes that he was not entirely a newcomer to the community, and he had even briefly encountered his potential sponsor, Jack, in a previous trip to the tattoo shop in which Jack worked. Atkinson used his background knowledge and experience to approach Jack in the most appropriate way:

> I knew that Wednesday was often a slow workday . . . and thought it would be an ideal time to re-introduce myself to [Jack]. . . . With some nervousness I approached Jack . . . and asked him if he remembered me . . . He nodded . . . and we began to talk about tattooing . . . I showed him some of my existing tattoo work . . . Showing your tattoo work . . . buys a certain amount of street credibility . . . . (Atkinson 2003: 74–5)

After discussing each of his tattoos, Atkinson revealed the purpose of his visit. As it turned out, Jack was amazed that someone wanted to do research on tattooing and tattoo artists and even more surprised that Atkinson had received funding to do the study. Jack's enthusiasm was apparent:

> [Jack] rushed to the back room, then brought back an armful of articles, books, and historical pieces on tattooing . . . and for about an hour and a half we pored through the texts . . . I left the studio feeling that . . . I had found a potential site to begin my venture into tattooing in Calgary. (Atkinson 2003: 75)

hung around and became familiar with the rhythms of work in tattoo shops before he approached his potential sponsor.

There is one caveat regarding sponsors. Individuals who are immediately welcoming to newcomers are often outsiders in their own social circle. You should, therefore, be cautious of aligning yourself with any individual who offers you an overly warm welcome. Becoming associated with a marginal member of a social group may make others wary of you and close off association with central members of the group (Warren and Karner 2010: 77).

Entering the Field

Once you have gotten permission to do your study, you will need to think about how to approach your setting for the first time. Of course, if you have been hanging around, the participants will already know and recognize you. Some of this advice, therefore, equally applies to earlier stages.

First impressions are important. If you have made an appointment with a gatekeeper or a sponsor, make sure that you are punctual. Also, remember that your dress and your demeanour should be appropriate to the setting. If the participants dress informally, you should too. Don't try to mimic their dress too closely if they are noticeably distinct from you. For example, if I were studying teenage girls, I would look ridiculous if I tried to dress like them; at the same time, I might dress less formally for such a setting than I would if I were studying an adult population.

Gaining the Group's Trust

When you first enter your research setting, you will likely be seen as an outsider. If you have gained entree through an individual who is not trusted by the majority of the group, you may find that some people in the setting will worry that you are a spy. For example, if you have been granted permission by a top-level gatekeeper such as an employer, some participants, particularly those in positions subordinate to the gatekeeper, may be very leery of you. If this is the case, you need to figure out how to gain the group's trust and convince them that you have not been sent by management to spy on them. Box 4.4 illustrates one researcher's successful attempt to gain the trust of his participants.

An effective way to gain trust and build rapport is to adopt the attitude of a learner or to take the role of an 'incompetent' (Lofland and Lofland 1995: 40). Asking questions at this stage will show that you respect the knowledge of your participants and communicate your genuine interest in their affairs. Of course, it will also help you to gain an understanding of the group and the environment.

Establishing Your Place in the Group

In the early days of your study, you will need to establish your role in the setting. As we discussed above, you will have some control over your level of participation, but the members of the group will define where you fit in and 'accord [you] a particular role or social place in that setting', a process of **incorporation** (Warren and Karner 2010: 85). This process involves negotiation between you, as the researcher, and the participants in the setting.

As you spend more time in the setting, your role may change. Gary A. Fine (1996), for example, started out his research in restaurant kitchens by standing in a place that was out of the way. As time went on and the cooks got to know him, they allowed him to perform small tasks, such as peeling potatoes.

Michael Atkinson (2003: 76–7) recounts that his initial encounter with Jack had 'a profound impact' on the role he adopted as he continued his study. In response to Jack's fervent interest in literature on tattooing, Atkinson chose to establish himself as 'a provider of academic information

---

BOX 4.4 ❀ BUILDING TRUST IN THE RESEARCH SETTING

When Gary A. Fine (1996) wanted to gain access to restaurant kitchens, he had to approach the managers of the restaurants for permission. With the managers' consent, he entered the environments, but he found that the kitchen workers were initially concerned that he might be a spy for the managers or that he might be conducting a time-use study that would result in lost jobs.

> Because [restaurant kitchens] are not public arenas, access is provided through management; as a consequence, researchers will have, even in the most optimal circumstances, a burden of trust to overcome (Burraway 1979). Whose side are we on (Becker 1967)? As a result, who I *really* represented was an issue, although one that became muted when it grew clear that I was not reporting to the management. . . . [O]ften, my role emerged in the context of joking and teasing but always with an underlying concern. . . . This [concern] became salient when I observed minor deviance, especially among low-status workers, who feared my power over their careers. (Fine 1996: 234)

Eventually, as Fine spent more time in the kitchen and the workers became more comfortable with his presence, they began to trust him and were less inhibited in their actions. As Fine notes, to be accepted by the group, he had to prove that he was aligned with their interests by establishing a reciprocal relationship:

> These workers trust[ed] that I [would] place myself on their side as a true, if limited, member of their group, embracing its underside. . . . As I gave them leeway, they returned the favour. (Fine 1996: 234)

---

on tattooing and [an] avid tattoo client' (2003: 76). Because Jack accepted him in this role, others within the community likewise accepted him and treated him as an informed participant.

Clinton Sanders (1994: 205), who conducted a similar study of tattoo culture, started by hanging around tattoo studios as one of a number of 'hangers-on' who lived in the area. In time, Sanders' role became more extensive. He writes:

> I routinely helped with the business of the shop. I made change for the amusement games, provided information about cost and availability of designs, stretched the skin of customers who were receiving tattoos on body areas other than arms or legs, calmed the anxiety of first-time recipients, and, in a variety of ways, made myself genuinely useful. (1994: 205)

By participating in the daily routines within the studio, Sanders gained first-hand experience of what daily life was like for his participants.

Making Observations and Taking Field Notes

Once you are in the field, you must be very attentive to your surroundings. Keep in mind that *you* are the research instrument—you must depend on your observations, what you see and hear, to produce results. If you have not been in your setting before, you may want to begin by mapping the location and identifying the subgroups and central figures within the population. As Goffman has commented, your initial observations in the field are particularly important: 'The first day you'll see more than you'll ever see again. And you'll see things that you won't see again. So, the first day, you should take notes all the time' ([1974] 2004: 152).

As you get to know people, you will begin to ask questions. Although you will have collected a lot of information about your setting and the people in it before you entered the field, the participants will know a lot more about what is going on than you do. Remember that the people you are meeting are the experts in their own lives; they know what is going on and can help you to understand. They are the only ones who truly know what certain things mean to them.

During these early days, you will be able to ask questions about what is going on as a naive, new participant. This is the easiest time to ask questions about things that are obvious or invisible to participants. After a while, the people in the setting will expect you to have learned these obvious things. You should also show interest in the people and their lives and demonstrate reciprocity by listening to stories and helping out with some simple tasks.

As you can imagine, it would be impossible to remember everything you learn in the field. Therefore, you will have to keep detailed records of what you see, hear, feel, and do. These records are called **field notes**, and they are absolutely essential to field research. Field notes are so important that Emerson, Fretz, and Shaw (1995: 1) refer to their production as 'one of the core' activities of ethnographic research.

Writing field notes will also help you to organize your thoughts. As Esterberg (2002: 73) has observed, 'writing is a way of making meaning'. As you write your field notes, you will begin to make sense of what you see because putting experiences into words inevitably requires some interpretation. Although consistent note-taking requires a lot of time and discipline, the process will become exciting when you begin to make meaningful connections within your setting.

The next two sections explain the two stages involved in creating good field notes: making **jottings** in the field to help you remember details and writing up your full field notes based on your jottings.

Making Jottings

When you start observing at your research setting, you should direct your mind to remember things at a later point. With practice, you can become quite good at this, but you will never be good enough to remember everything.

Box 4.5 ⚙ Advice for Making Jottings

- Record what you know has happened versus what you think has happened.
- Record your observations during or immediately after the event.
- Abbreviate your words and consider using standardized coding forms (we will discuss coding in detail in Chapter 7).
- Use a grid to represent different areas within the setting and make jottings on what happened in each area in the appropriate section of the grid to save time.
- Record even seemingly unimportant things.
- Use concrete words.
- Compile a lexicon of local terms used by participants.

For this reason, you should carry a notebook with you so that you can make jottings at any time. Jotting down brief notes—phrases, quotes, and key words—at your field site will help you to jog your memory when you go to write your full field notes later on. If you want to remember longer dialogues, you can make more extensive jottings to preserve the actual words that you hear. (See Box 4.5 for tips on making jottings.)

There is no single, correct way to take jottings. As you practise, you will develop your own style. Your jottings are not for anyone else to read, so the most important thing is that they work for you.

When, where, and how to write jottings depend on your research site. In some settings, you won't have any problem with overtly taking notes while you are observing. If you are sitting in a coffee shop, no one will feel uncomfortable if you occasionally write things down (although, if you seem to be staring and writing, staring and writing, you may make people uncomfortable). In other places, taking notes while the action is going on may be rude or inhibit natural social interaction. If you are at a party, people might think it weird if you take notes. The general rule is to take notes in a way that fits with your setting. Often, researchers withdraw to a quiet place to write jottings and then return to the scene. There is an old joke about ethnographers needing to take frequent trips to the washroom (Hammersley and Atkinson 1983: 147).

If you are in a setting where writing in a notebook fits in well, you may be tempted to write full field notes while you are observing. I advise against this practice because it is impossible to write and pay full attention to what is going on at the same time. If you are too involved in writing about one event, you may miss something else that is happening—just think about how often you have missed something your professor said because you were taking extensive notes on a topic that was just covered. Wait until you have left the field to write your full field notes.

Writing Up Full Field Notes

One of the most common questions students ask about writing field notes is what to include. The short answer is everything you can remember. It is probably impossible to have too much detail.

Recording as many details as possible is important because you never know what might be relevant later on. For example, when I was studying the retirement community, I noted that people often referred to 'ring around the collar' to make note of grease marks in the pool. I wrote the phrase down even though it did not seem important at the time. Later, I realized that the comment was representative of the residents' strong sense of ownership of the common areas in the community, and my notes about that phrase became important.

As you write your notes, avoid making statements that characterize what people do in a general way. Be precise. Avoid 'opinionated words which lend themselves [more] to [evaluation] than to detailed, textured descriptions' (Emerson et al. 1995: 32). If you are observing the checkout point at your university's cafeteria and someone pushes into the line, do not write that the person was very rude. Instead, write exactly how the person moved into line. Did she or he walk in front of someone while looking off to the side or avoiding eye contact in some other way? Did the person say anything to the individual he or she cut in front of? Did they seem to know one another? What did other people do when this event occurred? By providing concrete details, you focus on what people do rather than what you perceive them to be.

This is not to say that you shouldn't record your own ideas and reactions to what you observe. Just remember to clearly distinguish between what you actually observed and what you think or feel about it. Some researchers find it helpful to keep two different files: one for field notes and one for personal memos. Others like to separate field notes and memos into two separate columns in the same file. I prefer to put my reactions in brackets within the field notes because this allows me to see my thoughts in direct relation to my observations.

Similarly, when you write about what people say, be sure to distinguish between the words they actually use and your paraphrased notes. You can use quotation marks to note when you are writing down people's words verbatim. This distinction is important, for the terms people use to refer to events or to others may provide clues that will help you to identify concepts when you are analyzing your data.

What you write in your field notes will change over the course of your project. During the early days, your notes will be fairly general. You will likely focus on recording your first impressions, providing a physical description of your site, and describing the cast of characters you meet. As you get to know your setting better, issues and questions will emerge from your observations, and your notes will become more selective to reflect your growing understanding of what is going on. As time passes, you will come to recognize the events that are most important to the people who are in the setting. Notice what they stop to look at and what they talk and gossip about (Emerson et al. 1995: 28). Keeping good notes of these issues will help you to discern what is meaningful to those in your setting.

Another common question that students ask is *when* they should write their field notes. Often, in the early days of your study, you will find it difficult to allocate time to write because you will be worried that you might miss something important in the field. If you find yourself in this position, you need to begin by accepting that you cannot observe everything at all times. In addition, spending too much time in the field can lead to fatigue, and you may miss things even if you are physically present in your setting. As your study progresses, you will be able to find the rhythm of the setting and identify the periods with the least amount of action. These relatively quiet periods will likely be the best times for you to withdraw to write up your field notes.

It is important to write your field notes as soon as possible after leaving your setting. Once you have left the field, go directly to your computer and do not talk to anyone about what happened until your field notes are complete. As time passes, the 'immediacy of [your] lived experience fades, and writing field notes becomes a burdensome, even dreaded experience' (Emerson et al. 1995: 41). In contrast, when you write your notes soon after you return from the field, you will be able to include the 'idiosyncratic, contingent character' of what you observed (Emerson et al 1995: 14) and the writing process will be much easier. Writing your notes without delay helps to avoid the 'homogenizing tendencies of retrospective recall' and allows you to record 'vivid memories and images' (Emerson et al 1995: 14). Writing up your notes after each session will also help give you an overview of your day's progress and help you plan for the next session in the field. If you act promptly and take the time to write thickly descriptive field notes, you will end up with the data you need to find patterns in your social setting. (We will look at data analysis in Chapter 7.)

As you are writing up your field notes for the first time, remember that every researcher has a different system for organizing his or her observations. I've included a sample of my own field notes in Appendix B, for your reference, but you will need to develop a system that works for you. In general, you will almost always want to structure your field notes so that they provide a running chronology of events, people, and conversations. This means that you should record the precise time, date, and place that you made your observations. Also, try to use complete sentences to describe your experiences. This will force you to form complete thoughts on your observations and it will help you ensure that you have not left out any important details. Keep in mind that your writing must be clear—a reader should be able to visualize your experiences in the field after he or she has read your full field notes.

Warren and Karner (2010) refer to writing full field notes as drudgery. I would not go that far, but writing up your field notes does take discipline and effort to overcome the pull of procrastination. It also takes a lot of time to write good field notes. You should plan to spend at least as much time writing up your field notes as you did observing. Michael Atkinson (2003: 76), for example, notes that he spent three to six hours writing up his field notes after each period of observation. Because this process is so labour intensive, you should always keep back-up copies of your full field notes. This will prevent you from having to go back and recompose your notes if you happen to lose the files due to a computer error.

At some point, you will likely find that you have become too familiar with your setting and that you cannot make any observations that you have not already made. When you can no longer learn anything new from your setting, it is time to leave the field.

Leaving the Field

No project can go on forever, and you will eventually have to decide how to withdraw from your study. Conventional wisdom suggests that you should leave the setting in a manner that would not make the entrance of a future researcher difficult. In some situations, you can simply stop going to the site. However, if you have established relationships with your participants, you must take more care in deciding how you will leave the field. Think about how a good guest would leave. Express your appreciation for your participants' hospitality; do not simply disappear. In some situations, you may want to promise to share your findings or plan a return visit. If you make these promises, make sure you fulfill them. You want to leave your participants feeling positive about their experiences in your study.

Summary

In this chapter, we have explored aspects of field research. We looked at the development of ethnographic studies, primarily in North America in the past century. We discussed how to plan and prepare for a field study. We examined the four main levels of participation that researchers use in their participant-observation studies, and we learned the importance of creating a coherent story line and of establishing relationships with gate-keepers and sponsors. Finally, we explored what to do once you are in the field—how to interact with participants, take jottings, and transform your jottings into field notes. In Chapter 5, we will look at another form of data collection: the qualitative interview.

Key Terms

bargain	ethnography	observer as participant
Chicago School of Sociology	field notes	participant as observer
	gatekeepers	primary group
complete observer	ideal types	sponsors
complete participant	incorporation	
ethnocentrism	jottings	

Questions for Critical Thought

1. If you were conducting field research in your own city, what groups do you think you could easily get access to? What groups might be the hardest for you to access? How might you go about gaining entree into some of these groups?

2. If you had unlimited access and infinite resources, what social setting would you most want to study? What fascinates you about the setting you chose?

3. Which research role from the participant-observation continuum would you prefer to adopt in your own studies? What advantages and disadvantages are involved in the role you chose?

Exercises

1. With a partner, have a five-minute conversation without taking notes. Share with each other how much you remember from the conversation.

2. With a partner, go to a public site and begin making observations. Without consulting your partner, make jottings on what you see and hear. When you have finished observing, compare notes with your partner. Identify any differences between the notes and think about why you might have missed something that your partner noted.

3. With a partner, observe a setting without making any jottings. After you leave the setting, wait an hour and then write down everything you can remember. When you are finished, trade notes with your partner. Make a list of observations that your partner recorded but that you did not include in your notes. Were there any significant details that you had forgotten about? How many details do you think that you both forgot about?

Suggested Readings

Robert M. Emerson, Rachel I. Fretz, and Linda L. Shaw. 1995. *Writing Ethnographic Fieldnotes*. Chicago: University of Chicago Press. This book provides very practical advice for novice ethnographers. It focusses on how to take jottings and field notes.

Lesley D. Harman. 1989. *When a Hostel Becomes a Home: Experiences of Women*. Toronto: Garamond Press. This study provides an excellent overview of an ethnographic study. Chapter 3, 'Becoming a Volunteer', which deals with getting in and learning the ropes, is particularly useful.

Elliot Liebow. 1967. *Talley's Corner*. Boston: Little, Brown. This classic ethnographic study is a very readable exemplar of good field research.

William Foote Whyte. 1993. 'Revisiting *Street Corner Society*', *Sociological Form* 8, 2: 285–98. In this article, Whyte talks about how he went about carrying out this classic study. He muses on the methods he used in light of more recent developments in ethnography.

Related Website

The Qualitative Report
www.nova.edu/ssss/QR/index.html

This website, maintained by Nova Southeastern University, includes links to an online journal for qualitative research (*The Qualitative Report*), a weekly qualitative report with a list of notable new articles, and other useful qualitative research resources.

5

In-Depth Interviewing

Learning Objectives

- To understand the strengths of qualitative interviews
- To discover ways of identifying participants for a qualitative interview study
- To learn how to construct an interview guide and conduct an interview
- To learn how to transcribe interviews

Introduction

In the last chapter, we explored field research. In this chapter, we move on to another form of data collection: in-depth interviewing. First, we assess **standardized interviews**, or surveys, to better understand their limitations and the reasons why qualitative researchers prefer to conduct **in-depth interviews**. Then, we take a brief look at different types of and approaches to in-depth interviews. Finally, we learn how to design and conduct an in-depth interview study.

Interviews have become so common in everyday life that sociologist David Silverman (1997, 1993) has dubbed our society the 'interview society'. He points out that interviews are a centrepiece in the mass media, market research, and political polling. It is the rare person who has escaped being interviewed about some aspect of her or his life. Most of the time, the type of interview we encounter in our personal lives is the standardized interview, or survey.[1] As qualitative researchers, we are more interested in conducting *in-depth* interviews. To understand this preference, let us look at the assumptions underlying the use of standardized interviews and the inherent limitations in this type of data collection.

Standardized Interviews

Your telephone rings and, when you answer it, the person on the other end asks you to participate in a survey. If you say yes, you spend the next several minutes answering questions that require you to agree or disagree with a particular opinion, to rate things on a scale of one to five, or to select an option from a list of predetermined responses. You have just experienced being an interviewee in a standardized interview.

In general, standardized interviews reflect a positivist approach to research. Investigators use them to collect 'standardized information about a large number of respondents relatively cheaply' (Fontana and Prokos 2007: 21), often to test hypotheses. Standardized interviews are most useful when the researcher wants information that is unambiguous and knows the 'very thing' that she or he wants to uncover (Schwartz and Jacobs 1979).

This type of interview assumes that the researcher can minimize or eliminate bias by making everything in the interview uniform. It functions on a stimulus–response model that suggests that if you standardize the stimulus (that is, the questions and the way that the interviewer reads them), the variations in answers represent a true measure of what you are investigating (Mason 2002: 65). As such, a standardized interview consists of a standard protocol or a questionnaire that the interviewer always reads in the same way and in the same order so that the 'stimuli' will be the same across all the interviews. Even the introduction at the beginning of the interview is scripted. The interviewer is trained to treat every situation in a like manner (Fontana and Prokos 2007). If the respondent does not understand a particular question, the interviewer is not permitted to rephrase it. Typically, he or she will simply repeat the question (Esterberg 2002).

Questions in this type of interview are worded to collect structured data. Therefore, the questions are usually what we call **closed-ended** or **forced-choice questions**. In answering this sort of question, the respondent must choose his or her response from a list of answers provided by the interviewer. Ideally, the researcher tries to offer answers that are as exhaustive and mutually exclusive as possible. In other words, the researcher designs the answers to include all possibilities and avoid any overlap. Therefore, a question meant to discover a respondent's age cannot present the options as '20 to 40 *or* 40 to 80'—anyone under 20 or over 80 would be excluded, and a 40-year-old would not know which category to choose.

Limitations of Standardized Interviews

As you might expect, qualitative researchers have objected to the use of standardized interviews in sociological research (Box 5.1 discusses some common objections from the perspectives of feminist researchers). Qualitative researchers point out that standardized interviews can only provide a rough sketch of respondents' true situations and that they cannot uncover any unexpected data. They further note that the basic assumptions of standardized interviews—those assumptions that make these interviews useful when conducting quantitative research—stand in direct opposition to the qualitative researcher's goal of obtaining complex, participant-defined data.

Box 5.1 ❋ Feminist Critiques of Standardized Interviews

Feminist researchers have long questioned the effectiveness of standardized interviews to shed light on individuals'—especially women's—lived experiences. Ann Oakley (1981), for example, challenged the stance of the distant, neutral interviewer who does not spoil the stimulus–response model of the interview by deviating from the script. She argued that 'feminist interviewing' should strive for openness and engagement on the part of the interviewer and recognize the possibility of developing a relationship between the interviewer and the interviewee (Reinharz 1992).

Marjorie DeVault (1999) has challenged the taken-for-granted categories that researchers use in standardized interviews. She suggested that their language often does not capture women's experiences. This is especially evident in words such as *work* and *leisure*, which do not relate easily to women's lives because women's activities do not always fit into one or the other category and because much of the work women do is invisible.

Similarly, Linda Caissie (2006), who carried out a study of the Raging Grannies (a group of older women activists who use street theatre, outrageous costumes, and satirical songs as methods of protest), discovered that although academic literature would identify their activity as serious leisure, the Grannies disagreed. Their understanding of leisure was different from the definitions developed by leisure researchers. The Grannies' definition of leisure included relaxation and rest, play, entertainment, recreation, unstructured free time, frivolous activity, choice, and social activities—the opposite of work. In contrast, they defined activism as unpaid work, self-expression, a calling, a way of life, political protest, commitment to justice, fun, social action, resistance, and volunteering (Caissie 2006: 145–6). These two lists of characteristics barely overlap. As Caissie notes in her discussion, 'we need to ensure we "hear" the views of those participants whose beliefs and experiences point them to something other than the segmentation of aspects of everyday life' (2006: 174–5).

To begin with, the standardized interview takes for granted that all respondents will understand and relate to the questions in the way in which the researcher intended. In other words, it assumes **validity** across various social contexts (Mishler 1986). Yet, as we have learned, every person interprets language based on his or her personal knowledge and experience. As Elliot G. Mishler (1986: 22) has criticized, 'survey research is a context-stripping procedure' in which researchers 'pretend' that diversity in social contexts and meanings does not exist.

The standardized interview also presumes that the response options provided by the researcher will be exhaustive and that they will not inadvertently exclude other valid answers that the interviewee might provide (Schwartz and Jacobs 1979). Yet, given the opportunity, most individuals would offer an opinion that is more complex than the ones predetermined by the researcher. Consider the following question, which appears in a textbook as a good example of the simple and direct wording that standardized interviews use: 'Sugar is bad for health. Do you agree or disagree?' (Bouma et al. 2009: 77). Notice that the wording of this question assumes that it has a straightforward answer. Yet few of us would agree that *all* sugar is bad for *everyone's* health at *all* times. The respondent has no way to indicate a more detailed, middle-of-the-road opinion.

Similarly, standardized interviews assume that the researcher can construct mutually exclusive responses to the survey questions. While this might be possible when the focus is on determining simple facts—a person's age or the party an individual voted for in the last election—it is less feasible when dealing with complex issues. For example, a survey on equality in the workforce might ask whether respondents think that women make less money than men do because women work in lower-paid occupations *or* because of discrimination. As you can see, the wording of the question implies that the two possibilities are mutually exclusive. Yet both factors could, and sometimes do, work together to contribute to women making less money.

Finally, standardized interviews assume that it is possible for an interviewer to present the script in a manner that is neutral and consistent across multiple interviews. Yet no two interviews can ever be exactly the same, as no interviewer can control every aspect of his or her tone and body language. In many cases, the interviewer may make a mistake when reading the script or add details that are not included in the script. In fact, research has shown that interviewers change the wording of up to one-third of questions on an interview script (Bradbury, Sudman, and Associates 1979, cited in Fontana and Prokos 2007: 21). A few years ago, I was a respondent in a phone survey. When we were almost done, the interviewer asked if I was Professor van den Hoonaard and then told me that he had been a student in one of my classes. I am quite sure that these comments were not part of his interview script!

As you will discover in the following sections, in-depth interviews allow the researcher to not only overcome some of the difficulties associated with standardized interviews but also use the interview process itself as a source of data.

In-Depth Interviews

Unlike standardized interviews, the purpose of in-depth interviews is to allow people to explain their experiences, attitudes, feelings, and definitions of the situation in their own terms and in ways that are meaningful to them. To get a sense of what an in-depth interview can accomplish, consider the following example, which I've taken from my own study of women's experiences as widows.

On a warm spring day, as I make my way up the driveway to the house of my first participant, I see that the mailbox lists both the husband's and the wife's names on it. I make a mental note to ask the woman I am about to interview about the mailbox. Adding a new question would be a problem were I conducting a standardized interview. Fortunately, I am not.

When I reach the door I knock, and my participant welcomes me into her home. We chat a bit as I set up my recording equipment. Once we are both ready to begin, I turn on the tape recorder. I explain that I am interested in hearing about her experiences of being a widow:

> What I would like you to do now is tell me about your experience with losing your husband. You can start where you want and end where you want. Put in what you want and leave out what you want. I'm just interested in hearing about your experience.

After a few minutes of thought, the woman responds:

> What was it like to lose him? I suppose first of all, you have to say what it was like to have him . . . he was a very supportive person. He was quite romantic, in a way. We met in a romantic manner . . . during the war in London. We did our courting during the Blitz, so he actually saved my life once in the Blitz at some risk to himself. And then he was overseas, too. (D.K. van den Hoonaard 2001: 8)

Here, in the first moments of our interview, this woman has communicated the impact of the history of her marriage and relationship with her husband on her experience of being a widow. Had I designed a questionnaire based on the literature and my own hypotheses, I would never have thought to ask about the way she met her husband. I would have missed out on hearing about something that my participant felt was central to her experience.

This recognition of the importance of the participant's perspective is the hallmark of qualitative interviewing. In the next section, we look at several types of qualitative interviews and some approaches researchers take when thinking about the interview process itself. We then talk about how to plan and carry out an in-depth interview study.

Types of Qualitative Interviews

Qualitative interviews take several forms. Some include 'a series of predetermined but open-ended questions' and 'use a variety of probes that elicit further information' (Ayres 2008: 810). Others are more flexible and 'the interviewee determines the direction the interview will take' to allow the researcher to 'discover [the interviewee's understanding of] the topic of interest' (Firmin 2008: 907). Many researchers refer to the former type of interview as 'semi-structured' and the latter as 'unstructured' but, as Hammersley and Atkinson (1983: 112–3) have pointed out, all interviews have some structure. Just as all social interaction is structured by the individuals involved, interviews are structured by both the interviewer and the respondent.

Researchers design different kinds of interviews depending on their proclivities and projects. Some will design an **interview guide** that encourages the participant to develop a chronological account of her or his life. Others may create a list of areas that they want to cover and provide little direction to the person they are interviewing. Still others may start with one opening question and let the participant lead them where he or she will. For example, when I interviewed an acquaintance to discover more about the experience of being a vegetarian, my only plan was to start with a simple question: 'How did you happen to become a vegetarian?' His answers led to other questions, and we talked for over an hour. When it was over, my interviewee told me that he had not realized how much he knew about vegetarianism.

Interviews that take place in the throes of a field study tend to be highly informal. They happen on the spur of the moment. Harry F. Wolcott (1995: 106) suggests that even a 'casual comment or inducement as "what you were telling me the other day was interesting"' can initiate an informal interview. In some situations, these on-the-fly interviews are the only possibility. For example, when Will C. van den Hoonaard (2000) was on a lunch break at a cartography conference where he was gathering information for his study on women's experiences of becoming cartographers, he unexpectedly encountered a woman who was on the team that mapped the far side of the moon. Not wanting to miss an opportunity to gather information from this woman, he quickly improvised an interview. Figure 5.1 shows this encounter. Note that van den Hoonaard is making use of the only recording devices he had at hand—a pencil and a paper plate!

Regardless of how formal or informal the encounter is, the qualitative interview is 'a directed conversation that elicits inner views of respondents' lives as they portray their worlds, experiences, and observations' (Charmaz 1991b: 385). Such interviews are characterized by a relatively informal style in which the interviewer encourages 'people to describe their [social] world in their own terms' (Rubin and Rubin 1995: 2). Interviews, however, diverge from conversations in three important ways. First, the interviewer has the task of bringing the discussion back to the topic of the interview when it veers off track. Second, the discussion is lopsided—the researcher says much less than the participant says. Third, the investigator can never engage in passive listening. The interviewer must listen intently because she or he needs to identify ideas or potentially useful concepts to ask about in subsequent questions. Elaine Brody (2010) calls this 'organized listening'.

FIGURE 5.1 Spontaneous Interviewing

Source: Jesus Reyes.

Approaches to Qualitative Interviews

Traditionally, many in-depth interviewers have seen the interviewee as a vessel full of answers that the interviewer may access with a sympathetic demeanour and skilful questioning (Gubrium and Holstein 2001: 13). Thus, Firmin (2008: 907) writes that an 'unstructured interview . . . is designed to draw from the interviewee constructs embedded in his or her thinking'. Others have suggested that the purpose of the in-depth interview 'centres on the meanings that life experiences hold for the individuals being studied' (Warren and Karner 2010: 127). With this understanding, researchers approach in-depth interviews as a way to 'help to uncover the participant's views', to allow his or her perspective to 'unfold as the participant views it . . . not as the researcher views it' (Marshall and Rossman 2006: 101).

In-depth interviews do, indeed, help researchers to understand how participants understand their social worlds. However, they are also social events that do more than simply extract data that already exist inside individuals. In fact, in-depth interviews often encourage participants to think about their experiences in new ways and to formulate ideas and opinions that they did not possess before the interview began. Thus, an in-depth interview is an interactional process more accurately described as 'generating data' than 'collecting data' that is already inside a research participant, waiting to be mined (Mason 2002).[2] This approach to in-depth interviewing has been conceptualized as the '**active interview**' (Holstein and Gubrium 1995).

The Active Interview

Qualitative researchers are very aware that social reality is constructed through interpersonal interactions as much as it is through words. Therefore, when conducting in-depth interviews, we must pay close attention not only to what participants say but to how they say it and how they behave in relation to the interviewer. As James A. Holstein and Jaber F. Gubrium have noted in their influential book *The Active Interview*, interviews are 'meaning-making occasions' that allow us to 'reveal both the substance and the process of meaning making' (1995: 76–7). As such, Holstein and Gubrium encourage researchers to take the approach of an 'ethnographer of the interview' and analyze the interactional process through which the interview takes place (1995: 78). By recognizing the interview as an active social process, we take into account the importance of the strategies participants (and researchers) use during the interview. Thus, we can view the interview process itself as a source of data.

Let us look at an example that illustrates what we can learn by actively analyzing the interactions that take place during interviews.

When I was conducting my study of older widowers, the men I interviewed behaved in an overtly assertive manner. They interrupted my questions, referred to me as 'girl' or 'dear' or by a diminutive of my first name, and lectured me about a variety of topics (D.K. van den Hoonaard 2009). Although the men did not express their motivations in words, their behaviour demonstrated that they were trying very hard to display their masculinity to make sure that I understood that they were still 'real' men. In contrast, when I interviewed older widows, the women took on a more submissive role. They questioned whether they were 'doing it right' and worried aloud that they might be talking too much or 'gabbling', talking nonsense. The women also offered me tea to enact the hostess role with which they were more familiar and comfortable. Their actions revealed their unspoken fear of being perceived as incompetent in their everyday lives (D.K. van den Hoonaard 2005).

As you can see, I was able to gain a deeper understanding of both groups by observing how participants interacted with me in the interviews. In addition, I learned a lot by comparing the behaviours of the widowers to that of the widows. For example, I noticed that members of both groups demonstrated a level of discomfort with the interview situation that reflected their marginal social status. The differences in the ways the participants communicated and managed their discomfort told me a lot about what it means to be a member of each of these groups and the gendered social meaning of an individual's status as an older widowed woman or man. By approaching each situation as an active interviewer, I was able to use the social process of interaction that took place during the interviews as a source of data that helped me understand the way my participants experienced their everyday lives.

Conducting an In-Depth Interview Study

We are now ready to think about how to actually go about conducting an in-depth interview study. Once you have decided on a research question to be addressed through in-depth interviews, you need to decide whom to interview and you need to design an interview guide.

Identifying Participants

If you are familiar with quantitative research methods, you may know that researchers who conduct surveys and do statistical analyses have developed sophisticated techniques to identify a **random sample** of the population. This method makes sense when a researcher wants to interview a large number of people and has a goal of generalizing the study's findings to a wider population. In contrast, qualitative researchers are more interested in learning a lot about a relatively small number of people, so random sampling is not an effective way to identify participants for a qualitative interview. How do we decide whom to interview?

First of all, we choose people for the qualities they have, people who can provide the greatest insight into the topic at hand. For example, I was interested in finding out the social meaning that being a widow has for older women. I, therefore, decided to recruit women over 50 who had been widowed between one and 10 years. I also wondered if the experience of women who live in urban areas would be different from the experience of women who live in rural areas. In the end, I sought a 'sample' of women that was split, approximately 50–50, between urban and rural widows over 50.

When you are deciding whom to interview, keep in mind that you want to undermine the 'hierarchy of credibility', as we discussed in Chapter 3. You will learn more about people's lives if you avoid interviews with experts and interview the people whose lives you want to know about. Hence, J. Peter Rothe (1990) did not interview experts when he wanted to understand the everyday experiences of older drivers who had been in accidents. Rather, he invited the older people themselves to become 'partners in the search for empirical detail on their lives' (Rothe 1990: 4). He decided to interview older drivers who had been in serious accidents because they, rather than the experts, knew what the experience had been like.

Because qualitative research design is emergent, new ideas about whom to interview may occur during your study. For example, when I was interviewing widowers in the Atlantic provinces, I was a bit frustrated with their level of stoicism, their unemotional approach to the interview. I, therefore, thought that it might be useful to compare the reactions of these individuals to those of widowers from a more emotionally expressive culture. I remembered that, in my previous studies, I had met a number of older Jewish individuals who described the Jewish culture, especially among urban Jews, as being particu-larly expressive. Of course, I could not expect that all urban Jewish widowers would be more emotionally expressive than all other Maritimers, but includ-ing a significant sample of Jewish widowers in my study did give me a shot at a more expressive style of interview participation. Ultimately, the similari-ties and differences between the two groups were very useful in my analysis.

Once you have identified the types of individuals you want to interview, you must spend some time searching for participants who meet your criteria. One strategy that can help you find members of your target group is **snowball sampling**. When an investigator uses this strategy, she or he locates initial participants and then asks them if they know anyone who fits the criteria and who might be interested in participating in the study. For my study of widows, I started by identifying a few participants and then asking them to approach other potential participants on my behalf. If the potential partici-pant was interested, I phoned her to talk about the study and to invite her to participate.

Sometimes, you can approach an organization to help you find your sample. As we discussed in Chapter 4, Karen March (1995) and Claudia Malacrida (1998) both found interview participants through organizations with which they were familiar. Even if you do not have an established con-nection to the organization, you may find this approach useful. As a note of caution, if you choose this route when identifying participants, you may miss potential participants who do not belong to the organization you have chosen, and you may end up with a sample group that is too narrow in focus.

In other cases, you may need to contact a person in a position of power—for example, a warden in a prison or a supervisor in a nursing home—to gain access to participants. In such a situation, it may be challenging to assure the voluntary participation of your participants. For example, a resident of a nursing home or an inmate of a prison might not feel free to refuse participa-tion even if you assure her or him that participation is voluntary. In addition, these participants may not feel that you will be able to follow through on your promise of confidentiality. This sense of insecurity may have an impact on how they answer your questions. These potential complications need not prevent you from carrying out your research, but you should consider them both in the planning of your study and in the analysis of your data.

Of course, some groups are easier to find than others. For example, when I wanted to study older urban and rural widows, I found a journalist who was willing to write an article about my research for the local newspaper. By nine o'clock the morning after it appeared, I had already received five phone calls from women who were interested in participating. Within a week, I had 18 volunteers! This is quite a lot, considering that in-depth interview stud-ies often have samples of 30 or fewer (I ended up with 27). As time went on, I strategically recruited from rural areas to even up my sample.

Recruiting older widowers was more difficult. Because life expectancy in men is lower than it is in women and women often marry men who are older than they are, I knew that I would be recruiting from a much smaller population. In addition, based on my past experience, I knew that older men are less likely than older women to volunteer as research participants. I, therefore, spread as wide a net as possible. I used newspaper, radio, and television publicity. I asked friends and colleagues if they knew a widower to whom they could refer me. I also tried snowball sampling, which had worked with widows. As others have discovered (for example, Davidson 1999), snowball sampling is not an effective way to recruit older widowers. I did not find a single participant using this method.

As you can see, there are many ways to go about finding people to participate in your interview study. Yet, as you will discover, there are always some people who will not take part in research. We know that women are more likely than men to agree to participate and that higher levels of education correspond to greater willingness to participate. But it is likely that there are other consistent factors that lead to refusal to participate in a study. It is, therefore, useful to think about who refuses to participate and what you might not learn because you do not have the opportunity to talk to those people.

Nonetheless, whether finding people to interview is easy or difficult, you will locate enough people if you are persistent and creative. Next, we talk about the interview guide, which you will develop during the processes of defining your research question and recruiting your participants.

Designing an Interview Guide

When discussing qualitative interviews, we use the term *guide* rather than *script*, *questionnaire*, *schedule*, or *protocol* to refer to our written plan. The term *guide* reflects the flexibility of our approach. We can rearrange questions to suit a particular interview, and we can choose to add or omit questions depending on how appropriate they are for a particular situation.

The first step in designing your interview guide is to list the broad categories that are of interest to you in your study. The second step is to develop the **open-ended questions** that are relevant to these categories. These questions will be the most significant questions you ask during the interview process. When you are designing your questions, keep in mind that you should only address themes that are directly related to your research topic. Avoid asking questions on topics that are simply a matter of personal curiosity.

The next step is to compose your draft guide. Think about the order of your questions. Do they flow from one to the other? Although the order may change during each interview, listing the questions in a logical order in the guide will help keep you on track. Be careful not to include too many questions. Remember that the participant may give long answers to your questions. A 10-question guide may result in an interview that lasts 30 minutes or one that takes three hours to complete. Too many questions may lead you to rush through the interview instead of listening closely to responses and asking good follow-up questions.

Follow-up questions, or **probes**, ask the participant to elaborate, explain, or provide a story or example of what she or he has said. During the interview, you should listen intently to every answer and plan potential follow-up questions. A probe might be general (for example, 'Can you tell me more about that?') or it might be more specific (for example, 'You mentioned that your friends treat you differently since you made the Olympic bobsleigh team. In what ways?'). Although you will devise most of your follow-up questions in response you what your participant says during an interview, you should try to anticipate some potential follow-ups and include these questions in your guide.

As you look over your guide, make sure you have designed questions that you think your participants can answer. You can ask people about

- their experiences or behaviours;
- their opinions or values;
- their feelings;
- their factual knowledge;
- what they saw, heard, or felt; and
- their personal background.

Keep in mind that people can only tell you about their own experiences. So, for example, you can ask a widow how her relationship with her friends has changed, but you cannot ask her how widows feel about their friends in general.

Plan to start your interview with questions that the participant will find relatively easy to answer. Many people are nervous when they are being interviewed, so putting your participants at ease will help build rapport and make the interview both more informative for you and more enjoyable for the person you are interviewing.

As we have seen above, we cannot always anticipate what things a participant may find important or meaningful. Therefore, it is both useful and respectful to include questions that invite your participant to add anything that she or he thinks is important that you have not asked in the interview. When I conduct interviews, my last planned question is always 'Is there anything that I haven't asked you about that I should have?' This question has often opened an entirely new line of inquiry. In addition, because data collection is emergent, you should always be open to adding questions during the interview itself.

To help guide you through the process of creating your first interview guide, I've included an example from my own work in Box 5.2. Notice the conversational tone I use in phrasing my questions. Also notice that my questions

Box 5.2 ❖ Sample Interview Guide

This is the interview guide I used for my interview study of women's experiences as widows. During the interview itself, I followed up, or probed, whenever appropriate and skipped questions that the participant had already answered in response to a previous question. The list of topics towards the end of the guide is there to remind me to ask about those topics if they do not come up as responses to earlier questions.

Guiding Questions

- Where and when were you born?
- How long were you married?
- What I'd like for you to do now is tell me about your experience with being a widow. You can begin wherever you like and include or leave out whatever you choose. I'm just interested in finding out about your experience. Could you tell me about this?
- What are your most vivid memories from the first few days after your husband died?
- How would you say your life has changed since your husband died?
- What has been the most difficult aspect of your life since his death?
- Is there anything that particularly surprised you?
- Have you ever lived alone before?
- Has your relationship with your children changed since your husband died? How? What about your relationship with your friends?
- How would you say you have changed since your husband died?
- Do you remember the first time you thought of yourself as a widow?
- What are the most important things other people should know about the experience of being a widow?
- Are you doing okay financially?

Additional Topics

- Decisions
- Relations with men—wedding rings
- Weekends; difficult times
- Mothers as widows
- Church support

Final Question

- Is there anything that I haven't asked you about that I should have?

encourage the participant to give expansive rather than short or categorical answers. In the next section, you will find advice on avoiding some common mistakes that can negatively affect the quality of your interviews.

Common Pitfalls

There are a few errors that novice researchers often make when they write their guiding questions. If you are aware of these potential mistakes, and if you pay close attention to the tone, wording, structure, and content of your questions, you should be able to avoid them. The following advice will help you with this task.

Don't make your participants feel as though they are being interrogated. The tone of your questions should be open and inviting. As we noted above, you should use conversational rather than technical or formal language to establish your tone. Most of the time, you do not want the wording of your questions to make the interview participant feel defensive or put on the spot.

Avoid using questions that begin with the word *why*. Rather, ask participants *how* they came to think or do certain things. 'Why' questions are likely to elicit answers that focus on motivation, and research shows that many people respond defensively to being asked *why* they did something. In contrast, 'how' questions are more likely to draw out answers that capture both motive and process.

Never ask leading or loaded questions. Choose your words carefully to avoid encouraging the participant to give a particular response. For example, a question that begins with 'don't you think . . . ?' leads the participant to believe that there is a 'correct' response. Naturally, the participant will try to supply you with the answer he or she thinks you want to hear. A loaded question is an emotionally charged question that makes an unqualified assumption about an individual. For example, if you ask 'How many times have you smoked an illegal drug?' without establishing that the participant has ever smoked an illegal drug, you have asked a loaded question. Often, loaded questions imply guilt, and they may cause participants to feel that they are being accused of a wrongdoing.

Another type of question to avoid is the **double-barrelled question**. This type of question asks more than one thing at the same time—for example, 'Do you respect your mother and your father?' In actuality, this question has combined two separate questions: 'Do you respect your mother?' and 'Do you respect your father?' Even more difficult than double-barrelled questions are complex questions that are long, with several phrases. By the end of hearing the question, the participant will have little idea about what you have asked. Remember that the structure of interview questions should be simple and direct so that the participant knows what you are asking.

Finally, avoid closed-ended questions, especially ones that lead to one of only two possible answers. Examples include 'yes/no' questions and 'either/or' questions. These types of questions are likely to shut down the participant. The exception to this rule is that you may use closed-ended questions when you plan to follow up with a more open-ended question, such as 'How so?' You could, for example, ask members of a bobsleigh team if their parents supported them in their quest to make the Olympics and then immediately follow up with 'How so?' or 'What kinds of things did they do?'

Once you have located participants and written your interview guide, it is time to carry out your first interview. The next section provides some ideas about how to actually conduct the interview. Although you may feel a little nervous about conducting your first interview, you will find that interviewing participants can be the most pleasant, exhilarating, and fascinating part of doing qualitative research.

Doing Interviews

Thinking about the distinctive characteristics of in-depth interviews will help you prepare for your first interview. To begin with, there is an intrinsic sense of reciprocity between the interviewer and the participant in an in-depth interview. So, in exchange for the stories and insights your participant offers, you should feel free to share your own ideas and details about yourself if your participant is interested. Next, the interview process carries with it a fundamental understanding that your participant is the expert on his or her own lived experience. Therefore, you should always ask for clarification if you think that you have misunderstood something that your participant has said or if you believe that your participant's meaning differs from you own. Finally, the structure of an in-depth interview is highly flexible. This flexibility is a particular strength of qualitative interviews, as it allows you to deviate from your guide to probe into interesting topics as they surface.

When you are getting ready for an interview, you should focus on making a good impression. First, as when conducting a participant-observation study, make sure that you are dressed appropriately. You want to look professional but unintimidating.

Second, always be on time. If you are unfamiliar with the interview location, which is often the home of your participant, get directions and use a map or an Internet resource to plan your route. Give yourself plenty of time to travel.

Third, ensure that you allot enough time for each interview. The conversation may last 30 minutes or three hours, and you don't want to make your participant feel rushed. Remember that your participant is giving you her or his time to share information, so you must reciprocate by giving her or him as much of your time as it takes to complete the interview.

Fourth, check that you have everything that you need. This may include an information letter or a consent form, a copy of the interview guide, and recording equipment. Make sure that you know how to use your equipment and that it works. Bring extra batteries or an extension cord and tapes (if you are using a tape recorder) as well as a pad of paper and pens in case your participant does not agree to be recorded.

Once you get to the interview location, focus on setting your participant at ease and making her or him feel confident that you know what you are doing. I usually hand my information letter to my participant to read and make small talk while I am setting up my recording equipment. Make sure to place the equipment where it will pick up both sides of the conversation—you will look unprofessional if you have to adjust the microphone once the interview begins. In addition, always accept tea or coffee when it is offered, whether you want it or not. This provides a feeling of balance and informality to the interview. Once everything is ready, and you have discussed the contents of the information letter, the interview begins.

There are a number of things that you can do during the interview to encourage your participant to enjoy the encounter and give you expansive answers. You should try to communicate your interest through your body language. Sit forward and look engaged. You want your participant to know that you think that his or her comments are important. In contrast, sitting back with your arms folded, listening with a blank expression on your face, or speaking in an uninflected voice communicates a lack of interest.

In addition, nodding, saying 'hmm', and repeating part of or summarizing an answer will encourage the participant to elaborate or provide an example. You can also express genuine ignorance about what the person said, particularly in the case of jargon or a phrase that you are not familiar with. For example, one of the widows I interviewed told me that she appreciated the support of her 'church family'. I was unfamiliar with the term and asked her to explain it to me. She not only clarified her definition of the term, as referring to the members of her congregation, but also went on to explain how that group symbolized family to her.

You can also show that you are engaged in what your participant is saying by asking appropriate follow-up questions. To do this, you have to actively listen and think at the same time. It takes a great deal of concentration to conduct a rich interview, but the results will be well worth your effort.

Remember that it is your job to keep the interview on topic. Your participant may go off on a tangent that does not seem relevant, and you should be willing to listen when this happens, but it is always your job to bring the discussion back to the question at hand.

When you have run out of questions on a topic and plan to introduce a new one, use a transition to help your participant follow the development of the conversation. This transition may be as simple as 'moving on to another topic' or 'now I'd like to ask you about . . . '.

Finally, don't fear pauses. Although many of us are uncomfortable with silence during a conversation, silence can give your participant a chance to compose his or her thoughts. Hence, when a participant stops speaking or takes a few moments to respond to a question, it often helps to simply wait longer than you ordinarily would before speaking. Avoid the impulse to jump in and clarify your question. Often, this will only cause confusion, as you are likely to come up with a rewording that is more complex and convoluted than your original question. Only offer to reword the question if your participant asks for clarification.

After the Interview

After you have given your participant time to answer the final question of the interview, it is time to thank the participant and put the equipment away. Participants often want to chat for a while after the interview. Always make time for post-interview discussion. Sometimes, participants bring up an entirely new, but important, topic after the recorder is off. When this happens, I usually ask permission to turn the equipment on again to catch the comments on tape. In the days following your interview, you may want to send a thank-you note to your participant. If you promise to send a copy of the recording or a transcript, make sure you follow through.

As soon as possible, write your field notes. Include your thoughts on the interview process, comments on the demeanour of the participant, and descriptions of anything she or he did. If your participant offered to give you a tour of his or her home, describe the incident in your field notes. Of course, do not include any details that the person asked you not to record. You will also want to transcribe your interview in full.

Transcribing Interviews

Researchers have different approaches to creating interview transcripts. Some believe in transcribing the whole interview, word for word, while others transcribe only what seems applicable to their own study. I belong to the first group. After all, how can you know what you need to transcribe before you have done your analysis? I even transcribe pauses, laughter, crying, and significant changes in pitch and volume. In addition, I include my own words to contextualize what the participant has said, as context can provide deeper meaning for analysis. For example, if I ask a widower if he is interested in remarriage and he answers 'yes', my question has elicited his answer. If I ask a widower a more general question, such as 'what is it like to be a widower?', and he says that he is interested in remarriage, he has revealed that he associates remarriage very strongly with the concept of being a widower.

Transcribing can be a very time-consuming, tedious process, but it also bears fruit of a deep familiarity with your data and can include euphoric moments of discovery. One hour of an interview may require four to seven hours to transcribe, depending on the available equipment and the skill of the transcriber. Therefore, as with field notes, it is essential that you always keep at least one back-up copy of your interview transcripts in case you run into any unforeseen glitches. I learned the importance of backing up my transcripts when, not too long ago, I had a computer problem and lost my digital files. Because I had printed out hard copies of the transcripts as I went along, I was able to scan the pages and reconstruct my files. Had I not made a back-up copy, I would have lost hundreds of pages of data.

If you are lucky enough to have funding to pay for a transcriptionist, it is essential that you correct the transcripts yourself. This entails listening to the interview with the transcript in front of you, either in hard copy or on the computer screen, and correcting any errors that appear. This process will help you become familiar with the content of the interview, which will in turn make the process of analysis easier. I found that when I was writing *The Widowed Self: The Older Woman's Journey through Widowhood* (2001), I could 'hear' the interviews whenever I read the transcripts because I had listened so carefully when I was correcting the pages.

But intimate familiarity is not the only reason to listen to the recording. Because the transcriber was not present during the interview, she or he may miss a subtle meaning that you picked up on. Hearing the recording for yourself can also help you remember details that you forgot after you left the interview. In addition, the transcriber might mishear or misinterpret what the participant said. For example, when I was correcting one interview, I noticed that the transcript read, 'I must have met a thousand Africans in my life'. From what I remembered about the woman whose transcript I was working with, I would have been surprised if she had met even one African. When I listened to the interview, I discovered that what she had actually said was 'I must have made a thousand afghans in my life'. Now it made sense. A transcriber might also have missed a small word, such as *not*. This is a simple error, but the loss of such an important word could change the entire meaning of your interview.

Listening to a recording of your interview will also give you a chance to revise your interview guide to prepare for your next interview. You should include topics that unexpectedly came up and remove or edit questions that did not work well. It is not unusual to develop several versions of an interview guide during the life of a study.

There is one final benefit to listening to the interview—it will help you to identify your strengths and weaknesses as an interviewer. This is a very important step to take when you are conducting your first interview study. In reviewing the session, you are likely to hear double-barrelled questions, missed opportunities for follow-up and times you spoke too soon to fill an awkward silence. As you do more interviews and critique your own performance, you will hone your skills and get better and better as an interviewer.

Summary

In this chapter, we have looked at the distinctive aspects of qualitative interviews. We delineated the differences between standardized and qualitative interviews and saw how their different underlying assumptions suit them to uncovering different types of data for different purposes. Finally, we talked about how to identify participants, design an interview guide, and execute an interview. As we learned, the participant is central to generating data in the interview process. Once you have interviewed all of your participants, written up your notes, and transcribed your interviews, the next step is to analyze your data—a process we will discuss in Chapter 7. But before we learn about data analysis, let us turn to examining methods of data collection that do not rely on direct interaction with participants. Chapter 6 will discuss unobtrusive research.

Key Terms

active interview

closed-ended (or forced-choice) question

double-barrelled question

in-depth interview

interview guide

open-ended question

probes

random sampling

snowball sampling

standardized interview

validity

Questions for Critical Thought

1. Is there any group that you would like to examine in an in-depth interview study? How would you go about identifying individuals to participate in your study?

2. What would you do if you were presented with a sudden opportunity to conduct an interview 'on the fly'? What strategies might you use to guide your interview?

3. How would you dress if you were setting out to interview an executive about his or her work? What about if you were setting out to interview a fellow student?

4. How would establish yourself as a professional in an interview setting? How might your approach differ if you were interviewing someone significantly older or younger than yourself?

Exercises

1. Interview a classmate for ten minutes about her or his best or worst class experience. Listen carefully and follow up or probe when the opportunity arises.

2. Visit the website for CBC Radio (www.cbc.ca/radio) and listen to a podcast of an interview. Think about what makes it a good or a bad interview.

Identify good questions, double-barrelled and complex questions, leading questions, and loaded questions.

3. Develop a brief interview guide on a topic that you would like to study by doing in-depth interviews.

Suggested Readings

Marjorie DeVault. 1990. 'Talking and Listening from Women's Standpoint: Feminist Strategies for Interviewing and Analysis', *Social Problems* 37: 96–117. In this seminal article, DeVault illustrates the shortcomings of using standardized interview strategies when interviewing women. Her arguments have relevance for anyone considering an interview study.

Andrea Fontana and Anastasia H. Prokos. 2007. *The Interview: From Formal to Postmodern.* Walnut Creek, CA: Left Coast Press. This highly readable book traces the development of the interview as a form of data collection from its origins to the present. It clearly and succinctly discusses the assumptions and strengths and weaknesses of different forms of interviewing and has a particularly cogent discussion of gender and interviewing.

James A. Holstein and Jaber F. Gubrium. 1995. *The Active Interview.* Thousand Oaks, CA: Sage. This influential and accessible book argues for an approach to interviewing that recognizes that an interview is an interpersonal accomplishment. It uses examples to show how to use the 'how' of the interview as well as the 'what' to understand the phenomenon under question.

Related Website

Robert Wood Johnson Foundation, Qualitative Research Guidelines Project, Interviewing
www.qualres.org/HomeInte-3595.html

This web page provides brief descriptions of different types of interviews and useful summaries of when and how to use each type.

6 Unobtrusive Research

Learning Objectives

- To become familiar with unobtrusive measures
- To understand the difference between manifest content and latent content
- To become familiar with the variety of ways in which sociologists use content analysis

Introduction

Imagine that you wanted to identify the most popular exhibit at a museum. You could set up a field study in which you station observers throughout the museum to note how many people are at each exhibit and to record how long each person stays in each location. This might work, but it would be a very complex procedure and it would take a lot of time to gather enough data at each exhibit. You could also conduct a survey or set up in-depth interviews to ascertain visitors' opinions on which exhibit they found most interesting, but this method would also take up a lot of time and it might be difficult to convince enough people to take time out of their trip to the museum to participate in your study. Webb et al. (1966) report a much more creative approach that was used at the Museum of Science and Industry in Chicago: Researchers noted that the floor tiles around the chick-hatching exhibit needed to be replaced very often—about once every six weeks—while the tiles around other exhibits did not need to be replaced for years at a time. Hence, by taking the unobtrusive measure of looking at differential rates of erosion of floor tiles, researchers were able to ascertain that the chick-hatching exhibit was by far the most popular.

In this chapter, we look at a variety of **unobtrusive measures**—ways of amassing data without interacting with research participants—that researchers can use to carry out qualitative research. Unlike the qualitative methods we have discussed so far, unobtrusive methods do not involve interaction with participants. The researcher simply analyzes materials that already exist, and the process of collecting data does not affect the materials that are studied (Reinharz 1992: 147). Most often, unobtrusive measures are used in conjunction with other more interactive methods.

As you will discover, almost anything that has been created or modified by people can be a source of data. Many researchers have gained valuable insight into their research topics by examining materials as diverse as maps, archival records, letters, photographs, movies, advertisements, books, and even trash. Shulamit Reinharz (1992: 146–7) provides a list of 'cultural artifacts' that feminist researchers have used as 'texts' for research: children's books, fairy tales, billboards, works of fiction and non-fiction, children's artwork, fashion, postcards, Girl Scout handbooks, works of fine art, newspaper articles, clinical records, research publications, textbooks, and academic citations. In my own work, I have analyzed the contents of monthly newsletters, autobiographical writings, novels, movies, children's books, students' essays, and magazine articles. When searching for materials for content analysis, you are bounded only by the limits of your own imagination.

Researchers who engage in unobtrusive research understand that cultural artifacts contain meaning on two levels—one that is obvious and one that is more subtle. When analyzing **manifest content**, the researcher looks at content that is easily observed and immediately evident. When analyzing **latent content**, in contrast, the researcher focusses on uncovering implicit meanings. Most often, latent meanings provide the researcher with the deepest understanding of an artifact. Consider the following example from Manning and Cullum-Swan's (1994) analysis of the menus at a McDonald's restaurant. Part of their study involved analyzing the manifest content of the menus: the ways the food items were described, the ways the items were organized into different categories, and the way the items were listed within each category, in order from most to least popular. Once they assessed the manifest content of the menus, the researchers interpreted this content to uncover latent meanings. Through this analysis, they concluded that the menus 'convey messages that enable fast decisions and increase turnover' and that the categories of items, such as 'Value Meals' and 'Happy Meals', 'raise per person expenditure and minimize complex, ad-hoc item selection'; in short, the menu's design reflects an 'efficient, routinized, fast transaction-based food service' industry (1994: 471).

Before you continue, you should note that the structure of this chapter differs from that of the previous two chapters. Rather than go into depth about how to carry out research using unobtrusive measures, the chapter demonstrates through example. It, therefore, includes illustrations from a wide variety of sources to demonstrate the range of possibility. As we examine the striking variety of types of content that sociologists and others have studied, try to imagine other possibilities.

Analyzing Pre-existing Documents

Many researchers argue that it is essential to include documents in our studies if we are to understand contemporary society. After all, individuals and groups represent themselves, both to themselves and to others, through the documents they produce (Atkinson and Coffey 1997: 45). We can learn much about the people who have created a document by analyzing what they chose to represent in their creation. As Howard S. Becker (1986b: 127) has noted, representations are a translation of reality 'into the materials and conventional language of a particular craft'. In addition,

> [s]ince any representation always and necessarily leaves out elements of reality, the interesting and researchable questions are these: Which of the possible elements are included? Who finds that selection reasonable and acceptable? Who complains about it? [And who does not?] What criteria do people apply in making those judgments? (Becker 1986b: 126)

While these questions could easily apply to analysis of any cultural artifact, they are especially salient in relation to document analysis.

In highly literate societies, written texts provide particularly telling windows into social worlds. Think about how much statistical records, survey forms, letters, autobiographies, articles in professional journals and magazines, and even works of fiction can tell us about the interests and concerns of the individuals who created these documents. Glaser and Strauss (1967, cited in Pawluch 2009) have referred to such documents as 'voices in the library' waiting to be heard and used for our analyses. Let us look at ways that researchers can gather valuable information from such voices.

Statistical Records

When conducting a study, researchers often consult pre-existing statistical records to get a general sense of a topic. In addition, many researchers have repurposed or reinterpreted existing statistics to reinforce their own findings or theories. Émile Durkheim ([1897] 1951), for example, used official statistics related to suicide rates to demonstrate his idea that lack of social cohesion rather than mental illness led to an increase in unhappiness. This example illustrates a very traditional approach to the use of statistical records in sociological research.

More recently, we have realized that *sources* of statistical data can reveal as much about a social group as the statistics themselves. For example, when someone commits suicide, individuals might choose to report the death as resulting from natural causes or from an accident for a number of reasons. Often, these reports make their way into official records and affect the statistical rates based on these records. If we study the documents upon which the statistics are based, we might learn about the motives and interests of those who produced these documents. For example, in our example of suicide rates, document analysis could reveal that members of the clergy were reluctant to classify certain deaths as suicides because doing so would deny burial in a consecrated cemetery. Document analysis might also reveal that some families took measures to prevent the deaths of loved ones from being labelled as suicides to avoid losing life-insurance benefits. It might even reveal that officials chose to classify some suicides as natural deaths, perhaps to protect the reputation of prominent members of the community. Thus, an examination of the documents behind suicide rates could reveal much about the social stigma a society attaches to committing suicide. A study of the documents behind the statistics may reveal that these statistics are not as objective as they seem and could shed light on deeper meanings of such statistics.

Researchers can also gain insight into the ideologies behind previously conducted studies by analyzing the design of the forms used to collect statistical data. To understand what such analysis can reveal, let us compare how questions of race and ethnicity are treated on the American census (US Census Bureau 2010) to how such questions are treated on the Canadian census (Statistics Canada 2006). The American form first asks if the person who is filling out the form is of 'Hispanic, Latino, or Spanish origin'; it then asks 'What is [this person's] race?', followed by a list of options. In contrast, the Canadian form does not use the word *race*. Rather, it has three questions about *identity*: 'What were the ethnic or cultural origins of this person's *ancestors*?'; 'Is this person an Aboriginal person, that is, North American Indian, Métis, or Inuit (Eskimo)?'; and 'Is this person' . . . (followed by a list of racial, ethnic, and geographic designations). In addition, the Canadian form provides rationales for asking about ancestry and identity ('The census has collected information on the ancestral origins for the population for over 100 years to capture the composition of Canada's diverse population' and 'This information is collected to support programs that promote equal opportunity for everyone to share in the social, cultural, and economic life of Canada'). The American form does not give a reason for the questions related to race.

Because these studies were designed to address national interests, we can interpret differences in how the two countries think about ethnicity and race. These differences tell us much about differing national identities. The focus on 'ethnicity' and the rationales that appear on the Canadian census questionnaire suggest that Statistics Canada seeks to represent Canada to Canadians as a multicultural society that appreciates its diversity and seeks full participation from its diverse population. The explanations about what the information will be used for also suggest that Statistics Canada respects respondents as intelligent partners in the information-gathering process. In contrast, the American form focusses on 'race', a category loaded with

meaning across the history of the country, and does not offer any explanation as to why the census is being conducted.

We can also see similarities in the way questions of identity are presented.
For example, both forms expect individuals to identify with at least one race
or ethnic heritage. Both forms also invite the respondent to check one or
more boxes for racial or ethnic identity, which reflects social changes associated with increased rates of intermarriage among diverse groups. In the past,
the forms would have asked each person to check only one box. At the same
time, the Canadian form instructs Aboriginal individuals to skip the following question on heritage, suggesting that the creators of the form do not
think that the possibility of a mixed heritage applies to them. The American
form also makes assumptions about how individuals understand their own
identity. It states that, for the purpose of the census, Hispanic, Latino, or
Spanish origin does not designate 'race'. These observations relate to only
a few questions on the forms; a full analysis would surely yield fascinating
conclusions.

Maps

Maps provide a strong example of the sort of documents that represent not
'reality' itself but a translation of reality. Think of how your city is depicted
on a roadmap, and compare that representation to the geographical reality
you encounter every day. Howard S. Becker (1986b) uses the example of
San Francisco to illustrate this point. He notes that San Francisco is a very
hilly city. Yet, despite cartographers' ability to indicate hills on a map, these
hills are absent from the road maps most tourists pick up to navigate the city
streets. Becker points out that we can determine the intended user of these
maps based on this omission. These maps are designed for people in cars
who are not worried about having to hike up and down hills. These maps are
not designed for pedestrians, who might be quite chagrined to discover that
the short walk they had used the map to plan entails walking up and down
very steep hills.

I experienced the limitations of using a map to plan a physical journey
when I visited the city of Suwon in Korea. My friend and I, using the map
shown in Figure 6.1, planned to circumnavigate the city by walking on
top of the walls that surround it. The map did not indicate that the wall
includes many flights of steps that make the walk very challenging. Boy,
were we tired at the end of our trek! Clearly, this map was not designed
with us in mind. Yet the map does provide evidence that indicates the
intended users. Along the major streets, tiny icons indicate numerous bus
stops. This detail, in addition to the clear labelling on sites of interest,
suggests that the map was designed for tourists planning to navigate the
city by bus.

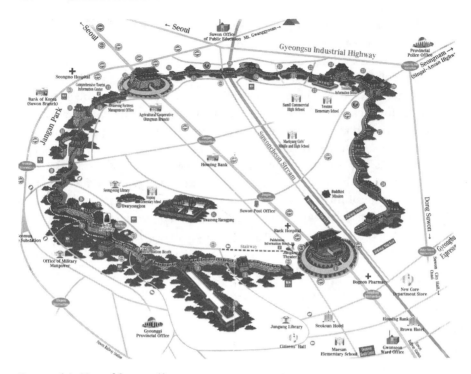

FIGURE 6.1 Map of Suwon, Korea

Source: Culture and Tourism Department of Suwon City Hall, Korea.

Letters and Autobiographies

Personal letters and autobiographical accounts can provide insight into individuals' lived experiences. Researchers W.I. Thomas and Florian Znaniecki understood this when they were gathering information for their in-depth study of Polish immigrants, *The Polish Peasant in Europe and America*, a five-volume work that they published beginning in 1918. In developing this groundbreaking study, Thomas and Znaniecki used a biographical approach that involved analyzing autobiographical materials, including letters between peasants in Poland and their relatives in the United States, in conjunction with public documents such as newspaper files and institutional records. Ultimately, this approach led the researchers to understand the lives of immigrants with greater depth than had ever been accomplished before, and this deep understanding led the researchers to identify the concept of '**social disorganization**'. This concept, which suggests that rapid social change can lead to the loss of norms and values, had an enormous effect on the development of sociological research. As Robert Faris noted, it 'turned scholars from humanitarian interest in social problems toward an analysis of the sociological processes of disorganization which cause them' (1967: 16–17). At this time, scholars began to distinguish between what C. Wright Mills ([1959] 1976) would later refer to as 'private troubles', which we can address on an individual basis, and 'public issues', which require social solutions (see Chapter 3 for a discussion of private problems and public issues).

The tone and words writers use in letters and autobiographies can often reveal as much as what the writers choose to discuss. For example, when Will C. van den Hoonaard (2011) conducted an analysis of letters from research ethics boards (REBs) to researchers, he found meaning in the overall impression each document made. He describes the letters as a form of 'institutional display' and argues that the writers adopt a 'voice of authority' by using the passive voice and 'words of insistence' (such as 'please clarify'). This style of writing makes it very difficult for the recipients of the letters (that is, researchers) to argue or resist the decisions of the REB. This 'voice of authority' gives the impression of appealing to 'irrefutable, higher ethical principles'.

As Hammersley and Atkinson note (1983: 130), autobiographical accounts can also help researchers identify sensitizing concepts. I found this to be the case when I analyzed published autobiographical accounts of women's experiences of widowhood. These texts made me aware of the concept of **'identity foreclosure'** and that the women were experiencing 'identifying moments' (D.K. van den Hoonaard 1997). I was then able to address issues related to identity foreclosure when I carried out interviews with my participants. In addition, I noticed that the more recent autobiographies had an advice-giving tone, indicating a societal shift towards an increasing desire for self-help resources.[1] As sociologists, understanding broad social changes can help us understand our research participants within a broader social context.

Professional Publications

Journal articles and scholarly publications can provide broader coverage of a topic than a single researcher might otherwise be able to accumulate on his or her own. By analyzing ongoing discussions and controversies in professional publications, researchers can also follow changing social trends. For example, Dorothy Pawluch (1996) wanted to trace changes in pediatricians' self-perceptions and understanding of their profession. Her initial intention was to base her study primarily on interviews, but she found that published materials provided more insight into the topic. By examining 'articles, discussion, and debates in their professional journals', she identified changes in what pediatricians did and the medicalization of broad aspects of children's lives. Box 6.1 describes the approach she took and the excitement of discovery she experienced as she read these periodicals.

BOX 6.1 ❖ DISCOVERY IN THE LIBRARY

At the time that Dorothy Pawluch was doing her study, pediatricians were starting to expand the territory of their practice by defining more aspects of childhood—for example, sibling rivalry—as having a medical explanation. Yet, not all pediatricians were comfortable with this new direction, as Pawluch's research quickly revealed. Pawluch describes her process of analyzing articles and letters in professional journals using a 'crude but effective' system involving 'a series of margin notations':

> Where I was able to articulate why I thought the observation was significant . . . the notation would be accompanied by a conceptual note . . . I would [later] try to 'translate'. . . what I had found into more analytical language. . . . The note was probably attached to a letter that a pediatrician had written . . . complaining about . . . a discussion of some subject [perhaps sibling rivalry] . . . about which the letter writer did not think pediatrics ought to be concerned. . . . With growing conviction, I [realized] that I would find the story behind pediatricians' involvement with medicalization of childhood in these documents. There was no 'eureka moment', only a growing sense that 'the field', as it were, lay in the pages of the materials I was reading. (2009: 318–30)

Thus, Pawluch's 'exciting discovery'—the existence of widespread controversy surrounding the changes in the profession—lay in the letters to the editor and articles in the professional journals of pediatricians rather than in her interview transcripts or field notes.

Analyzing Documents of Social Institutions

Social institutions produce masses of documents—including mission statements, strategic plans, forms, and letters—that researchers can use as sources of data. Dorothy Smith, in developing a research method called **institutional ethnography (IE)**, has argued that such documents can 'produce and sustain standardized practices' and establish 'relations of ruling' (Smith 2005, cited in McCloskey 2008: 44). In other words, bureaucratic forms 'represent people, establish priorities, and dismiss specific events or individuals' (McCloskey 2008: 44). To see how bureaucratic documents 'rule' the experiences of individuals who live and work in institutions, we will look at two IE studies that combine document analysis with participant observation to examine social life in nursing homes.

First, let us revisit Timothy Diamond's (1992) study of life in nursing homes, which we first encountered in Chapter 3. In one component of his study, Diamond examined the process of charting (Diamond 1992: 130–67).

Diamond used a combination of participation and analysis of residents' charts to demonstrate how these texts misrepresented the actual work that nursing assistants did. Along with their 'official' work—the physical tasks that authorities monitored through the charts—nursing assistants talked to, comforted, and cajoled residents. Diamond describes how this complex relational work was reduced to a tick mark on a chart. Officially, 'if it wasn't charted it didn't happen, but much more happened than got charted' (Diamond 1992: 137). Hence, the documents rendered invisible much of the work the nursing assistants did in the institutions:

> The chart demanded that whatever happened as a human encounter be eliminated from the recording of the event. Recording the work in the charts came to be no more than jotting down numbers and check marks, transforming it out of social contexts into a narrative of tasks . . . [the work] became simply menial and mechanical as recorded. (1992: 164)

Diamond's juxtaposition of the actual work the nursing assistants did with the way it was shrunk down to unskilled labour in official documents provides a powerful picture of the social world of nursing homes.

Next, let us turn to Rose McCloskey's (2008) Canadian study on the transfer of nursing-home residents to hospital emergency rooms (ERs) via ambulance. Like Diamond, McCloskey used a combination of first-hand observations and document analysis to complete her study. McCloskey notes that her analysis of the patients' 'care plans' revealed a greater interest in demonstrating 'the facility's ability to identify residents' needs' than in actually addressing those needs (2008: 114). In addition, the standardized forms that ambulance personnel complete and the standard ER records showed the system's interest in bureaucratizing the care of patients. As McCloskey observes,

> Standard texts and protocols provide ER practitioners with the legitimacy necessary to think and act in a mindless fashion. Mindless strategies satisfy the ER's need for timely responses to complex circumstances and help to ensure objectivity is upheld. (2008: 119)

McCloskey's findings regarding the use of forms to selectively record aspects of experience are similar to Diamond's. Her study, like Daimond's, captures how documents of social institutions can contribute to 'relations of ruling' and establish the dominance of bureaucracy in the nursing-home setting.

Analyzing Media Content and Reflections of Reality
News Media

News coverage can frame our understanding of our social world and can communicate the importance, or lack of importance, of issues, people, and events. Therefore, it is not surprising that researchers use material from the news media as a source of data. Below, we will examine some examples of how researchers have analyzed articles from popular newspapers and magazines.

If you pay attention to the news, you may be under the impression that we are in the grip of a crime wave. There is heavy coverage of violent crime, and many politicians are promoting a 'tough-on-crime' agenda that only makes sense if the incidence of crime is increasing. But, if you look at actual statistics, you will discover that the crime rate has been falling for years. What is going on? Altheide and Michalowski (1999) provide a possible explanation in their study on the use of the term *fear* in a daily newspaper, *The Arizona Republic*, from 1987 to 1996.

Altheide and Michalowski (1999: 478) used the concept of **frames** to conduct their analysis. As they note, frames shape media articles by determining 'what will be discussed, how it will be discussed, and above all, how it will not be discussed' (1999: 478). These frames contribute to particular definitions of the situation, which, as we have seen, have consequences for individuals and societies.[2] Altheide and Michalowski observe that media reports frequently use a 'problem frame', which they describe as 'a secular alternative to the morality play' and characterize as having a 'narrative structure, universal moral meanings, specific time and place, and an unambiguous focus on disorder', to 'satisfy the entertainment dimension of news' (1999: 479). They further note that this frame often generates reports about fear.

Altheide and Michalowski describe their method as both a 'mapping' of 'where the word and related references to fear occur throughout news reports' and a 'tracking' of 'changes in usage, particularly with different topics and issues, over time' (1999: 477). Through this mapping and tracking, the researchers were able to identify the top three topics associated with fear in newspapers: children, crime, and schools. Tracking the use of the term over time revealed that *fear* was more prevalent in the news at the time of their study than it had been a few years earlier. In their conclusion, Altheide and Michalowski comment that 'fear is a larger part of our symbolic landscape at a time when the social terrain is comparatively routine, predictable, and safe' (1999: 500).[3]

Clarke and Binns (2006) also used the concept of frames in their analysis of the portrayal of heart disease in the 20 magazines with the highest circulation in Canada. Looking at manifest content, they identified three frames: medical, lifestyle, and social-structural. They found that the medical frame was dominant. It portrayed 'supreme optimism', describing 'medical interventions . . . as if they occur in highly optimistic contexts and have only positive consequences'. Medicine was depicted as good and heroic, while the body was characterized as 'bad' (2006: 42–3). The lifestyle frame encouraged individuals to take responsibility for their own health by adopting a 'list' of healthy habits. Yet, as Clarke and Binns also observed, when celebrities with heart disease were discussed, the articles attributed their conditions to external factors such as the unavoidable stress of their jobs rather than to individual lifestyle choices. Least common were articles that used the social-structural frame, despite the fact that many studies have shown that income is one of the strongest predictors of health status.

Juanne Clarke (2006) conducted a similar study on the portrayal of Alzheimer's disease in magazines. She found that even though there is much uncertainty about the causes, diagnosis, and treatment of Alzheimer's, the medical frame was dominant. As a result, the articles focussed on the perspectives of doctors and health professionals rather than on those of individuals with Alzheimer's.[4] She also found that the articles described Alzheimer's almost entirely in its 'later stages and in language that exacerbates fear' and that the little hope a reader might find in the articles is located in pharmaceutical and other medical interventions. Clarke concluded that fear is exacerbated by the lengthy lists of possible causes and potential therapies, and hope is then presented as lodged in the medical model. Hence, the medical frame serves to reinforce the power of medicine and pharmaceuticals as the appropriate and benign instrument of social control (2006: 274).

Linda Caissie and I have recently embarked on a content analysis of *Zoomer Magazine* (see Caissie and van den Hoonaard 2009). In 2008, the Canadian Association for Retired Persons 'relaunched' its magazine. In doing so, it changed the name of the magazine from *CARP Magazine* to *Zoomer Magazine* in an attempt to shift its readership to include younger people. People '50 and over' used to be its constituency. The cover now suggests its readers are 'men and women 45 and up'. This magazine is attempting to create a new identity for baby boomers, whom it refers to as 'zoomers'—'boomers with zip'. Our study looks at how the magazine encourages those on the cusp of old age to acquire this new identity and the emerging social meanings related to aging. So far, we have analyzed the covers of the magazine, advertisements, and the 'From the Founder' column. As our study continues, we will look at the articles in the magazine as well as the table of contents to develop a comprehensive understanding of the identity the magazine is constructing. So far, we have found that the early issues of *Zoomer* are Toronto-centric, encourage so-called zoomers to see themselves as forever middle aged, reinforce a culture of beauty and youth, promote consumerism as a means to aging successfully, and ignore social and economic inequality. In terms of frames, *Zoomer Magazine* uses a lifestyle frame, rather than a biomedical or social-structural frame, to approach issues related to aging.

Advertisements

Almost everywhere we go, we see advertisements. We see them so frequently that we tend to take their often bizarre content for granted or at least accept it as normal. As Shulamit Reinharz (1992: 152) commented, 'most [North]

Americans are accustomed to seeing giant females in various states of undress smiling and caressing products such as whiskey, foods, and records'. Yet, as we have seen, qualitative analyses have the potential to shed light on items that are so familiar that they are almost invisible.

As Reinharz's comment might suggest, advertisements have been a favourite source of data among researchers interested in gender roles and ideals. Ads often depict 'cultural ideals to which the media and the marketplace would like us all to aspire . . . [to the] type of body and appearances marketed to . . . and often sought after by teenage girls or boys, or adult women and men' (Warren and Karner 2010: 178–9). Erving Goffman (1979, cited in Holder 2010) did an early analysis of 'gender displays' in advertising. He found that, compared to men, women were presented in a diminished capacity, objectified, over-feminized, and portrayed in insular terms. Goffman also noted that when women and men were posed together, the men were portrayed as central, strong, and dominant in comparison to the women.

Jean Kilbourne has made a series of powerful films that analyze images of women in advertising: *Killing Us Softly* (1979), *Still Killing Us Softly* (1987), *Killing Us Softly 3* (2000), and *Killing Us Softly 4* (2010). Through skilful analysis of a wide array of advertisements, Kilbourne identified a number of recurring themes that exploit the female image. She found that many ads are sexist and violent, promote an ideal of beauty that is not achievable for the vast majority of women, reduce women to body parts or otherwise objectify women, and/or make women seem helpless.

Other researchers have looked at how men are represented in advertisements. For example, Toni Calasanti and Neal King (2007) examined the portrayal of masculinity in Internet ads created by companies that promote products claiming to keep one looking and/or staying young. In particular, they analyzed ads on websites that sell anti-aging products. They concluded that the ads 'include revolutionary depictions of old people forestalling or even defeating the physical incursions of age . . . by affirming a masculine heterosexuality that subordinates women and treats youth as the ideal phase of development' (Calasanti and King 2007: 367). The researchers also noted that the standard for successful aging that these advertisements provide, similar to those standards presented in ads that promote beauty ideals for women, is unattainable for most men.

In another study, Lee, Kim, and Han (2006) explored advertisements through a cultural frame. They compared the portrayal of older people in television advertisements in South Korea and the United States. They found that there was an underrepresentation of older people in advertisements in both countries, although older people were more likely to play major roles in South Korean advertisements than in American advertisements. As well, although there were stereotypical representations in both countries, the images in South Korea were more positive.

Fiction

While fictional representations, by definition, depart from reality, they still reflect certain aspects of our world and our experiences. Thus, as Hammersley and Atkinson (1983: 131) suggest, researchers can analyze the 'themes, images, [and] metaphors' used in fiction to become aware of and 'sensitized to cultural themes pertaining to sex, gender, family, work, success, failure, commitments, health and illness, the law, crime, and social control'.

To get a better sense of how researchers can draw meaning from fictional representations, let us look at a study I conducted with Will C. van den Hoonaard in which we analyzed the portrayal of airports in fictional children's picture books and in fictional films for adults. We chose to compare these two media because they represent 'some of the most generalized ways to offer anticipatory socialization to large numbers of people' (1991: 3).

Children's literature is often didactic, with the aim of educating children about some aspect of the world. Thus, we were not surprised to discover that the five books we examined (all published between 1967 and 1982) focussed on preparing children for the 'airport experience'. We found that the books took three principal approaches to achieving this goal. First, they introduced children to unfamiliar technologies. We found that almost 42 per cent of pictures in the texts dealt with repairs and plane maintenance. These pictures most often showed cockpit scenes; tarmac and runway activity such as loading food, luggage, or freight; fuelling procedures; and safety-related technologies such as metal detectors, wind socks, weather stations, runway lights, and control towers. Second, the books introduced children to the organization of airports. The images here included organized crowds acting towards a common purpose such as arriving at the terminal by means of ground transport, buying tickets, waiting in lounges, and securing their luggage at check-in points; a smaller number of images depicted activities associated with disembarking and leaving the airport after the flight. Third, the books introduced children to the laws and control measures that govern people's behaviour in airports, with 12 per cent of images relating to this concern.

Notable was the absence of images depicting children interacting with the airport environment. The images showed children reading and waiting, but there were no images of children playing with airport social organization (perhaps running down the very long hallways, crawling, or climbing on chairs), no instructions for what children should do if they become lost in an airport, and no mention of friends or family members who might greet children after their flight.

What about the portrayal of airports in Hollywood films? We discovered that airport scenes were often used to facilitate major changes in characters' lives and that, by extension, these scenes functioned to prepare audience members for dealing with major changes in their own lives. We noticed that the iconic airport scene in *Casablanca* (1942), perhaps the earliest airport scene in a feature-length movie, set the stage for later films. In particular, this scene exhibited the classic elements of what van Gennep ([1909] 1960) called **'rite of passage'**, elements that recur in many subsequent airport scenes. The rite of passage includes three stages: separation from one's former status and role; transition (or liminality) when one is sanctioned to be different, to not follow accepted norms; and incorporation, during which one assumes a new identity. These three stages were present in all nine movies we studied.[5]

When we compared the portrayal of airports in children's books to that in movies, we found that both representations depicted caricatures of airports, but that these caricatures were drawn to reflect very different aspects of real airports. While the children's literature idealized the experience, the movies equated airport experience with disruption and change. Both the children's books and the movies offered anticipatory socialization to their intended audience, but the former did so on a literal level (preparing children for their first trip to the airport), while the latter did so on a metaphorical level (preparing adult viewers for dealing with significant life changes).

In a separate study, I analyzed fiction for a somewhat different purpose. I looked at novels and movies to identify common stereotypes and conceptions of widowers. I found that there are generally two characterizations of widowers in these media. The first, more common, is that of the young widower whose wife has died violently, often in an accident or at the hands of a murderer, or 'passed away' after struggling with a disease. This young man is often a romantic character. You might think of Tom Hanks' character in *Sleepless in Seattle* (1993), whose wife died of cancer, or the widower in Stephen King's *Bag of Bones* (1998), whose wife died after having a brain aneurism. The second characterization is that of the lost older man, such as Jack Nicholson's character in *About Schmidt* (2002), whose life falls apart as he retires and becomes widowed almost simultaneously.

Television

Television is a unique medium in that it brings together fictional and non-fictional representations of reality in various ways. In a two-hour period of watching television, a viewer might take in a scripted sitcom about college students, a 'reality' show about life as a former rock star, a news program discussing local and global events, and a documentary on global warming, all the while being bombarded with advertisements at regular intervals. If the viewer chooses to 'flip' between channels, he or she may be exposed to any number of influences in two hours. With this in mind, some researchers have analyzed how television programming, in all its forms, reflects widespread conceptions of social issues.

Diana Rose (2004, 1998), for example, has looked at how mental illness is portrayed on television in the United Kingdom. Rose looked at mental illness as it appeared on prime-time TV, whether on news programs, documentaries, soap operas, dramas, or situation comedies. She found that mental illness is frequently associated with danger and violence. Rose also discovered that 'people with mental illness tend to be filmed alone and with close-up or extreme-close-up shots whilst others are filmed medium-close-up to medium-wide and they are often not alone in the shot' (1998: 223). Rose further documents a theme of community neglect of the mentally ill, which points to concern with the failure of public policy, a major topic of discussion at the time of her study.

Analyzing Physical Objects

While analysis of physical objects might not be appropriate to all studies, everyday objects can provide the astute researcher with more information than you might think. I first realized how much objects can reveal while I was collecting garbage with an organization that has 'adopted' a stretch of road near my home. We have been going out twice a year, for the last 10 years or so, to pick up items that people have dumped onto the side of the road. We always spend some time comparing what we have found and thinking about what it might tell us about our community. For example, we find many 'Tim's cups' along the roadway. Most likely, this indicates the popularity of Tim Hortons among drivers in our community, but it may also suggest, among other possibilities, a correlation between drinking Tim Hortons' coffee and throwing cups out of moving vehicles. Some parts of the road seem to almost grow beer bottles, suggesting that these locations may be near sites where people come to drink beer in the nearby woods. The most interesting thing I have ever found was an 'anger journal' that had belonged to a man who had been ordered to keep the journal after he had been charged for abusing his wife—possibly, he threw it on the side of the road in a fit of anger.

My group has never done a systematic analysis of what we have found, but we certainly could analyze how many pieces of what kind of garbage we pick up and where they are placed (for example, we tend to find less garbage in front of houses). We might even start by thinking about what the presence of the 'Adopt-a-Highway' program says about the community. Surely, a community would not need such a program if people did not regularly litter or if residents did not care about the litter along the road.

Jeff Ferrell (2006) has done a systematic study of what people have thrown out. He calls his work a 'close ethnography of objects lost and found' (2006: 4). Ferrell's methods of 'data collection' included dumpster diving, trash picking, and street scavenging. Through his careful sorting, counting, and categorizing of what other people had discarded, he 'developed a critical, grounded understanding of contemporary consumption and its relation to collective wastefulness' (2006: 6).

Ferrell found two kinds of garbage that tell a great deal about contemporary society. First, he came upon what he calls an 'overwhelming, inundating, surplus' of things that were 'useful, functional, desirable, [and] many times unused and unmarred' (2006: 16–7) that indicated the wastefulness and extreme consumerism that are characteristic of our culture. In his analysis, Ferrell provides a wealth of evidence to make the case for the prevalence of overconsumption in our society (see Box 6.2).

Second, he found a type of curbside trash that is the 'residue of significant life changes'. These include the thrown-out objects that result from 'significant life changes' such as divorces and deaths. This sort of garbage includes 'the material residue of shared meaning . . . : bronzed baby shoes, diplomas, wedding photos, ticket stubs, [and] old newspaper clippings'. Ferrell refers to these items as 'material postmortems' (2006: 19). This second type of trash indicates our desire to rid ourselves of unhappy reminders of the past after we go through a major change in our life.

While my group found Tim Hortons cups, Ferrell, who did his study in Texas, found bullets 'everywhere [he] scrounge[d]' (2006: 59). In all the years I've been picking up trash in New Brunswick, I have never found a single bullet, and I live in deer-hunting country. Such factors indicate very different ways of life.

BOX 6.2 ⊛ MEANING IN TRASH

In *Empire of Scrounge*, Jeff Ferrell systematically documents many instances of finding perfectly good, often unused, merchandise thrown out as though it were useless. Early in the text, he notes the surprising contents of one particular pile of trash, which he found on a street running behind a strip of mansions in a highly affluent neighbourhood:

> Working my way through the bags and boxes, I discovered that they were full of pretty party favours, decorations, gift wrap, used paper plates and paper cups, and expensive baby gifts. Many of the gifts, in fact, were still sealed new in their gift boxes—the absurd aftermath of a baby shower meant mostly for show. (Ferrell 2006: 20)

Although Ferrell is probably correct in his interpretation of the 'trash' from the baby shower, it is also possible that the expectant mother in this particular case had a miscarriage after the shower and that the mountain of trash is actually evidence of a sudden tragedy. This possibility exposes a limitation of using material objects as data. They are not direct evidence of what has happened and what it has meant.

Summary

In this chapter, we have surveyed some of the myriad approaches to content analysis. We also discussed the benefits and challenges of using pre-existing data rather than data generated by other more participatory methods. As we have seen, researchers often do content analysis with a critical eye. One source of content that we have not addressed in depth is the Internet, but we will look at Internet-based research more closely when we discuss virtual ethnography in Chapter 9, 'New Directions in Qualitative Research'. In the next chapter, you will learn about how qualitative researchers analyze the data they obtain in their studies.

Key Terms

frame	latent content	unobtrusive
identity foreclosure	manifest content	measures
institutional	rite of passage	
ethnography (IE)	social disorganization	

Questions for Critical Thought

1. Keeping in mind Jeff Ferrell's study of trash, think about the kinds of things that you routinely throw out and where you discard them. What conclusions might an 'ethnographer of trash' come to about your way of life based on what she or he would find in your trash?

2. Even though romance novels are considered low-status forms of fiction, many women read them voraciously. How might you design a content analysis of this genre to explore how it presents the perfect relationship, the perfect man, and the perfect courtship? What might such a study tell us about widely held conceptions of 'romantic' relationships? Think about the possible frames a romance novel might use to construct a definition of the situation about romance.

3. If you were to do a study of student life at your university, what texts would you include in your analysis, and why?

Exercises

1. Do an analysis of the student evaluation form at your university. (You should be able to get a copy from the registrar's office at your university.) Make a list of the topics of each question and think about what the list tells you about how the university wants to represent itself to itself, to its faculty, and to its students. If you were to design your own questionnaire, what items

would you include? What do the differences between the official form and yours tell you about divergent ideas about what matters in a university class and the goals you have contrasted with the university's goals?

2. Look at a copy of each of four different magazines—for example, *Maclean's*, *Chatelaine*, *National Geographic*, and *Men's Health*. Examine the ads carefully and answer the following questions: To what kind of audience is the magazine addressed? What does the magazine suggest are the interests and the preoccupations of its readers? How does the magazine demonstrate how men and women relate to one another? What messages about race, ethnicity, or age do the images imply? Are there any striking patterns in the photos? If so, what might these patterns suggest?

3. Watch five hours of scripted television shows and analyze how aging and older characters are represented. Consider depictions both in the shows themselves and in the advertisements that run during each show. What does the manifest content tell you about the types of characters represented? What does the latent content tell you about how the audience is meant to perceive the characters?

Suggested Readings

Jeff Ferrell. 2006. *The Empire of Scrounge: Inside the Urban Underground of Dumpster Diving, Trash Picking, and Street Scavenging*. New York: New York University Press. Jeff Ferrell spent eight months living off what he acquired by going through dumpsters and other sources of discarded goods. This book is his account of the community of those who live off the streets as well as an 'ethnography' of the material objects. His photographs and prose provide an intriguing account that would lead anyone to question contemporary consumer society.

Dorothy Pawluch. 1996. *The New Pediatrics: A Profession in Transition*. New York: Aldine de Gruyter. This study traces the evolution of the field of pediatrics as the dangers of life-threatening illnesses for children receded. It is a model of how to use professional publications in analysis.

Related Websites

YouTube
www.youtube.com

There are several videos on YouTube that provide excellent coverage of how researchers have used unobtrusive measures. In particular, you may want to check out Jeff Ferrell's short video about dumpster diving and clips from *Killing Us Softly 4*, Jean Kilbourne's latest installment of her analysis of advertising's image of women. You can also view videos of various advertisements and analyze them for yourself. (The ads produced by Dove for its Campaign for Real Beauty provide interesting alternatives to the approaches to aging and beauty that advertisements more commonly display.)

How to Read Ads

www.ltcconline.net/lukas/gender/background/howto.htm

This website provides advice on how to interpret ads. The approach is based on the tripartite approach Katherine Frith developed in her 1998 publication *Undressing the Ad: Reading Culture in Advertising* (New York: Peter Lang).

7 Trust the Process: Analyzing Qualitative Data

Learning Objectives

- ⊛ To become familiar with the process of data analysis
- ⊛ To understand how to go about coding
- ⊛ To grasp how to develop and use themes, sensitizing concepts, and generic social processes in your analysis

Introduction

Qualitative research, whether it involves field work, in-depth interviews, or document analysis, yields mountains of data that can intimidate any researcher, novice or experienced. The most basic fear of all qualitative researchers is that they won't find anything in their data. I have this feeling every time I do a study. But there are always things to find, usually more than a single study can address. So, it is very important to **trust the process** and to have faith that there are important themes in your data and that you will have the insight and skill to find them and tie them together in meaningful ways. Although data analysis involves what Lofland and Lofland (1995: 181) have referred to as 'routine activities'—for example, writing up full field notes, transcribing interviews, correcting transcripts, reading and rereading transcripts and notes, and **coding** data—the process is open ended and creative, with high points of excitement that accompany unexpected insights.

There are different ways to go about analyzing qualitative data, and the choice depends on the researcher's theoretical perspective, professional interests, and research questions. I do my work from a symbolic interactionist perspective, so I tend to highlight how my participants understand their everyday lives and how they go about explaining them to me. When I conduct interviews, I take an active-interview approach and, therefore, pay close attention to how the interaction has played out in the interview. In addition, because I have an ongoing interest in issues of gender, I always keep an eye out for how gender identity affects a person's understanding of her or his social world.

Although you may follow an approach that reflects your perspective, never begin with predetermined concepts, hypotheses, or theoretical frameworks. Some novice researchers, overwhelmed by the amount of data they uncover, are tempted to choose a hypothesis and then search for items in their field notes or interviews that support that hypothesis. Resist this impulse. As Maria Mayan (2009 93) points out, if you were to give in to this temptation, you would be importing a deductive approach into your research and would 'squash any opportunity for new ideas or notions of the phenomenon' you are studying. Your process may then come to resemble Cinderella's stepsisters' attempts to force their big feet into her tiny glass slipper by cutting off their toes. You do not want to mutilate your data to fit your preconceived notions.

Many researchers engage in **reflexivity** as they interpret their data. They recognize that their own experiences and status (their gender, age, class, profession, etc.) affect the way that participants interact with them. For example, as I thought about my interviews with older widowers, I took into account that I, as a middle-aged woman, was the type of person with whom some of the men might be interested in forming a romantic relationship. Thus, I had to accept that some of my participants may have been trying to impress me during the interview process. Many researchers also consider how their own perceptions and experiences influence their interpretation of the data (Dowling 2008).

Although there are a number of software packages on the market to use in qualitative data analysis (for example, NVivo), I will not discuss them in this chapter for two reasons. The first is that they do not do the conceptual work for you. It is essential that you learn how to analyze data on your own before you turn to a data-management tool for help. Jumping into the software too soon is like using a calculator before you learn to add. If you do not understand the process, you will not have any way of knowing if your analysis makes sense. The second reason is an extension of the first: when you code data using a software package, especially if you are a novice researcher, you may cut off options too early in the process and lose some of the flexibility that is the strength of qualitative research. If you do choose to use one of these programs, remember that you will likely have to either go back to your data to develop new **codes** as you go along or risk compromising your analysis by sticking to decisions you made too early in the coding process. In my own research, I use a word-processing program when I am analyzing my data, and I find it works very well. Interestingly, Warren and Karner (2010: 222) note that most published qualitative researchers prefer to use a word-processing program rather than a data-management program to help them organize their data.

Unlike data analysis in quantitative research, which begins only after all of the data have been collected, analysis goes on throughout the life of a qualitative study. As you may have noticed, we have already discussed some of the early steps in data analysis (for example, writing up full field notes and transcribing interviews). In addition, we will continue to discuss certain aspects of analysis in Chapter 8 as we discuss the process of writing up your research. In this chapter, we look at processes most central to analysis. First, we consider how memos can help you keep track of your ideas related to analysis throughout the research process. We also learn about coding interview transcripts and field notes, using stories and sensitizing concepts to gain a deeper understanding of your participants' perspectives, and identifying and analyzing generic social processes to get at the heart of your material. Finally, we discuss how you can join the broader research conversation and make a real contribution to the field.

Beginning with Memos

Analysis starts as soon as you begin to collect your data. For this reason, you should keep a notebook with you at all times to jot down **memos**. You never know when an idea will hit you, and you do not want to lose any valuable insight. In your notebook, record anything that might help you understand your data later on: your own preliminary ideas, connections you make while in the field, references to articles or books that may contain useful information, and so on. Also record any pertinent comments others make about your research, as such comments can help you approach your research topic from a wider perspective. For example, when I was interviewing widowers, many of my friends and colleagues commented that widowers get married too soon after their wives die and that widowers do not know how to cook or do housework. These comments led me to investigate how widowers think about repartnering as an intrinsic part of widowhood.

Once you leave the field, transfer your notes to a computer file. This process will force you to make sense of your notes and provide you with a back-up copy in case you lose your notebook. Make sure to date each memo and note what you were reading or thinking about or doing at the time you got the idea. Box 7.1 includes sample memos from my study of old men's experiences as widowers (see D.K. van den Hoonaard 2010). Several of the memos contain ideas and questions that occurred to me while I was reading interview transcripts or listening to the recordings of interviews; others are meant to reminded me of literature I wanted to keep in mind as I did my analysis.

You will find it useful to read through your memos on a regular basis while you are analyzing and writing up your data. This perusal will remind you of your early ideas as you work. As Charmaz (2006) notes, good memos may help you flesh out concepts or theoretical explanations that will help you understand your findings.

As time goes on, you will want to consult your field notes or interview transcripts and begin the process of coding.

Box 7.1 ❊ Sample Memos

26 April 2002

From interview with 'DL'

- Thoughts about being a widower—incl. stereotypes
- Participants' tendency to turn topic of interview to their own accomplishments
- Is having a woman something that is just part of being a man?
- Note: he doesn't mention his wife when he talks about his son's dyslexia—she's an invisible presence in his interview

28 April 2002

From interview with 'TK'

- This idea that women are chasing men—is this similar to the idea that young men are pursued by women who want commitment the men don't want to give?

30 April 2002

From interview with 'WN'

- Cautionary comments about men rushing into new relationships and his own 'correct' way of dealing with things
- Uses language of being trapped if married to the wrong person
- Do men talk more about what they do and women more about what others do, in terms of how the experience works out?
- Was he invited out for coffee because he was a man? Is there any way to find out?

3 May 2002

From interview with 'FL'

- Finances—he bought a computer program to figure out finances—vs women who find a person, usually a male relative or financial advisor, to help them
- 2 aspects of parenting—functional (e.g., getting food on the table) and emotional
- Widower identity—does not seem to exist and some men look for other ways to self-identify to avoid the ambiguity of calling themselves widowers. So, if there's no image, then self-identifying is empty.

8 May 2002

From interview with 'GA'

It seems that, for women, not looking for another man is a badge of honour in some ways—she is loyal to a man who was wonderful. For men, it may be that not being interested in other women or not being able to find one may be a weakness—they're too attached to their wives. Hmm.

11 November 2005

Revisit Sarah H. Matthews, *The Social World of Old Women*, the chapter on maintaining a precarious self-identity. In this chapter, she identifies strategies old

(continued)

women use to distance themselves from the self-identity as old women . . . maybe this would work in identifying strategies men use to maintain a sense of masculinity.
- p. 82: 'justifying labels'
- maybe p. 83: attaching new meaning to old activities

Coding Interview Transcripts and Field Notes

Analyzing qualitative data is labour intensive, and it requires time for you to think and let ideas percolate. There are no real shortcuts to interpreting data. Lofland and Lofland (1995: 185–6) liken analysis to the solving of a puzzle and explain that finding theoretical propositions in the 'chaos of "mere data"' can be exciting and exhilarating. They exhort us to 'go for the high!'

Once you have typed out your interview transcripts or field notes, it is time to read them through. When you are finished reading them, read them again, think about them, and read them again, all the while writing memos. Andrea Doucet (2007: 278–84) finds it useful to focus on a different aspect with each pass when she is analyzing data from interviews. First she reads each transcript with attention to the story that her participant is telling and tries to understand 'what is going on here'. Then she 'reads [her]self' into the story and thinks about her own reactions to what the participant said and did in the interview. Her third reading is an 'I' reading, during which she focusses on how the person speaks about her or himself. This reading sheds light on how the participant sees and presents her or himself in the social world. In later readings, she looks at the location of the participant in her or his social network and in wider social structures.

As you analyze your data, you will be trying to refine your research questions. Remember that because analysis occurs throughout the research process, your research questions will change across the life of your study. Thus, Howard S. Becker (1998: 121) suggests an approach that involves finding a question in the data: 'The data I have here answer a question. What question could I possibly be asking to which what I have written down in my notes [or transcripts] is a reasonable answer?' Similarly, Kathy Charmaz (2001: 678) advises that we ask of our data, 'what is happening here?' The approach suggested by Becker and by Charmaz reminds me of the quiz show *Jeopardy*: The data provide the answer, and you have to figure out the question.

To determine the questions that your data answer, you will begin by coding your data. The word *code* may be intimidating and make it seem as though developing codes is a complex business, but there is no need to over-complicate it. Codes are simply names for the topics, activities, events, and people that come up in your transcripts or field notes. While the term *coding* is borrowed from quantitative analysis, where words and ideas are translated into numbers, we do not reduce data to numbers in qualitative research. Coding, in our case, simply means finding terms or phrases to categorize chunks of the data so that we can work with them. When you code, you first identify the themes that appear in your data. Later in the process, you will look for and develop more detailed sub-themes and concepts.

The first step in coding is called '**open coding**', a process closely associated with **grounded theory** (Glaser and Strauss 1967, Charmaz 2006). Open coding involves labelling the themes that you find in your transcripts or field notes. At this early stage, do not try to narrow down what you are looking for and do not limit your codes to what seems relevant to your research questions. You should not decide on your codes in advance, or you may lose the richness of your data and, in fact, misrepresent them. Kathy Charmaz (2006) encourages speed and spontaneity for this initial coding because it can spark creative thinking. Later, you will revise and improve on these initial codes.

While you do not want to narrow your focus too much in advance, you will find that your background knowledge and experience shape the types of information you find. This is natural, and it can lead you to become aware of things that other researchers might not have found, given the same data. For example, if you are familiar with your research topic, you may notice that some theme seems to be missing from your transcripts or field notes. If you have strong reasons to believe that a theme is important even if your participants have not discussed it, re-read your notes or transcripts to see if you can find any clues as to what is going on.

I have often gained insight into my participants' experiences by investigating themes that seem to be missing. In my interviews with Iranian Bahá'ís who came to Canada as religious refugees, I noticed that none of the people I interviewed discussed the issue of racism. Yet, I knew that at least some of these people must have experienced some racism. I, therefore, **problematized** the issue and looked for clues in the data to explain the absence of discussions on racism. I found that the participants had described many examples of extreme persecution in their country of origin, and these experiences led them to minimize any less severe problems they had in Canada. As a result, they downplayed the racism they encountered in their new surroundings and excused racist behaviour as understandable or characteristic of only a few individuals. In the end, questioning the absence of the theme of racism in the interviews led me to a deeper appreciation of the creativity the participants used to find a place for themselves in their new communities. Similarly, when analyzing my field notes in my retirement-community study, I noticed that there were very few instances where new residents and original residents of the community appeared to be friends. I also observed that there were few friendships between widowed and non-widowed people and between snowbirds (residents who were only in the community in the winter) and full-time residents. These absences led me to investigate how and why newcomers, snowbirds, and widowed persons became socially marginal in the community.

As you begin your process of coding, try to analyze your data in manageable pieces. If you are working with field notes, you might want to look at your notes for each session and identify a few recurring themes. When looking through transcripts, try to identify a few themes that characterize each interview. Sharon Kaufman (1986) used this method for her classic study *The Ageless Self*. In describing how she found themes in her transcripts, she explains that the theme of an interview is a topic or issue that comes up over and over again. For example, in my own research, one widow whom I interviewed repeatedly brought up the poor relationship she had with her stepchildren. This topic became the theme of her interview.

At this early stage, you do not have to worry about how everything fits together. Trusting the process means taking one step at a time. Trying to do everything at once would, indeed, be overwhelming. You will likely find that your early codes are 'numerous and varied' (Lofland and Lofland 1995) because they identify the issues that your participants brought up. In addition, you may find that individual items, events, or stories fit into several thematic categories. As you accumulate more data, you will also likely realize that you cannot develop all the topics that show up in your notes or transcripts. All of this is fine—the most important themes and questions will become clear to you as your analysis progresses.

Once you have coded each transcript or set of field notes, your next step is to bring the material together. This requires assembling the data related to each particular theme in one place. If your transcripts or notes are quite long and your research question is broad, you might find it useful to think of organizing your themes into chapters, as in a book. So, for example, when I was analyzing my data on women's experiences of widowhood, I grouped sections of my interview transcripts under headings such as 'What does it mean to be a widow?', 'How do widows' relationships with their children change?', and 'What kinds of new things do widows learn to do?' Next, read over each transcript or set of field notes (again!), make a file for each theme, and then copy all the data related to each theme into the appropriate file. You should also note where each chunk of data came from so that you can always place it in its original context.

As you are compiling your data into thematic chapters, you will also continue to develop memos on your ideas for how to organize your data,

---

Box 7.2 ⚙ **Memo: Ideas for Chapter on Widows' Relationships with Men**

- Experience with men—new ways of relating
- Comments about male guests and gossip ('J', 'M', 'R', 'D')
- For the widows who had a relationship ('D', 'C') this was a theme of the interview
- Strategies for male companionship—safe ways to go about it ('A' with ballroom dancing; 'D' and 'I' at church)
- Men's attitudes
- Wedding-ring issues
- Kids' attitudes about remarriage

---

both within each chapter and throughout your written analysis as a whole. Box 7.2 includes my ideas for a chapter on widows' relationships with men. At this point, you may also decide on a tentative outline or table of contents to use when you are writing up your study (see Chapter 8), but keep in mind that the table of contents is not set in stone. Its purpose is to help you think about the overall narrative or way that you can explain what you have found.

Once you have finished sorting your data into open codes, you are ready for the next step—**focussed coding**. During this phase, go through the material that relates to each broad, open code and re-code for specific aspects of the theme. So, for example, in the widowhood study, after pulling together all the data related to the theme of learning new things, I did focussed coding and made separate files for the more specific sub-themes of learning to do new things, in general; learning to live alone; learning to drive/learning to drive alone; and changing self-concepts related to learning to do new things. Then I worked with each file separately.[1]

During this process, you will winnow out less useful codes and begin to focus on a select number of more productive codes (Lofland and Lofland 1995: 192). As you go through the data more closely, you will discover concepts and have ideas that escaped your attention when you were reading to identify your initial codes (Charmaz 2006: 50). By staying very close to the data, you can avoid the mistake of 'imputing your motives, fears, or unresolved issues to your respondents and . . . data' (Charmaz 2006: 53).

As you are coding your data, remember that a primary goal of qualitative research is to understand the participant's situation from his or her point of view. Because the participant is the expert on his or her own situation, you can understand the data only if you know what the data mean to each participant. Next, we will look at two approaches to understanding your participants' situations in-depth: analyzing **stories** and developing **sensitizing concepts**.

Stories

A story is a refined version of events. Often, when someone tells a story, he or she has told that story before and has, with each telling, crystallized the meaning that the narrative holds for him or her. Telling a story is usually purposeful; there is a moral to the story that addresses the issue at hand, and the teller wants the listener to understand this moral. Many people even adopt a story-telling tone to communicate the importance of the story.

Often, you will learn the most about a participant's situation and self-perception by listening to what Kenyon and Randall (1997: 46–7) have referred to as 'signature stories'. These are tales people like to tell about themselves or situations that they like to narrate. Signature stories reveal something about what makes us tick, about turning points in our path, about why our life has turned out the way it has. They also indicate something about our fundamental beliefs, convictions, and habits. If you think about it, you probably have particular stories that you like to tell about yourself, perhaps to create an impression about the type of person you are and to develop a moral self for your listeners. Whether you are aware of it or not, these stories contribute to the process of what sociologists often call 'impression management' (see Goffman 1959).

In interpretive research, we can analyze stories to understand how our participants understand their place in the world and how they interpret their own status in relation to others.[2] Consider what the following story tells about the man, a widower, who told it to me:

> If you follow all these money grabbers' wishes. Like I went to [the store]; I knew [my wife] used to have [their] credit card. And she had [their customer-loyalty card]. So I went in one day, probably two months after [her death] to try and transfer her . . . points to my name. No way in hell. No, they wanted a copy of her will to see that I was going to get her stuff. They wanted her death certificate, and they wanted her medical and doctor's certificate. So that kind of ticked me off. I was getting kind of ugly at that point. It was stupid. I knew she was dead . . . well, they say, 'well, maybe you kicked her out and you're trying to take all her stuff.' And all this stuff. And I said, 'well, does she owe you any money?' They wouldn't tell me that either. So finally, I said to the girl, 'well, I hope she does . . . You're going to have to find her to get it.' And I never heard from them after that. (D.K. van den Hoonaard 2010: 59)

In telling this story, the man has established himself as a heroic individual who is willing to take on big business, the 'money grabbers'. In contrast, he describes the store's representatives as oppressive and unjust, falsely accusing him, the victim, of kicking his wife out and then attempting to steal from her. Finally, he turns the situation around, suggesting that he has the power in the relationship because the store might want something from him in the future.

Now, compare the previous story to the following one, in which one of my participants, a widow, relates an accomplishment:

> Well there's one thing for instance, and it's so simple, like you know when the hydro goes out on the VCR and the clock, you know, it's blinking twelve o'clock, twelve o'clock, I never ever, now this is so simple, I never adjusted that thing, and I just didn't even know how to open this little box there. . . . I left it for about, oh it must have been about a week blinking. Well, I put a book up so I wouldn't see it. [So you wouldn't see it.] Yeah, I put a book up and said I don't know how to do it. So one day I went downstairs and I took my glasses and I said, 'I'm going to fix this thing or else it's going to be unplugged'. So I sat down and I got the instructions out and I just went step by step and I thought this was a major, oh I did a major job on that. Finally, I got it. And it was just the idea, I had never done it and I had never even looked at the instructions. And a child, of course, could do it. But it was a big achievement there.

Here, the woman telling the story doesn't depict herself as a hero, but rather as an average person who persevered when faced with a difficult task. The woman's purpose in telling the story was to explain how she had developed a sense of confidence that she had not had before.

Sensitizing Concepts

Researchers develop sensitizing concepts to help them understand their participants' world views. Herbert Blumer (1954, cited in W.C. van den Hoonaard 1997: 29) first articulated the idea of sensitizing concepts as 'holding pens'—tools to group similar data together—that we can use to 'frame' the activity we are studying. For the most part, as with the codes we discussed above, sensitizing concepts come from our data themselves rather than from ideas we have before we collect our data.

The first step in developing a sensitizing concept is to look for concepts that the participants in the study formulate for themselves. As you are assessing your data, ask yourself, 'What is this person talking about?', 'Is the idea or process important?', and 'What does this idea or process mean to this person?' Look for words, phrases, and ideas that your participants used frequently, especially those that are not in common usage outside of the group involved in the study. Don't take any terms for granted. Rather, question how participants use them and what they imply about social life. To get a better understanding of how researchers identify, develop, and use sensitizing concepts in their research, let's look at some examples from real-life studies.

When I was interviewing widows, I noticed that many of the women repeatedly used two phrases when they talked about their relationships with their friends: 'keeping up appearances' and 'couples' world'. The women used the first phrase to explain that if they wanted to keep their friends, they had to give the impression that they were doing okay. If they seemed too depressed or talked about their husbands all the time, their friends would drop them like 'a hot potato'. They used the second phrase to capture their feelings of discomfort and exclusion in many social settings due to their status as a single person. One widow emphasized the meaningfulness of the phrase when she told me 'it's a couples' world', defined what she meant, and then repeated, 'I tell you it's a couples' world'. These two concepts contributed to my theoretical understanding of the changed status women experience when they become widows.

In her study of Inuit residents in Arviat, Nunavut, Lisa-Jo van den Scott (2009) identified the concept of 'Southern clothes' as central to the experiences of the residents. The only access this town has to the rest of Canada is on four daily flights. Van den Scott notes that, at the airport, one can easily determine who is leaving and who is not by the way each person looks. She writes,

> Travellers' hats are off, hair is often styled, shoes have now replaced boots. . . . It is commonplace for travellers to leave their Arctic parkas behind and to walk, or run, to the plane through the cold. (2009: 215)

The locals refer to this attire as 'Southern clothes', but van den Scott notes that the concept connotes more than simply a change of style. It refers to 'a way of reaffirming and performing identity and differentiating between [Nunavut and the South]' (2009: 215).

While studying shrimp fishermen in Iceland, Will C. van den Hoonaard (2009a) noticed that the fishermen used the term 'going south' when they talked about going to Reykjavik, which is located in southern Iceland, to negotiate with marine biologists about fishery regulations. The fishermen called this process 'going south' even if they lived south of the capital and were, therefore, actually travelling north to get there. As van den Hoonaard notes, this sensitizing concept

> opened the way to [his] understanding the nature of the relationship between peripheral groups and the 'centre'. . . . The interactions between the shrimpers and the marine biologists echoed the wider characteristics of a society which must constantly deal with the periphery and the centre. (2009a: 101)

Thus, this concept helped van den Hoonaard understand not only the situation of the individuals central to the study but the situation of the wider population as well.

Consulting the Literature

Some sensitizing concepts are very broad and relate to many social contexts. Thus, as you read literature related to your study, you may come across previously identified sensitizing concepts that help you understand the situation of your own participants. When this is the case, remember to create a memo to record the source of your inspiration. This memo will help you in case you want to go back and consult the literature at a later time, and you will need this information if your idea proves fruitful and you end up using the idea in your final written analysis (we will discuss writing up your study, which is an extension of the process of analysis, in the next chapter).

One example of a generalizable sensitizing concept is '**civil inattention**'. Erving Goffman first identified this concept in his influential text *Behavior in Public Places* (1963), in which he analyzed 'ordinary human traffic and the patterning of ordinary social contacts' (4). Goffman developed the concept of civil inattention to explain individuals' habit of subtly acknowledging the presence of others but not focussing on them too intently, thus avoiding any feelings of threat or confrontation (1963: 84).[3] This concept has broad application, as most of us use some form of civil inattention every day—while walking down a crowded street, eating at a restaurant, or even attending a class. Thus, you can see how the concept Goffman developed might be adapted to various situations; indeed, many researchers have used the concept of civil inattention to gain an understanding of their participants' behaviours. Let us look at some other examples.

Arlie R. Hochschild (1979) was the first researcher to develop the concepts of 'emotion work' and 'feeling rules'. She described these concepts in her study of flight attendants and the commercialization of emotions, in which she discovered that the attendants work to make themselves feel a certain way (they engage in emotion work) so that they can display the feelings they are required to have while they are working (feeling rules). Many later researchers have found these sensitizing concepts useful in understanding their own participants. In my study on widows, for example, I found that these concepts informed my understanding of the ways in which my participants described their efforts to 'keep up appearances'.

In their influential text *Awareness of Dying* (1965), Glaser and Strauss identified a series of related concepts to capture the continuum of how much dying patients know about their terminal status. These concepts include 'closed contexts', when the patient is completely in the dark; 'suspicion', when the patient suspects that he or she is dying but no one else will admit the situation; 'mutual pretense', where everyone knows about the impending death but pretends otherwise; and 'open context', when everyone involved both knows and admits to knowing that the patient is dying. Today, these concepts are well known among researchers, and they have been adapted to a variety of other situations. For example, Karen March (1995) used these concepts to help her understand and explain the situation of adoptees who were attempting to control stigma associated with their identities of being adopted.

Scott and Lyman's (1981) concept of 'accounts' provides yet another example. According to their definition, an account is a 'statement made by a social actor to explain unanticipated or untoward behaviour', behaviour that is socially unacceptable at some level. Jacqueline Low (2004), who studied the experience of people who use alternative health therapies, expanded on the initial concept and identified three categories of account in her participants' narratives: the mistaken identity account, the ignorance of others account, and the biographical account.

As you can see, the more reading of others' work you do, the more potential concepts you will have to help you understand your data. Of course, all the concepts you use have to 'earn their way into your analysis' (Glaser 1978, cited in Charmaz 2006). Hence, if a concept does not present itself based on the data you have, do not include the concept in your analysis.

As your analysis proceeds, you will continue to re-evaluate your previous findings in light of your new understandings. Eventually, you will have accumulated enough data to identify generic social processes that relate to your study. In the next section, we will discuss how to go from codes, concepts, and themes to results you can use in your final write up.

Bringing It All Together: From Codes to Generic Social Processes

Once you have coded your data, identified major themes and sub-themes, and located sensitizing concepts, it is time to think about what it all means, to address what Esterberg (2002: 166) calls the '"so what" question'. You need to think about how your various themes and concepts relate to one another and make connections among them. One way of doing this is to interpret them in light of social processes.

Identifying generic social processes within your data can help you describe and explain how things happen and why people do the things they do. To identify such processes, look for commonalities in the ways your participants approach and interpret their situations. Doing background reading on the types of processes other researchers have analyzed in their studies can also inspire you to identify such processes in your own data. While you should never try to make your data fit with a particular generic social process, being aware of such processes can help you understand what is going on in your participants' social world.

The best way to grasp how researchers can identify and use generic social processes in their analysis is to look at examples from previous studies. As you read through the examples below, note how some researchers have identified the broader implications of their findings by comparing what they have discovered about their participants to individuals' situations beyond the limits of their study. Such comparisons often present themselves at the end of the analysis process, once the researcher has gained a full understanding of his or her data.

Mary L. Dietz (1994) studied how individuals become and stay involved in the world of professional ballet dancing. In her analysis, she identified commonalities in the ways her participants engaged in the generic social process of getting involved in activities or social worlds. Her work highlights how people first become involved in ballet, usually as small children, and the contingencies that keep them involved and move them into a professional track. She concludes that the process results in the dancer identity overwhelming and engulfing the individual's previous identity. She also notes that being and staying involved requires a commitment similar to one required for those in professional sports, but that involvement in the world of professional ballet dancing rarely results in fame or high salaries.

Antony J. Puddephatt (2003) conducted a study in which he explored, through participant observation and interviews, interactions within a community of amateur chess players. In his analysis, he noted that the players had common approaches to the generic social process of performing activities. He identified the shared practices of strategic interaction that chess players use and suggested dimensions of that interaction, including how people create an image (image work) by masking their intentions and fears and by keeping their attack plans veiled. He then connected this process to the way hustlers and magicians use deception and image work in their activities.

In her study on the use of alternative therapies, Jacqueline Low (2004) identified a shared approach to the process of problem solving among her participants. Her participants saw 'taking control' and 'being subject to self-control' as ways of solving the problem of 'achieving wholeness and balance'. Low notes that solving the problem by taking control involved wresting control from medical professionals, asking questions, getting second opinions, and finally trusting practitioners enough to hand over control to them. Being subject to self-control involved doing independent research and making lifestyle changes.

Daniel and Cheryl Albas, whom we first encountered in Chapter 2, provide an exemplary illustration of how identifying and analyzing concepts and social processes can lead researchers to draw meaningful conclusions in their studies. As you may recall, the Albases have spent many years studying student life in its various aspects. In analyzing students' approach to exams, they identified the concept of magic and then observed how magic fits into the social process of dealing with uncertainty. They write:

> One of the most fascinating yet difficult features of the study to understand was the . . . extent to which students employed magical rituals and charms . . . seemingly irrational and bizarre behaviour, for example, the student who

reported that she always studied in the presence of one of her torn toenails . . . because it 'brought her good luck'. . . . This led us to start collecting, classifying, and evaluating the occurrences our students told us about . . . material items (e.g., lucky sweaters) or behaviour (e.g., ritual formulae or prayer) prescribed for luck or to be avoided (e.g., don't let anyone wish you good luck or don't sit near anyone wearing something pink). . . . We define magic as action directed to the achievement of an outcome with no logical relationship between the action and the outcome itself. (Albas and Albas 2009: 109)

Thus far, we can see that the Albases have identified a concept to help them understand the students' behaviours around dealing with the uncertainty of exams.

Once they had made their primary observations, the Albases problematized the concept of magic by thinking about the social context and how the magic they had observed differed from magic in other situations. They then did background research on other settings where people have been known to use magic. First, they looked at preliterate societies. In those contexts, the rituals were performed publicly, passed down from one generation to another, and widely shared. Second, the researchers investigated more contemporary groups who use magic, such as actors, soldiers, and athletes. They found that members of these groups share knowledge about their rituals—for example, most actors know to refer to the 'Scottish Play' rather than *Macbeth*, and most hockey players are aware of the common superstition associated with shaving during the Stanley Cup playoffs. The researchers found that in these contexts, magic had a more collective orientation. In contrast, the students' rituals were made up by each student, practised on an individual level, and kept secret.

As the Albases' example suggests, reading material related to your study can help you contextualize your data and uncover the wider implications of your findings. Reading a variety of sociological studies can also help you find connections between your own findings and the findings of other researchers. When you take the next step of writing up your research, the topic of Chapter 8, you will include such comparisons in your write-up. By relating your findings to those that have come before, you join the research conversation already in progress in the literature and contribute to an increased understanding of social life. As we discussed in our introduction to generic social processes in Chapter 2, this is the 'generalizability' of qualitative research.

Summary

In this chapter, we have looked at how to transform mountains of data into research findings. We discovered that qualitative data analysis is an ongoing, labour-intensive process, but the mantra of 'trust the process' encourages you to have faith that, with enough effort, you will find valuable connections among your data. We learned that coding can help you identify these connections and that memos can help you keep track of your insights and ideas. We saw how stories and sensitizing concepts can lead you to understand your participants' situations from their points of view. Finally, we encountered illustrations of how researchers have used concepts and generic social processes in their analyses. At this point, it is time to start writing up your research. As you will learn in Chapter 8, writing is an extension of the process of analysis because you continue to gain further insights and generate more ideas about your data while you write.

Key Terms

civil inattention	grounded theory	reflexivity
codes	memos	sensitizing concepts
coding	open coding	stories
focussed coding	problematize	trust the process

Questions for Critical Thought

1. Do you ever use the kind of 'magic' that the Albases described as a 'private ritual'? What other social settings might you investigate to find different interpretations of the concept of magic?

2. Are there feeling rules that apply to how you should react when receiving your grade on a final exam? What are those feeling rules? Do you find yourself doing emotion work to conform to these feeling rules?

Exercises

1. Think about a social group that you are interested in studying and of which you are not a member. Based on your experiences with members of this group, develop a sensitizing concept that could help you understand their social world from their perspective.

2. Think about a group you belong to and write a list of words or ideas that a researcher could use as sensitizing concepts in a study of the group. Did you find this task easier than the one given in the previous exercise? If so, why do you think this was the case?

3. Do some open coding of an interview transcript or a set of field notes. Write down, in memo form, any ideas you had while doing the coding that might help you understand your data.

Suggested Readings

Kathy Charmaz. 2006. *Constructing Grounded Theory: A Practical Guide through Qualitative Analysis*. Thousand Oaks, CA: Sage. Charmaz is one of the foremost contemporary writers on the use of grounded theory. The concrete suggestions and examples she includes in this text are invaluable for thinking about data analysis whether you use grounded theory or not.

Will C. van den Hoonaard. 1997. *Working with Sensitizing Concepts: Analytical Field Research*. Thousand Oaks, CA: Sage. This book, which belongs to Sage's research methods series, provides practical advice on how to identify and work with sensitizing concepts.

Related Website

Qualitative Research in Information Systems, Association for Information Systems
www.qual.auckland.ac.nz/

This website includes an overview of various methods of collecting and analyzing qualitative data. It provides a useful discussion of varied philosophical approaches to analyzing qualitative data as well as links to other websites and publications.

8   Writing Up Qualitative Research

Learning Objectives

- To discover and trust the process of writing
- To become familiar with the parts of a qualitative research report
- To understand the need to start writing early and to write several drafts
- To develop an engaging style of writing

Introduction

In Chapter 7, we talked about learning to trust the process of data analysis. Your analysis continues as you write up the results of your research. As you write, you will gain further insights and create more ideas about your data. Once again, you may be questioning your ability to bring together all of the data you have collected in a meaningful way. Once again, I urge you to trust the process, this time the process of writing.

Writing a report requires you to stay close to your data while learning to connect with what others have written. Even if this is your first study, you are joining the research conversation when you write it up and share it. This chapter offers advice that will help you create a worthwhile contribution to this conversation. You will learn how to develop the various parts of your report. You will also encounter tips on how to engage your reader and keep your message clear. As you will discover, the writing process is creative and exciting, but it can also be frustrating if you do not know where to begin. Therefore, let us first turn to some advice on how to get started.

Getting Started

Many of us find it difficult to start writing. We might sit and stare at the computer screen or a blank piece of paper for a very long time trying to find just the right opening sentence. Howard S. Becker (1986a: 43–67) suggests that many people have a great deal of trouble writing because they believe there is 'One Right Way' to construct a report. Hence, they believe that there is only one way to get the writing process started, and they spend an inordinate amount of time looking for the perfect opening sentence and the one correct way to write it. This sort of thinking can make starting very difficult.

To overcome such difficulties, begin by recognizing that there are many ways to write a good report. With practice, you will discover the method that works best for you. When I was a student, I was taught that before I started writing, I should do all my research, make a good outline, and only then, only when I knew exactly what I was going to say and in what order, start writing. Since then, I have, through experience, discovered that those directions do not work for me. Instead, I find it helpful to start writing early. I like to get my thoughts down on paper so that I can reflect on them and adapt them as my research project progresses.

Begin Early

Many researchers have identified the benefits of putting their thoughts into writing early in the research process. Becker (1986a) recommends writing a first draft *before* you have all your data, while Harry F. Wolcott (1995) suggests starting to write even before you begin your research. Wolcott calls this early writing **prewriting** and points out that such writing can help you identify what you already know, what you only *think* you know, and your own biases. He further suggests that you might discover at this stage that your study is secretly 'intended only to validate a personally held position', in which case you might as well write a polemical piece and skip the research (Wolcott 1995: 201).[1]

Beginning to write at an early stage can also help you avoid the all-too-common situation of having to rush through your final draft because you have run out of time. Inevitably, if you take such a hurried approach, you will end up with a poorly written report. Remember: good writing, like good analysis, takes a lot of time and effort, but the work you put into your report will always pay off in the end.

Make Mental Preparations

Many books on writing note that you should find a way to mentally prepare yourself for the process of writing. Often, this involves separating yourself from distractions in order to focus on the task at hand. Thus, many writers like to find a quiet place, such as a library, where they can be alone with their thoughts. At the same time, every writer has different needs. For instance, I have a colleague who prefers to write in his local coffee shop. For him, the privacy and ambient noise of this public space help him to concentrate. As with all aspects of the writing process, you should find the conditions that best facilitate your own ability to write.

You may also find that certain rituals help you stay focussed on your writing. As we discussed in Chapter 7, Albas and Albas (2009) have found that many students develop magic rituals to help them with their studies. Becker (1986a) has observed that academic writers often use magic to facilitate their writing. After talking to his graduate students, he noted that many had 'peculiar habits' associated with writing—for example, one woman felt that she 'could only write on yellow, ruled, legal-sized pads using a green felt-tip pen' (1986a: 2–4). Similarly, Dawne A. Clarke (2010: 103) has found that university professors use rituals to help them write. She notes that one of her research participants can write only when she is wearing pyjamas, while another can write only in a rented motel room with country music playing in the background, and yet another can write only when using one special pen. Clarke explains that there is a 'mystique around writing' that leads us to control the parts of the process we can with these superstitious practices. If you have a ritual that helps you to mentally prepare for the task of writing, by all means, use it.

Focus on Your Reader

You can also mentally prepare yourself for the writing process by identifying your reader's expectations. As a student, your primary reader is often your professor, and you may naturally feel anxious about submitting a report to someone with such authority. This anxiety can be particularly intense if you do not know your professor very well or if your professor has a reputation, deserved or not, for being a hard marker. Talking to your professor in person may lessen your fear because it will help you to get to know your intended reader and what he or she expects from you.

You should always follow the guidelines your professor gives you about format and style. At first, you may object that the prescribed format is too artificial and restrictive, but this is one area of preparation where you should not simply go with whatever works best for you. Think of your professor's requirements as the rules of a sport: as a player of the sport, you agree to abide by the rules. Hockey players do not argue with their coaches or officials that the offside rule in hockey should not apply to them because they do not like it; they simply follow the rule as much as they can and pay the price when they are caught offside.[2] Just as different sports have different rules, different professors have different formats that they will require you to use. When you follow the format that your professor asks for, she or he will have a better first impression of your report. Knowing this and understanding what your professor expects is a surefire way to reduce your anxiety about writing. Also, being able to adapt to different formats will, in the end, make you a more flexible and versatile writer.

Envisioning your intended reader as you write can also help you ease into the writing process. Remember that your reader is a real person and that you want to keep his or her attention on your report. We will talk later in the chapter about certain stylistic choices you can make to engage your reader, but for now you should simply remember that you must make a good impression. Also remember that your report is only one among many that your professor will be reading, so you must make sure that it will grab your professor's attention and provide an enjoyable read. When my students hand in their reports, I often hold up the stack of papers and jokingly tell them that all this reading is how they get even for all the hard work they put into their reports. They usually laugh because they have not thought about how many reports their professors have to read!

Writing Your Report

Published work usually reads as if it were written in a single attempt and in a linear fashion. It seems as though the author started with the first sentence of the introduction and then simply continued writing until she or he got to the end. Any honest author will likely tell you that this was not the case. Most often, writers go through many drafts before coming up with the final version. If you were to look through the files on my computer, for example, you would see three or more files for each chapter of any book I have written—each file reflects at least one draft of the chapter. In addition, most experienced writers will tell you that you should write the introduction to your work last. In fact, I wrote Chapter 1 of this textbook after I finished writing all the other chapters. This way, I was aware of the content before I wrote the introductory material. While I began the writing process by developing a table of contents and a brief description of each chapter, the creative process of writing shaped the chapters in ways I could not have anticipated.

The next sections of this chapter give advice on how to write the different sections of your report. I've covered the sections in the order in which I suggest you write them—findings, literature review, methods section, conclusion, then introduction—but you may find a slightly different order that works for you. Later in the chapter, we will discuss the order in which they should appear in your final report.

The Findings: Working with Your Data

Many qualitative researchers begin their first draft by organizing their findings, in whatever state they are in, into a preliminary order. This usually involves piecing together a rough list of themes or a tentative table of contents. As you write about the various themes, you will continue to think about how they hang together, and you will likely revise your list as you proceed. Luckily, with the help of computers, you can move what you write as many times as necessary until everything makes sense.

Once you have a general conception of how everything might fit together, focus on the theme of your research that is most interesting to you and that you have something to say about (Lofland and Lofland 1995: 205, Charmaz 2006: 156). Pull together all the material you have for that particular theme. If you have followed the advice on analyzing your data given in Chapter 7, you will have already started a file with data that pertain to this theme. If you have not already done so, read the interview segments and/or field notes through several times and then start to fine-tune the sub-themes by bringing together all the quotes or excerpts you have that relate to each sub-theme.

Next, try writing a paragraph about the theme. The paragraph does not have to be well organized or have a good beginning or end at this early stage. As Kristen Esterberg (2002: 202) notes, you do not have to know exactly what you want to say before you begin; you will 'discover it as you go along'. Esterberg suggests that if you are stuck, you can always start with a phrase such as 'This section is about . . .' and go from there (2002: 202). Once you have written a paragraph or two, you can start working with your data and shaping the section you have started on. You will find that the writing process will help you to see clearer connections in your data and to discover new categories or ones that you have overlooked. When this is happens, go back to the data. As Kathy Charmaz (2006: 154) notes, 'learning to trust in the writing process . . . is like learning to trust the . . . analytic process: our writing, like our analysis, is emergent'.

I use this approach in my own writing. For example, when I was getting ready to write the chapter of *The Widowed Self* (2001) that talks about the theme of widows learning to do new things, I made separate files for each of the following sub-themes:

- learning to do new things, in general;
- learning to live alone;
- learning to drive and learning to drive alone; and
- changing self-concepts related to learning to do new things.

Then I worked with each sub-theme separately. Box 8.1 includes my notes on learning to drive, and I developed my outline for the section on driving based on these notes. Once I had the outline, I started writing and chose quotations from the interviews that illustrated my points. As I went along, I honed the sub-topics even more. Occasionally, I went back to the data when a new idea emerged in the process of writing.

As you might expect, it is very important to choose strong, representative quotations or excerpts to include in your write-up. Next, we will examine

BOX 8.1 ❈ NOTES ON WIDOWS AND DRIVING

Comfortable Driving	Limited	No Driving	Bought Car
'D', 'R', 'G',* 'S', 'TH',* 'C', 'RC',* 'MT', 'F',* 'A', 'I', 'J'	'B': challenge of finding her way around; went to Toronto	'K': used to drive	'S': went with husband
	'J': only drives in town	'L': daughter discourages her from driving; used to drive before marriage	'BH': ignored at first
	'E': learned to drive since husband's death		'A': story about gauge light
	'JS': learned to drive when husband was sick	'J': eyes bad; used to drive	
	'I'*: does not drive long distances	'E': used to drive until husband teased her (at 21 yrs)	'I': ignored at first, called dealer whom she knew

*commented about being fortunate to know how to drive or that others should learn how to drive

Note: I've used initials in place of names to protect the anonymity of the women who participated in the study. In my final write-up, I used pseudonyms to represent each participant.

how to select the best quotations from your notes and how to use these quotations to the greatest effect.

Including Excerpts

Choosing excerpts from interview transcripts and field notes can be one of the most fun parts of writing up qualitative research. It gives you a chance to go back through your notes and reconnect with your participants—this time, from a more informed perspective. Focus on selecting excerpts that will illustrate a point you want to make and draw the reader into your study. As Sally Thorne (2008: 185) notes, 'the best examples will typically be those that not only show the point you are making but also do so in some utterly human and interesting manner'. In addition, ensure that the excerpts you use are characteristic of your data. You can highlight an unusual point of view, but you must note that that particular excerpt is not typical of your data in general.

When using quotations, try to keep them short and to the point. As Laurel Richardson has observed, 'readers are more likely to read short, eye-catching quotations' than long ones (1990: 41). You may find it helpful to smooth out the quotation to make it more direct, but you must be careful not to alter the speaker's meaning. While starts and stops are common in spoken conversations, a long excerpt that starts, stops, and changes direction can be very difficult to follow in written form, where there are no verbal inflections to enhance the meaning. When you do adjust a quotation, you should use an ellipsis (. . .) to indicate where you have removed words, and you should place square brackets ([ ]) around any words or comments you have inserted.

Using the words of your research participants gives power and emotional depth to your report. It also helps the reader understand the participant's perspective. Take a look at the first quotation I used in *The Widowed Self* (you may recognize this quotation from our discussion of in-depth interviewing in Chapter 7):

> What was it like to lose him? I suppose first of all, you have to say what it was like to have him because that would mean that you have . . . he was a very supportive person. He was quite romantic, in a way. We met in a romantic manner . . . during the war in London. We did our courting during the Blitz, so he actually saved my life once in the Blitz at some risk to himself. And then he was overseas, too. (D.K. van den Hoonaard 2001: 8)

In using this quotation, I wanted to show that the participants understood their situations as widows not only in terms of what had happened since their husbands died but also in terms of their experiences with being married. I also wanted to move the reader. By carefully choosing an informative and 'utterly human' quotation, I accomplished both of my purposes.[3]

You can also use quotations to illustrate similarities and differences among your participants. Several short quotations in a row can be a useful rhetorical device to emphasize similarities. For example, when I was writing *By Himself*, my study of widowers' experiences, I wanted to illustrate how consistently the widowers I interviewed described their need to avoid spending too much of the day in their houses 'sitting around'. For them, not leaving the house during the day symbolized giving up on life. I used several brief quotes, one after another, with the phrase 'sitting around' highlighted in italics, to emphasize the point:

> I'm not just *sitting around* the house moping.
> It's better to be busy than *sitting around* doing nothing, *sitting around* and thinking.
> Now I don't want to *sit around* . . . what am I going to do with myself?
> I didn't just want to *sit home*. . . .
> Just come in here and *sit down* or lay down on the couch and give up. [emphasis added] (D.K. van den Hoonaard 2010: 127)

You may have noticed that sitting around sounds like and is a sensitizing concept (see Chapter 7). Including sensitizing concepts in your report brings in theoretical observations. As Kathy Charmaz (2006: 173) has noted, your theory is more accessible when you weave it into the narrative.

An effective way to illustrate differences within the group you are studying is to present two or more quotations in close proximity to one another and then conduct a compare-and-contrast analysis on the quotations. For example, in *By Himself*, I wanted to explain that widowers in Atlantic Canada and widowers in Florida have different comfort levels with women's assertiveness in pursuing a romantic relationship. To illustrate this point, I included quotations that demonstrate that the different cultural contexts led to different interpretations of very similar actions. The men in Atlantic Canada were put off and intimidated if women seemed to take the initiative:

> I've really learned that widows are lonely and they're really looking for a man . . . if you said the wrong thing. If you've said anything at all, it might make them think that . . . you're maybe interested in them. And that, uh, you'd better watch out. (D.K. van den Hoonaard 2010: 95)

A contrasting quotation from an interview with a Florida widower whose girlfriend had been very assertive in establishing their relationship makes the point:

> After, she decided that she liked me . . . She came over a lot more than I realized. I didn't mean to make a regular routine of it. I just asked her out once; and before I knew it, here she's coming in like she's my girlfriend . . . she pushed herself into it. (D.K. van den Hoonaard 2010: 98)

As you can see, these quotations illustrate how different definitions of the situation affected widowers' interpretation of women's similar behaviour.

The way you introduce and comment on quotations is as important as your choice of the quotations themselves. As the writer, it is your job to tell your readers what you want them to see in the excerpts so that you and they share the same interpretation (Stoddart 1991: 246). If you simply drop the quotation into your report without explaining why it is there, you are asking your readers to do too much work, to read your mind. Box 8.2 provides a good example of how to frame your excerpt with your own commentary. The example starts with an orienting paragraph that explains what the quotation is about, follows with an indented quotation, and ends with my analytic commentary. Notice that I have not asked the reader to do the work of interpreting the text.

As go through your notes to find useful quotations, you should begin assigning **pseudonyms** to your participants. Pseudonyms allow you to maintain confidentiality while humanizing the participants. Some researchers ask the people they interview to choose their own pseudonyms. Clarke (2010) chose names from the television show *Coronation Street*. I try to choose names that sound authentic to the population I am discussing. Therefore, I would not use the name 'Tiffany' for an older widow or 'Christine' for an Iranian Bahá'í refugee.

Once you have written up your findings, or at least begun your discussion of your themes, it is time to turn your attention to planning and writing the

---

Box 8.2 ❉ Excerpt and Commentary

For men, becoming widowed is definitely *not* an 'expectable event' (Martin-Matthews 1991). In fact, when I asked participants if there was anything that surprised them about their experience with being widowed, seven explicitly answered that simply the fact of being widowed was the most surprising. One man made the following observation:

> No [surprises] . . . Because I *never* thought about it . . . You know, my wife, it was a standing thing that I was going to die a long, long time before her . . . It *never* entered my head, or I *never* even thought about what I was going to have to do when I was alone. No plans, I *never* dreamed that . . . I *never* even thought about what it would be like . . . That wasn't a part of what was supposed to happen. [emphasis added]

. . . Even the men whose wives were ill for some time before they died had still believed that, somehow, they would die first. The repetition of the word *never* in the quotation above underlines the complete lack of anticipation of becoming a widower for this man. [He] and other widowers had not imagined in their wildest dreams that they might find themselves in this position. This unexpectedness contributes in important ways to many men's uncertainty about how to relate to themselves as widowers.

Source: Deborah K. van den Hoonaard. 2010. *By Himself: The Older Man's Experience of Widowhood.* Toronto: University of Toronto Press, p. 22.

---

rest of your report. At this point, I usually turn to the literature review, but you may choose to work on your methods section.

The Literature Review: Connecting to the Literature

As we discussed in Chapter 3, literature reviews serve a different purpose in qualitative studies than they do in quantitative research. Rather than reading to develop hypotheses, the qualitative researcher reads to situate his or her particular study in relation to the research that others have done. Thus, when you are writing your own literature review, you should demonstrate that you are familiar with what others have said and that your work allows you to have a conversation with other researchers. You should use the literature review to establish the rationale for your study by 'claiming continuity [or gaps] in the existing literature' (Stoddart 1991: 244) and to remark on the intriguing questions the literature raises (Kamali 1991).

Connecting to the literature will help you discover the broader implications of your findings. In many cases, you will discover that your findings connect to previous research in ways that you could not have anticipated. Yet you can only make these connections if you are familiar with a range of past studies. Thus, you should try to read as broadly as possible. Becoming familiar with other researchers' work will also help you discuss your own work in terms that are familiar to other sociologists. In turn, these established terms will give you a foundation on which you can build your own analysis. Remember, your job is not to reinvent the wheel.

In my own research, I've found that my extensive reading has led me to make unexpected connections. For example, when I was thinking about how my participants acquire the identity of a widow, I noticed that they talked of an awareness that came suddenly like 'a punch in the stomach'. Their way of talking reminded me of how Kathy Charmaz (1991a) described the *identifying moment* that chronically ill people experience. Thus, in my literature review, I referred to Charmaz's study to help me make sense of my own findings. Similarly, when I was developing the concept of 'keeping up appearances', I thought of Arlie R. Hochschild's (1979) discussion of the *emotion work* airline stewardesses do to ensure that they present the feelings that they are expected to display. In both of these examples, you can see how reading studies on topics that did not at first appear related to my own led me to make significant connections to the literature and join the research conversation already in progress.

When you are writing your literature review, you should be careful to avoid two common problems that many students have. The first is relying too heavily on external sources. The second is summarizing rather than integrating what you have read. Let us look at ways you can avoid these problems.

Avoiding Common 'Lit Review' Traps

When I was a student, one of the biggest problems I had in dealing with my sources was that the authors I was reading all wrote so much better than I did. I found myself quoting them far too often. The result was a report that contained a bunch of quotations strung together with very little of my own input. I might as well have photocopied everything I read and handed it in to my professors. You may have the same difficulty. After all, the articles and books you have read were far from first drafts, and their authors are often experts in the field. How can you escape the temptation to rely too heavily on your sources?

First, as Kirby et al. (2006: 247) suggest, you should have a 'firm grasp of your data analysis' before turning to the literature. They comment that if you go to the literature too soon, the sheer authority of the printed page may overwhelm your own analysis. In that case, you may feel that you have a glass-slipper problem that is similar to the one you get when you try to make your data fit with a pre-existing hypothesis or theoretical framework (see Chapter 7).

Second, you should write a rough draft of your literature review without consulting the literature itself. I used to write the literature section of my reports in a completely different room from where I had my notes and articles. It was the only way I could avoid the temptation to rely too heavily on quotations. As much as possible, try to use your own words to express what others have written. Phyllis Creme and Mary Lea (2008: 121) provide 'linking words' that you can use to begin your summary: for example, you might say that the researcher 'discusses', 'points out that', 'illustrates', 'claims that'.

Organizing the literature review also challenges many students. You may be tempted, as are many others, to describe each item you have read separately, one after the other. This approach reminds me of listening to a small child tell me about a movie he or she has seen. Rather than highlighting the most important points in the plot, the child will start with what happened in the first scene and talk for hours without drawing any connections among the various parts of the movie. I have usually stopped listening after a few minutes and have no idea what I have heard by the end. You want to avoid boring your reader. As Kristen Esterberg (2002: 211) points out, discussing each study on its own, without pointing out how it relates to other studies and to your own findings, will bore you as you write it and bore your readers as they read it.

The best way to avoid this trap is to organize the literature by theme. This approach forces you to think about and discuss how the studies relate to one another and to your own work. It will also help you maintain your reader's interest by drawing connections for the reader rather than asking him or her to do the work of interpreting how everything fits together. In addition, forcing yourself to synthesize what you have read demonstrates that you have understood and are able to make sense of it. As a student, your literature review tells your professor that you are familiar with and comprehend what other researchers have said about your topic and theoretical approach.

The Methods Section: Describing What You Did

The methods section of your report may be the easiest part to write because, for the most part, all you have to do is describe what you have done. You can write it at any point. I often work on the methods section when I am waiting for inspiration on another part of my report.

The methods section of your report accomplishes three things. First, it tells the reader how you carried out your research. Second, it orients the reader to the setting and the participants involved in your research. Third, it situates your research in a particular research tradition and gives credibility to your findings.

As you discuss the way you conducted your research, ask yourself 'what happened?', and organize your response in a chronological order. Describe how you planned your study, carried out your research, and analyzed your data. Also note any unanticipated events you encountered and how you dealt with any setbacks. For example, when I was writing my methods section for my study on widows, I noted that a gatekeeper did not allow me to observe a support group, and I explained what I did to compensate.

There are many ways that you can use the methods section to orient the reader to the study's setting and the research participants. If you have done field work, provide a brief description of your setting. If you conducted interviews, explain how you decided whom to interview, describe how you recruited your participants, and include your impressions of the participants. You may also want to include some demographic information about your participants. To orient the readers of my book about widowers, I provided a description of social life in the Atlantic provinces and in the Florida retirement community that I studied. I also furnished general information about the participants' ethnicities, lengths of marriage, levels of education, and ages.

To situate your research in a particular tradition, you should draw parallels between what you did and what other qualitative researchers have done before you. As we have seen, qualitative methods are highly adaptable, creative, and flexible, but they also involve the use of 'sanctioned procedures' (Stoddart 1991: 245). In most cases, therefore, you can draw on the body of literature to support and explain the strengths of the methods you used in your study. In addition, you can add credibility to your study by clearly describing how you collected and worked with your data. The professionalism you show in this section will reassure the reader that your approach was systematic, that your analysis was sound, and that your findings are not simply based on anecdotal evidence.

The Conclusion: Summing It All Up

In your conclusion, you will sum up what you have written and explore the implications of your study. A brief summary will give your report a finished quality: This is what I said I was going to do, this is what I've done, and this is its significance. When the reader has finished reading the last sentence, she or he should have the feeling that the report has an end, that it does not simply fade off into space.

When you are writing your conclusion, imagine that you have to answer the 'so-what?' question: 'Okay, I have done all this research, and I have identified these themes, but so what? Why does it all matter?' You can begin by explaining how your research relates to existing literature. If appropriate, you can identify points of agreement or disagreement. Differences do not necessarily mean that you are right and other researchers, wrong, or vice versa. The conclusion or discussion of your report provides a place for you to discuss what may have contributed to these seeming discrepancies.

You can also identify the limitations of your study and acknowledge its shortcomings in your conclusion (Kirby et al. 2006: 248). Discussing these limitations gives you the opportunity to suggest further areas of research that might fill in the gaps in your own study. You might also mention interesting themes that were beyond the scope of your report but could inform a future study.

Your conclusion should not be very long, and it should not present any new data. If you are tempted to include new data, go back and find a better place to put them. If you cannot find an appropriate place, leave them out.

Once you have finished writing your conclusion, it is finally time to write your introduction.

The Introduction: Creating a First Impression

The introduction provides the first and most lasting impression of your report. It, therefore, should draw the reader in and orient him or her to your study. Mitchell and Charmaz (1996: 151) explain that the first paragraph should 'pull us into the story and convince us to continue' because it 'invites, entices, and involves the reader to stay with the story'. The best introductions start with an 'attention-getting' opening (Emerson et al. 1995: 198). Recognizing the importance of the opening sentence, Marjorie DeVault (1999: 187) explains that she puts a lot of thought into devising a sentence that 'feels genuine and bold . . . that will open space, and claim attention for [her] voice'. Box 8.3 includes exemplars of opening sentences that make the reader want to continue. When I read opening lines like the ones in this box, I figure I am in for a great read.

Once you have grabbed the reader's attention, identify the question or topic your report addresses and your rationale for studying and writing about your topic. Your rationale may include evidence that the topic is important or that researchers have not studied it in the past. You can also simply give the reason that your particular setting or group of people intrigued you in the first place. You will also include a brief description of the data and the theoretical approach you took while conducting your study.

In the final part of your introduction, provide an overview of the report, a road map that will help the reader to follow your argument as it develops. For some reason, many students resist including this road map in their reports. It could be that they have not followed the dictum to write the introduction last and cannot map something that does not yet exist. Howard S. Becker (1986a: 51–3) suggests that perhaps writers think they need to 'reveal items of evidence one at a time, like clues in a detective story' and then come up with the denouement at the end. His suggestion is to put the last 'triumphant paragraph' first so that readers can know where the report is going and connect each part to the overall argument as they are reading.

BOX 8.3 ❖ OPENING SENTENCES THAT DRAW THE READER IN

A midnight run shatters the night air. Thirty Harley-Davidson motorcycles stretch out for a quarter-mile, thundering down the highway.
—Daniel R. Wolf, *The Rebels: A Brotherhood of Outlaw Bikers* (1991)

They both came of age at the height of segregation. Sixty-five, a lifelong Chicagoan, Slim is a black mechanic in a back-alley garage in the ghetto. Bart, white and ten years older, is a retired file clerk who grew up in the rural South. Both are regular patrons of the Valois 'See Your Food' cafeteria.
—Mitchell Duneier, *Slim's Table: Race, Respectability, and Masculinity* (1992)

It was a crisp Canadian day in late autumn when I met Sam for our second interview in a Tim Hortons coffee shop near his home in the Ottawa suburbs. A soft-spoken stay-at-home father of two young children, he is one of over 100 Canadian fathers interviewed as part of this study of primary caregiving fathers.
—Andrea Doucet, *Do Men Mother?: Fathering, Care, and Domestic Responsibility* (2007)

Food reveals our souls. Like Marcel Proust reminiscing about a madeleine or Calvin Trillin astonished at a plate of ribs, we are entangled in our meals.
—Gary Alan Fine, *Kitchens: The Culture of Restaurant Work* (1996)

When a man's wife dies, he enters a foreign country, one which offers few images of what it means to be a widower. The images with which he might be familiar, those in popular culture, surely do not refer to him.
—Deborah K. van den Hoonaard, *By Himself: The Older Man's Experience of Widowhood* (2010)

I love a mystery, but not in the form of a research report. I want to know where we are going, and your professors do, too.

As we have seen, your introduction should pull in your reader. But to maintain your reader's interest, your writing must be clear and engaging. In the next section, we will discuss some techniques that you can use to make your writing more readable.

Matters of Style

As with any other skill, the more you practise writing, the better your writing will become. You will find that taking the time to edit and rewrite your work will help you develop your writing skills. In addition, reading others' work—novels, short stories, articles, book-length ethnographies—will help you discover your own voice, build a rich vocabulary, and accustom yourself to the conventions of punctuation, grammar, and usage. Below, you will find some concrete advice on how to improve your writing. First, we talk about using simple language. Then, we discuss using the active voice and the first person in your writing. Finally, we end with some hints about how to polish your work.

Simple Writing

Many students find themselves seduced by the idea of using academic language and **jargon** to display their intelligence. I can recall one student who used so many obscure words that I felt as though he was giving me a vocabulary test. This student so deeply resented my advice to write simply and clearly that he dropped the class! Nonetheless, every modern guide to practical writing stresses the importance of writing simple prose. Let us think about what this means.

The best way to simplify your writing is to avoid the 'jargon trap' (Van Manaan 1988: 28), or what Becker calls 'writing in a classy way' (1986a: 31). Relying on unnecessary jargon is a way to 'strike a pose' (Van Manaan 1988), to 'sound like [and] maybe even be' a certain kind of person (Becker 1986a: 31). There is an elitism hidden in this kind of writing that makes it inaccessible to anyone who is not familiar with the jargon. You gain nothing if your writing is accessible only to your little club, particularly if your professor is not a member. The best way to avoid the jargon trap is to use a conversational tone and avoid 'being overly flippant, judgmental, arrogant, emotional, or self-absorbed' (Thorne 2008: 183). Write your report in such a way that someone who knows very little about your topic could understand what you have written.

In addition to avoiding jargon, you can keep your writing simple by composing relatively short sentences. If you find yourself getting lost in long, convoluted sentences, you can bet your readers will also be lost. It is easy enough to turn a long, complex sentence into two or more shorter sentences. Writing in the active voice and the first person will also make your writing clear and inviting.

The Active Voice and the First-Person Perspective

Almost every text on writing urges us to use the **active voice** rather than the **passive voice** as much as possible when we write. Why? First, as Howard S. Becker (1986a: 79) notes, using the active voice 'almost always forces you to name the person who did whatever was done'. Why is this important? Consider the following sentence, which is written in the passive voice:

The interview was conducted.

What is wrong with this sentence? It doesn't reveal *who* conducted the interview. Was it the lead researcher? A research assistant? Another participant? As you can see, omitting the doer in this case could affect the way your reader interprets the situation. Of course, we could include the doer of the action while maintaining the passive voice, but such a construction would sound awkward and unnatural:

The interview was conducted by the researcher.

Now, compare this sentence to the following sentence, which conveys the same information but is written in the active voice:

The researcher conducted the interview.

As you can see, this sentence is more fluid and interesting.

Another common problem in student writing is avoidance of the first-person perspective in formal reports. Many students believe that first-person pronouns establish a tone that is too informal for academic work. In contrast, they see writing in the third person as a way to make their work more detached and, therefore, more scientific. Yet, is a sense of detachment necessary in a research study? Certainly not in a qualitative study, where the researcher is often in direct contact with his or her participants. Compare the effects of the following two sentences:

Third-person: The researcher noticed that the participants hesitated when she asked them about their experiences with gambling.
First-person: I noticed that the participants hesitated when I asked them about their experiences with gambling.

The first sentence is factual, but it is dry. The second sentence is just as factual, but the writer's role is clear and the sentence is more active and engaging.

So, you can see the benefits of writing in the active voice and using the first person. Yet, I offer one warning. When you write in the first person, do not allow your voice to become so prominent that the story of your research becomes about you rather than the setting or the participants. If your report becomes an 'egocentric revelation' of your research process, you have strayed into what Van Manaan (1988) calls a 'confessional tale'.

After you have written your drafts of each section, you will begin to put the finishing touches on your report.

Cleaning It All Up

Regardless of the order in which you wrote the sections of your report, there is a fairly standard order that your professor will expect you to use in your final submission: introduction, literature review, methods, findings, and conclusion (sometimes called a discussion). Almost always, you will attach a cover page to the front of your report, and your bibliography or references section will go at the end.

When you are polishing your final report, you want to make sure that all of the parts are cohesive, that the report hangs together as a 'whole rather than a series of disconnected bits' (Creme and Lea 2008: 158). As you move from one section to the next, use bridging sentences to help your reader follow the transition. You also add cohesion to your report by using consistent formatting. Make sure that you use a single font for your running text and that you use the same style for all headings. Also, use standard spacing—your report should be double spaced without extra spaces between paragraphs.

As you edit your report, you also want to look for typographical errors, grammatical mistakes, awkward wording, and missing citations. When I'm looking for such errors, I usually print a copy of my report so that I can see what the final version will look like on paper. Then, I carefully go through it—word by word, sentence by sentence, and paragraph by paragraph. I look closely at my punctuation and make sure that the subjects and verbs of my sentences agree, that the verb tenses are consistent, and that I have caught and corrected all my typos. Never rely on your word-processing program's spelling and grammar checker to do the job. It will often miss typos such as *form* instead of *from*. As a professor, I find that when students do not use proper grammar and spelling, I cannot always decipher what they are trying to say.

At this stage, you also want to look for extraneous words and meaningless expressions that can complicate your writing. Howard S. Becker (1986a: 80) uses a 'simple test' to look for unnecessary words: 'I check each word and phrase to see what happens if I remove it. If the meaning does not change, I take it out.' Also look for vague expressions and words that allow you to avoid making a definite statement or claim. For example, in the Maritimes, rather than saying that it is hot outside, we might say that it is not overly cold. This roundabout way of communicating works well in informal contexts, but it will only obscure your meaning in a formal report. Some particularly vague words include *somewhat*, *relatively*, and *basically*. You never lose the meaning of your writing when you remove these words. In fact, you make the meaning clearer.

You should also remove any unnecessary repetition. While you were writing your report, you may have inadvertently made the same point twice, and now is the time to correct this mistake. Unnecessary repetition will not only make you look like a careless writer, it will also bore your reader by forcing her or him to revisit a point that she or he has already encountered. In addition, look for expressions that you use too often, as they can make your report feel repetitious. For example, a while ago I noticed that I was using the word *hence* too often in my writing; now, when I edit, I make sure to delete *hence* if it appears too often.

Finally, when you think you are just about finished, show your report to a friend who is willing to read it. Ask him or her to tell you if something is not clear or does not make sense, if the organization is not logical, if there is unnecessary repetition, or if there are any mistakes in referencing. Remember that you should only include external sources that you have mentioned in your text in the bibliography or references section.

A Word about Plagiarism

So far, I have not said anything about **plagiarism**, although your professors worry about it a great deal. Simply stated, plagiarism is taking someone else's ideas and passing them off as your own, even if you do so inadvertently. Many professors have noted that plagiarism has become more common in recent years. Some have posited that the ease of cutting and pasting content from the Internet and other electronic sources has made it difficult for many students to grasp the idea of giving credit where credit is due. Plagiarism has become such a widespread issue that most universities have developed elaborate materials to help students avoid committing the crime of plagiarism. Penalties for plagiarism typically range from a failing grade on an assignment to a failing grade in the entire class.

So, how to you avoid committing such a crime? In short, you must reference any source that you quote word for word or that you paraphrase. You can easily avoid committing plagiarism by citing your sources as you write and keeping the file for your bibliography or references section up to date.

Summary

We have looked at how to go about writing up your research report. I have encouraged you to start early, to have fun choosing the best excerpts to include in your work, and to write more than one draft. As you write your first research report, you may find it useful to consult the checklist located in Appendix C of this text. As you will discover, the more you write, the more you will develop your skills as a writer. Go forth and write!

Key Terms

active voice   passive voice   prewriting
jargon   plagiarism   pseudonyms

Questions for Critical Thought

1. What are the barriers you face when you are getting ready to write an academic paper? What are some ways you can overcome those barriers?

2. Do you use any 'magic rituals' to help you get started writing? Do they work for you?

3. Think about the best assignment you have ever written. What did you do that contributed to its quality?

Exercises

1. Without looking at your data, write a paragraph that summarizes your research findings. If you have not yet conducted your own study, write a paragraph that summarizes what you learned in your last lecture class without looking at your notes.

2. Look through an interview transcript or a set of field notes and identify the best excerpts. What made you choose those excerpts?

3. Choose a journal article that discusses a qualitative research project and that you find well-written and informative. Write a short analysis of the article, paying close attention to the ways the author addresses the presumed readership, uses excerpts as evidence, connects to the literature, and discusses the methods he or she used to conduct the research. What changes would you make to improve the argument of the article?[4]

Suggested Readings

John Lofland and Lyn H. Lofland. 1995. 'Chapter 10: Writing Reports', in *Analyzing Social Settings: A Guide to Qualitative Observation and Analysis.* Belmont, CA: Wadsworth Publishing Company. The chapter provides concrete advice on how to write a report as well as a useful checklist for novice writers.

Howard S. Becker. 1986. *Writing for Social Scientists.* Chicago: University of Chicago Press. This book not only offers practical advice, but it also includes sociological discussions about why writing is challenging for all of us. Becker is well known as a clear and engaging writer, and this book is a pleasure to read.

Related Websites

HyperGrammar, The Writing Centre, University of Ottawa
www.writingcentre.uottawa.ca/hypergrammar/

This website explains the rules of grammar in very clear language. You can use it for easy reference when you're not sure if your grammar is correct. It contains sections on a variety of elements including parts of speech, punctuation, and building phrases, clauses, sentences, and paragraphs.

How Not to Plagiarize, University of Toronto
www.writing.utoronto.ca/advice/using-sources/how-not-to-plagiarize

This website contains concrete and useful advice to help you avoid inadvertently plagiarizing someone else's work.

9 New Directions in Qualitative Research

Learning Objectives

⊛ To become familiar with emerging trends in qualitative research
⊛ To discover how researchers have included these trends in their qualitative studies

Introduction

Over the past few decades, there has been a great deal of innovation in qualitative research methods. These new approaches reflect a fragmentation of the research community as well the development of new media and technology that researchers can use to conduct research. This chapter will familiarize you with the most pervasive of these new approaches. You will find descriptions of each approach and examples of how researchers have used these approaches in their studies. This chapter is by no means comprehensive, but it does provide a taste of several new methods that are being used by qualitative researchers: discourse analysis; narrative analysis; auto-ethnography; ethnodrama, or performance ethnography; visual sociology, including photo elicitation; and virtual ethnography.

Discourse Analysis

Discourse analysis is an interpretive approach influenced by the writing of Michel Foucault, a French philosopher. Foucault believed that language is not only a tool that describes reality but also a 'social practice, a way of doing things' (Wood and Kroger 2000: 4). Foucault suggested that discourse—the language we use to describe ourselves and our world—controls the way we define and think about our and others' places in the world. In short, he suggested that discourse constitutes, rather than reflects, social life. Hence, discourse limits how we can think about the world, and Foucault believed that powerful components of society control the way we talk about phenomena and, thereby, define them (Rabinow 1984). These powerful components might be dominant populations within a society or any individual or group with enough sway to influence public discourse. If we think about the concept of the definition of the situation, we might say that discourse constructs the possible definitions of the situation and, therefore, has real consequences. The discourse we use to name and describe an object portrays it as 'having a very different "nature" from the next' object (Lafrance 2009: 199).

Let us think about how the words people use to describe themselves shape their social reality. In the past, the majority of Canadians referred to and thought of themselves as *subjects* of the British Crown. By defining themselves as such, these individuals established their identities as subservient to England and its monarchy. Later, as Canada began to see itself as a separate country, most Canadians began to call themselves *citizens*. In adopting this term, they began to see themselves as participants in the country's social and political life, and they emphasized their constitutional rights and obligations. More recently, many Canadians have begun referring to themselves as *taxpayers*. This term encourages people to see their social power in terms of money, and popular discourse focusses on government as accountable to the taxpayers because it uses their money. The term notably excludes those who do not make direct financial contributions to the government—for example, children, individuals on social assistance, some older people, and parents who care for their children at home and do not participate in the labour force. Therefore, the government becomes accountable only to those we recognize as paying taxes, even though others contribute to society in various ways. Thus, you can see how an analysis of the national discourse on Canadian identity can reveal much about the dominant population that has the power to control the discourse. Such analysis also reveals that not everyone has such power.

Researchers who engage in discourse analysis understand that a definition is relative to the social group that constructed it. Thus, different social groups often have different discourses related to the same topic. For example, in New Brunswick, where I live, people refer to their ancestors who left the States during the Revolutionary War as *Loyalists* because they were loyal to Britain. Most Americans call these same individuals *deserters* because they refused to fight against the British. Both terms refer to the same people, but they hold very different connotations. Each term serves the ideology of those who use it. Researchers can tell a lot about the dominant ideologies within a social group based on the group's shared discourse.

Often, prevailing discourses are so deeply rooted in our understanding of our social world that we do not question where they originated or who controls them. Consider the widespread acceptance of the biomedical discourse. As the language and terminology of doctors, pharmaceutical companies, and medical specialists have taken hold, the biomedical discourse has come to influence more and more of our interpretation of ourselves in terms of medical conditions. For example, in 1966, a doctor named Robert Wilson identified menopause, which was previously accepted to be part of the natural aging process, as a 'hormone deficiency disease'. Since that time, this term and the discourse that surrounds it have shaped our conception of women over 50—these women now see themselves and are seen by society as not entirely healthy. By examining the roots of such discourses, researchers can identify those who control the discourse and how their interests affect the way we interpret ourselves and the world around us.

Michelle N. Lafrance (2009) has done a discourse analysis of the experience of women who have been depressed. As she conducted interviews with her research participants, she identified discourses that construct men as dominant and women as subservient. She also considered the dominant biomedical discourse of depression as a medical condition. She found that her participants strove to meet a 'good-woman ideal' that was impossible to achieve, while the 'dominant understanding of depression as a biomedical problem' hid women's oppression and made them feel as if their suffering was 'not real' (2009: 174). She concludes:

> . . . women who are depressed face pervasive delegitimation and silencing forged by both discourses of femininity and biomedicine. The interlocking discourses were similarly implicated in the silencing of a host of health problems that are particularly common among women. . . . Thus, the effect of this interlocking set of discourses is to marginalize and silence women's pain. This silencing maintains the status quo and the hegemony of both patriarchy and its bedfellow—biomedicine. (Lafrance 2009: 174–5)

Lafrance's research is an excellent example of discourse analysis. In analyzing her data, Lafrance clearly focusses on how language has shaped women's experience with and understanding of depression. Discourse analysis often identifies and critiques everyday concepts and demonstrates how they serve the interests of those in power, those at the top of the hierarchy of credibility.

Narrative Analysis

Narrative analysis has become a very popular approach in a variety of fields, and it takes many forms. In all cases, researchers who use narrative analysis recognize the centrality of stories in the way people understand and talk about their lives. Sociologists focus on the stories people tell, the ways in which tellers structure their stories, the identity of the audience, and the social context or narrative environment within which stories develop (Gubrium and Holstein 2009). In narrative analysis, the stories themselves are the object of research (Riessman 2001). Some scholars even suggest that, in essence, 'people are stories' (Kenyon and Randall 1999). Also, as David R. Maines (1993) has pointed out, narratives can constitute social acts.[1]

Stories can be particularly powerful when they extend beyond the individual to reinforce a group's identity or values. Hence, towns, countries, and ethnic or religious groups often have prototypical stories they tell and retell. For example, the purpose of the Seder in Jews' celebration of Passover is to tell the story of the group's escape from slavery in Egypt through the responses to four questions that address the general question, 'Why is this night different from all other nights?' The four questions ask

> Why is it that on all other nights during the year we eat either bread or matzoh, but on this night we eat only matzoh?[2] Why is it that on all other nights we eat all kinds of herbs, but on this night we eat only bitter herbs? Why is it that on all other nights we do not dip our herbs even once, but on this night we dip them twice? Why is it that on all other nights we eat either sitting or reclining, but on this night we eat in a reclining position? (Kosher4Passover 2010)

These questions and the story they evoke are well known to everyone participating in the ritual, and they strengthen the bonds between participants by reminding them of their shared identity. In addition, the way the story emerges—in a social setting, among an audience of fellow Jews, in response to questions that are always asked by the youngest boy at the table—reinforces the purpose of the story.

Researchers can also combine individuals' narratives to build a 'collective story', to 'narrativize the experience of a social category' (Richardson 1990: 24–5). If they do a good job of building the collective story, individuals who are members of the category will respond with 'That's my story. I am not alone' (Richardson 1990: 25). Collective stories illuminate 'the intersection of biography, history, and society' (Riessman 2001: 697). Gay Becker (1997) developed a collective story out of the narratives of people who had experienced sudden disruptions in their lives. She created this story by bringing together personal narratives on such topics as infertility, midlife disruption, stroke, late-life transitions, and the experiences of ethnic minorities. In her analysis, she argues that narratives help people make sense of disruptions caused by illness or personal misfortune, as people use narratives to shape their experience and to create continuity. She also suggests that this collective story has reverberations beyond the focus of her study, into the wider culture of America, as the attempt to create continuity is an important value in American culture.

I tried my hand at narrative analysis to interpret the stories widows told about their husbands' deaths (see D.K. van den Hoonaard 1999). I looked at how the women structured the stories, the content of the stories, and the context in which the women developed their stories. I identified three themes, or stages, common to all of the stories: learning that the husband was dying, taking care of the husband, and meeting the husband's death. Box 9.1 includes quotations to illustrate each of these themes. Notice how the first-person narration provides force to the

BOX 9.1 ⁙ NARRATIVE ANALYSIS: STORIES AND THEMES

THEME ONE: LEARNING THAT THEIR HUSBANDS WERE DYING

So I said, when he came out to the car. I said, 'What did they say?' He said, 'Oh, we'll talk about it when we get home.' . . . So we went home . . . and he said, 'I have cancer.' Like that, I felt. I felt like, you know, I can't move.

THEME TWO: TAKING CARE OF THEIR HUSBANDS

We realized our time was short. So we made the best of it. . . . We did some trips and enjoyed ourselves. And probably had the most serene and loving kind of relationship . . . it was a time given to us especially.

THEME THREE: MEETING THEIR HUSBANDS' DEATHS

A very peaceful death for him . . . he wasn't aware of anything. . . . We had gone to bed later on a Friday night . . . we were laying [sic] there, and he had his arm under my pillow and his other arm around me . . . And about five minutes before he had said, 'I love you so much.' And then he said, 'I've got to move.' And I said, 'Have I got your arm pinched?' . . . And he said, 'No, I'm dizzy.' And that was it.

Source: Quotations from D.K. van den Hoonaard. 1999. 'No Regrets: Widows' Stories about the Last Days of their Husbands' Lives', *Journal of Aging Studies* 13, 1: 59–72.

story and how the story includes plots, characters, and time. Once I had analyzed all of the stories, I concluded that they served as a bridge that eased the women's transition from the status of wife to that of widow, from a higher to a lower status.

Jaber F. Gubrium and James H. Holstein (2009) remind us that narratives always occur within a social context. They argue persuasively that analyzing a transcribed narrative (for example, a story taken from an interview) without being aware of the environment or interactional context in which the story was told can provide only a partial understanding. They further comment that particular circumstances, or narrative environments, influence whether or not a story will emerge and the shape it will take. An example of a narrative environment is an Alcoholics Anonymous group meeting. Norman K. Denzin, in *The Alcoholic Self* (1987), demonstrated how the AA environment shaped the stories that members told about themselves—at meetings, members constructed their stories so that they told the story of AA in the process. Similarly, Jaber F. Gubrium (1986), in his study of Alzheimer support groups, found that different groups valued different kinds of stories about caregiving, and the stories members told during the meetings reflected the values of each group.

As Mitchell Duneier (1999) notes, in a research setting, the social force of the narrative environment is often greater than the influence of the researcher. Duneier calls this the 'Becker principle', after Howard S. Becker, who taught that social situations 'practically require people to do or say certain things [or tell certain stories in particular ways] because there are other things going on that . . . are more influential in [their day] than a researcher' (Duneier 1999: 338). Thus, while we must always be aware of the influence of our presence as a researcher, we can reasonably assume that participants will generally say and do what seems appropriate in the setting despite our presence.

Autoethnography

Researchers sometimes use narratives to tell their own story. They refer to this practice as **autoethnography**. In autoethnography, the researcher includes his or her biography as a part of what he or she is studying. According to Carolyn S. Ellis (2008), a prolific author of autoethnographic works, autoethnography involves the researcher shifting back and forth between the social and cultural and her or his inner experience. Autoethnographies take many shapes and often appear in the form of a personal narrative. These narratives can be powerful, and they can transport the reader into the experience of the author. I still remember reading Ellis' 1993 article about her brother's death in an airline crash. I found the article riveting; it provided a window into her enormously devastating experience. Ellis argues that the telling of her story in the first person connects her 'lived experience' to the sociology of emotions and avoids the ordinary approach of sociologists that assumes that 'WE study THEM' (1993: 724), as if researchers somehow escape the social processes that they study. In contrast, the autoethnographer is at the centre of the story she or he is telling.

JoAnn Franklin Klinker and Reese H. Todd (2007) carried out a joint autoethnography to study their individual experiences of 'an emerging social phenomenon, middle-aged women leaving comfortable lives to explore new horizons'. Both women started careers as university professors and 'accepted the challenges of commuter marriages' in mid-life (2007: 166). In a process they eloquently describe as conducting 'interviews with our memories [that] reconstructed our past selves', each researcher wrote about her past and how it led to her decision to become a professor (2007: 169). The two researchers had conversations about their experiences, compared notes, and identified many similarities in the two stories. Klinker and Todd, citing Holt (2003), observed that autoethnography involves 'highly personalized writing' in which 'authors draw on their own experiences to extend understanding of a particular discipline or culture' (2007: 169). In their analysis, the authors connect their own experiences to the sexism and ageism that women, in general, face in contemporary culture. They also note that their study led them to recognize that cultural influences had had more of an impact on their personal experiences than they had originally thought.

Autoethnography has led to much creativity among its practitioners. Researchers have used a variety of unusual formats, including poetry and drama, to tell their stories. Laurel Richardson (2007), for example, has recently published an autoethnographic book that comprises the journal entries in which she recorded her experiences during the last 10 months of a close friend's life. She writes:

> *Last Writes: A Daybook for a Dying Friend* tells two interlocking stories. The first . . . is a friendship story in which I tell of the last ten months of my best friend's life and our thirty-five-year complex and sometimes difficult friendship, a deep friendship between two women. The second story is the story of the writing. (Richardson 2007: 9)

In taking this dualistic approach, Richardson acknowledges the importance of both her experience itself and her process of interpreting that experience.

Ethnodrama

It is not only autoethnographers who have experimented with new ways of communicating their research findings. Some ethnographers develop their research into **ethnodramas**, or performance ethnography. They choose this medium 'to create the most credible, vivid, and persuasive portrait of the participants' culture and lived experiences' (Saldaña 2008: 283). Performance ethnography is particularly effective when the researcher is looking to disseminate information to a specific audience or to the general public in an emotion-generating manner.

Pia C. Kontos and Gary Naglie (2006) developed an ethnodrama to bring life to their study of personhood in Alzheimer's disease. Their findings, which they generated from field work, challenge the assumption that those with cognitive impairment have no sense of self. They argue that their ethnodrama 'opens a space' for people who care for others to see the 'humanity of persons with dementia' and thereby facilitate more 'humanistic approaches' to care practice (2006: 302). They suggest that this mode of communication makes their research accessible to a broad spectrum of people and that the emotional engagement of the audience may overcome resistance to new ways of thinking.

Visual Sociology

Visual sociology entails the use of images as data. With the ubiquitousness of images in our daily lives—in magazine and newspaper articles, on billboards and in other advertisements, and in videos, to name only a few of the most common sources—it is no wonder that there is an increasing interest among sociologists to incorporate images into their research methods. Yet the approach is not entirely new. In the inaugural issue of the journal *Visual Studies*, which was published in 1986, Tim Curry notes that the American Sociology Association devoted a session to visual sociology in 1974, and the International Visual Sociology Association (IVSA), which publishes *Visual Studies*, was founded in 1981. According to IVSA's website, the organization's mandate is to

> promote the study, production, and use of visual images, data, and materials
> in teaching, research, and applied activities, and to foster the development and
> use of still photographs, film, video, and electronically transmitted images in
> sociology and other social sciences and related disciplines and applications.
> (IVSA 2010)

The organization has come a long way since 1981. If you look at the first issue of its journal, you will find that it looks like a low-budget newsletter. Yet, a brief review of a recent issue will reveal that the publication has grown into a full-fledged international journal. This transformation testifies to the increased interest in visual sociology over the past few decades.

Howard S. Becker (1986b: 232) suggests that sociologists who want to work with visual materials need to approach these materials in a 'studious way'. Becker (1986b: 246–9) has summarized the steps a sociologist might use to ensure that he or she transcends a superficial, snapshot approach when using photography in his or her research methods. First, the sociologist-photographer takes pictures of 'almost anything he [or she] sees in the situation . . . trying to cover whatever seems in a commonsense way to be worth looking at'. This step is similar to the field researcher's initial step of making rough jottings when first entering a social setting. These early photographs help the researcher identify who is in the setting, what they are doing, and anything that does not seem to make sense and thus requires more investigation. Second, after studying the first photos, the researcher comes up with questions to pursue with his or her camera. Again, this step is similar to the field researcher's use of his or her early notes to develop research questions. Third, the researcher asks people in the setting about what he or she has seen. In particular, the researcher can learn a great deal by showing participants the photographs and encouraging them to talk about the images and to suggest other things they think should be photographed. Often, a researcher records such comments on video. As the study progresses, the researcher uses his or her theories about what is going on to photograph things or people he or she 'might otherwise have ignored'.

Visual sociologists use images to study a wide range of topics. Beverly Yuen Thompson (2010), for example, used a combination of field work, interviews, participation, photography, and video recordings to complete her study of heavily tattooed women. Her research questions were 'What is it like to be a heavily tattooed woman?' and 'What is it like to be a woman tattoo artist in a field dominated by men?' Over three years, she filmed and interviewed 70 women to complete her study. The result was the film *Covered: Women and Tattoos* (2010), which makes a powerful statement about the stigma associated with being a tattooed woman. The film also reveals the amount of work that Thompson put into using images in her study; she did not simply take a few photographs and hope that she interpreted them correctly![3]

Mitchell Duneier (1999) used photography in his ethnography of sidewalk magazine and book vendors in Greenwich Village, New York. He recruited Ovie Carter, a professional photojournalist, to take pictures 'to illustrate the things [Duneier] was writing about' (1999: 12). Duneier comments that he noticed things in the photographs he would not have seen otherwise. In addition, he included photographs of the vendors and the neighbourhood in which they worked in his published account of the study, *Sidewalk*. If you take a look at *Sidewalk*, you will see how the pictures make the study and its participants come alive as they could not have through the written word alone. The visual aspects enrich the ethnography and have contributed to its effectiveness.

Visual sociology also contributes to an understanding of material culture. For example, Hernan Vera (1989) used visual examples to carry out his study of windows in Holland, which 'are big, left uncovered day and night, and passionately decorated' (1989: 215). In his study, Vera photographed the windows, had informal conversations with Dutch acquaintances, made presentations on his ideas about the windows, and carried out formal interviews with researchers and government employees who had similar interests. He found that the windows allow residents to keep track of the comings and goings of their neighbours, while they allow passersby to see what is going on inside the home. As my Dutch husband has remarked, the windows demonstrate that the residents have nothing to hide. As Vera concludes,

> Interpreted as a work of art . . . the Dutch window appears not as behavior adapted to physical and symbolic constraints, but rather as actions serving the purpose of individual and familial expressions . . . . [They] call our attention to the need of conceiving material culture in terms of the purposive acts we accomplish by adapting our objects to our practical and expressive human needs. (Vera 1989: 232)

The photograph in Figure 9.1 shows a street-level view of an apartment building in Holland. Notice that you can see into almost every apartment. The photograph suggests that the practice of leaving windows mostly uncovered is widespread in the country.

FIGURE 9.1 Dutch Windows

Source: Will C. van den Hoonaard.

There are also visual sociologists who focus on studying images in popular culture, particularly those in the media. This type of research is called **cultural studies**. Researchers who work in cultural studies use items such as magazines, movies, and websites to identify representations of culture. Researchers can analyze images in the media to uncover changing social attitudes. For example, in the past few decades, we have begun to see more interracial couples in advertisements; this change indicates the general population's increasingly positive attitude towards interracial couples. Most often, researchers look for common themes in visual representations to identify cultural ideals—ideals to which we are all supposed to aspire. For example, in a typical study, a researcher might analyze images of women in magazine ads and identify the narrow appearance norms of youth and extreme slenderness that are today's ideals for women. Researchers can also find evidence of cultural ideals by looking at contrasting representations. For example, when Linda Caissie and I were looking through *Zoomer Magazine* to gather data for our study on how the magazine frames the aging process, we noticed a photo of a depression-era old couple on the website of *Zoomer Magazine* (www.zoomermag.com) (see Figure 9.2) that stood in stark contrast to the photos in the magazine. While the majority of the photos promoted a young-looking, consumerist ideal for today's baby boomers, the depression-era photo provided a negative reinforcement of this ideal by showing readers an image to which they would not want to aspire (Caissie and van den Hoonaard 2009).

Photo Elicitation

Photo elicitation is a method of data-generation often used in visual sociology. In this method, researchers display photographs and ask participants to comment on what they see. Sometimes, researchers take the photographs

FIGURE 9.2 Depression-Era Couple

Source: US Library of Congress, LC-USF34-046511-D.

themselves but, as Marisol Clark-IbáÑez (2004) observes, this practice is more useful for deductive, theory-driven research than for inductive research because the researcher may take photos that grab his or her attention but are not particularly meaningful to the participants.

For qualitative researchers, it is more productive to ask the participants to take photographs that they find meaningful. Often, the researcher will give each participant a disposable camera and ask her or him to take photographs. The researcher either asks the participants to take pictures of anything they find interesting or suggests that they focus on a particular aspect of life that relates to the research question at hand. This task serves two purposes: It starts the participants thinking about the topic and allows them to bring into the research what is meaningful to them (Keegan 2008). After the participants have taken the pictures, the researcher develops the film and then sits down with each participant to talk about why she or he took each picture and what it means to her or him. This method is sometimes referred to as 'photovoice' because the photos help participants express what they want to say. Clark-IbáÑez (2004) explains that discussing photographs often leads to rich, personal narratives.

John L. Oliffe and Joan L. Bottorff (2009) used photo elicitation in their study of men who had prostate cancer. They asked the men to take photographs as if they were mounting a photographic exhibition called 'Living with My Prostate Cancer' and then discuss the pictures during an interview. Oliffe and Bottorff report that the 'planning, introspection, and reflection' the process required led the men to develop fresh perspectives on their illness. The process also helped the men overcome their reluctance to discuss their emotions by engaging them in a familiar activity and encouraging them to take charge as experts on the photographs.[4] Further, the photos elicited telling narratives about dichotomies, such as survivorship and mortality, that the men interwove with 'details about fear, uncertainty, bravado, and hope' (2009: 853). For example, one man took a photograph of a cemetery and revealed that when he was first diagnosed, he worried about being carried into the cemetery, but as time went on, he came to think about the cemetery in terms of having survived. Finally, the process allowed the participants to set the agenda for the interview and thereby resulted in truly inductive research. Oliffe and Bottorff observe that a simple prompt, such as 'tell me about this photograph', might result in a 20-minute commentary about the 'meanings embedded in the photograph' (2009: 853).

Virtual Ethnography

Conspicuously absent from most of our discussions so far has been the impact of the Internet on qualitative research methods. While I could write an entire book on the topic and all its permutations, here I will simply provide a taste of how qualitative researchers can use the Internet as a source of data.

Virtual ethnography is the in-depth study of a group or culture that exists in an online environment. The discipline emerged in the 1990s when sociologists and others noticed that virtual environments provide spaces in which online communities develop. Virtual ethnographers use various media such as email, message boards, and wiki spaces to study these communities. The ethnographer's sense of what is appropriate and meaningful in a particular site or online community guides the form and types of engagement she or he will use in the study (Hine 2008). Virtual ethnography requires the same labour-intensive, systematic approach as all qualitative research and, as with any ethnography, the researcher has the goal of discerning the distinctive characteristics of the particular culture, its norms, and its social hierarchies. He or she also seeks to learn the jargon as well as how the community recognizes and identifies insiders and deviants and establishes its boundaries.

Virtual ethnography also presents challenges unique to the online environment. First, the researcher must be aware that deception by participants seems to be fairly common online. Therefore, the researcher cannot be sure that what people say about themselves bears any resemblance to their reality offline. Yet, when the researcher's goal is to study an online culture, this is not an issue because what matters is the definition the members of the culture have of each other. Second, the researcher must decide whether to 'lurk' or to participate. It is quite common for many members of a list to lurk, to read messages without ever being visible. If the virtual ethnographer decides to participate, he or she must also consider how to develop an appropriate online persona. This step might include creating a signature, an avatar, and even a website (Hine 2008). These preparations mirror those that any ethnographer must consider before approaching a social setting or community.

Nancy K. Baym (2000) carried out an early virtual ethnography of an online discussion group organized around watching soap operas. Baym, a soap-opera fan herself, did participant observation of this discussion group for three years in the early 1990s. At the centre of her study was the question of how soap-opera viewers 'use the mass media to structure and articulate [their] relations with one another and to make the world intellectually meaningful, aesthetically pleasing, and emotionally compelling' (Baym 2000: 9, quoting Jenson and Pauly 1997: 163). She writes that two methods drove the research: discourse analysis and online surveys. Baym notes that she took a careful, systematic approach to her research:

> One of the most troubling shortcomings of the many analyses of online community to date has been their reliance on personal anecdote and hypothetical theorizing in place of close study. . . . A central goal of this study has been to demonstrate the advantages of empirical grounding . . . we cannot understand [the] complex dynamics [of online communities] by just thinking about them. (Baym 2000: 198)

In 1992, when she gathered most of her data, she systematically collected over 32,000 messages in a 10-month period. She quickly decided that she needed to refine her focus, so she chose to examine a subgroup that was made up of fans of the soap opera *All My Children*. She notes that the participants were eager to share their insights with a fellow viewer. She also observes that the members she studied defied the stereotypes of soap-opera fans as bored, uneducated women with nothing better to do with their time than sit around and watch television. Rather, she discovered that many of the members were educated professionals who participated in meaningful, analytical discussions on the topic of soap operas.

Summary

In this chapter, we have taken a tour through some of the newer approaches to qualitative research. We have seen new ways of gathering data, new ways of interpreting them, and new ways of communicating results. The landscape has become very rich, indeed. I hope that you have enjoyed learning about these new approaches, and I encourage you to read more about the studies in which researchers have used these innovative methods. Perhaps you will even try some of them for yourself. As you venture forth to conduct your own studies, remember that doing qualitative research of any sort takes much work and dedication, but it also involves thrilling discoveries and exhilarating experiences. Enjoy.

Key Terms

autoethnography
cultural studies
discourse analysis

ethnodramas
narrative analysis
photo elicitation

virtual ethnography
visual sociology

Questions for Critical Thought

1. Which of the methods discussed in this chapter seem to hold the most promise? What is it about them that led you to this conclusion?

2. Think about an online community on which you might do a virtual ethnography. What is it about the group that you find sociologically interesting? How would you go about approaching the group?

3. Do you think autoethnography has a valid place in academic research? Why or why not?

Exercises

1. Using an interview transcript, see if you can identify the particular discourses the research participant uses. What do these discourses tell you about what kind of person the participant thinks he or she is?

2. Select a photograph that you like and that you find meaningful. You may select a photo that you have taken or one that you find, perhaps on the Internet. Study the photo for five minutes. Actively look at everything depicted in the photo, and give each element a name. Identify relationships between the elements, and try to make sense of these relationships by creating a story that explains what you see in the photo.[5]

3. Look closely at a group of photographs you have taken at an event. How would you explain the event to another person while you were showing the photos?

Suggested Readings

Nancy K. Baym. 2000. *Tune In, Log On: Soaps, Fandom, and Online Community.* Thousand Oaks, CA: Sage. This virtual ethnography includes both a fascinating discussion of the online discussion group Baym studied and a clear description of how Baym went about carrying out her research.

Lisa Given, ed. 2008. *The Sage Encyclopedia of Qualitative Research Methods.* Los Angeles: Sage. This encyclopedia contains many entries on the latest approaches to qualitative research. Each entry suggests further readings where you can find examples and in-depth discussions.

P.C. Kontos and G. Naglie. 2006. 'Expressions of Personhood in Alzheimer's: Moving from Ethnographic Text to Performing Ethnography', *Qualitative Research* 6, 3: 301–17. You have to read this article to get a sense of how moving an ethnodrama can be. Even if you do not have the slightest interest in Alzheimer's disease, you will see the power of performance ethnography. The article includes a very good description of the transformation of data into drama.

Related Websites

Centre for Interdisciplinary Research on Narrative
http://w3.stu.ca/stu/sites/cirn/index.aspx

This useful website includes an extensive bibliography of narrative theory, practice, and research from a variety of disciplinary perspectives. It also hosts the online journal *Narrative Works: Issues, Investigations & Interventions*.

International Visual Sociology Association
www.visualsociology.org

This is the website of the International Visual Sociology Association. It provides links to the association's journal, announces meetings, and includes discussions on research and teaching.

10 Ethics on the Ground: A Moral Compass

Will C. van den Hoonaard

Learning Objectives

- ⊛ To develop a moral compass to guide you through the qualitative research process
- ⊛ To understand the importance of promoting respect for persons, concern for human welfare, and justice in qualitative research

Introduction

In this final chapter, we discuss the ethical dimensions of qualitative research. First, we encounter the three ethical principles that form the basis of many official research ethics codes—respect for persons, concern for human welfare, and justice. We discuss these principles as they are set out in Canada's official guide to conducting ethical research, the *Tri-Council Policy Statement: Ethical Conduct for Research Involving Humans* (CIHR, NSERC, and SSHRC 2010). Then, we move on to explore how you can take an ethical approach in your own research and how ethical considerations relate to what you have learned in the previous chapters. We also delve into the real-life experiences of researchers as they grapple with ethical issues while they plan, conduct, analyze, and write up their research. As you will discover, the purpose of this chapter is not only to underscore the general principles of ethical research but also to help you develop a moral compass that will allow you to steer your way through qualitative research.

Ethical Principles of Research in Canada

In Canada, ethical considerations for researchers working with human participants are laid out in the *Tri-Council Policy Statement* (TCPS). This work has been jointly created by Canada's three federal research bodies: the Canadian Institutes of Health Research (CIHR), the Natural Sciences and Engineering Research Council of Canada (NSERC), and the Social Sciences and Humanities Research Council of Canada (SSHRC). The **ethics codes** laid out in the TCPS are teaching researchers to sharpen the ethical dimensions of their research. Today, all Canadian researchers, including student researchers, who conduct studies involving humans, must submit their research plans to their university's **research ethics board (REB)** for approval. The TCPS specifies how REBs must review research plans.

Initially, the government was inspired to create these codes to protect the public against medical research of questionable ethics. Thus, the first version of the TCPS (CIHR, NSERC, and SSHRC 1998) was directed more towards biomedical research, and it did not explicitly discuss ethical concerns in qualitative studies. Thus, in 2010, the agencies released a heavily revised version of the publication with an aim to better reflect the issues faced by qualitative researchers. The new TCPS (CIHR, NSERC, and SSHRC 2010) has a separate chapter devoted to qualitative research that, read as a whole, serves as a guide to conducting qualitative studies in general.

The TCPS states that it is the researcher's duty to preserve the dignity of her or his participants. To help researchers meet this goal, the document identifies three ethical principles that stand at the core of all research projects involving human participants: respect for persons, concern for human welfare, and justice. Box 10.1 provides brief definitions of these principles.

Applying the Principles of Ethics to Qualitative Research

At this point, you may be wondering exactly how you can ensure that you respect the dignity of the participants in your own qualitative research studies. Here is some proven advice to help you build your moral compass.

First, enter the research situation with an open mind. As a qualitative researcher, you should never expect your participants to confirm your own assumptions, and you should never invent or rush in to explain your participants' motives. Remember that you are not the expert on the situation. You have no way of knowing what a particular experience is like for a participant, why they do the things they do, or why they *think* they do the things they do. You must allow participants to explain their situation and their motives in their own words.

Second, ask 'how' questions rather than 'why' questions. As you learned in Chapter 5, 'why' questions can make participants feel defensive, as if their motives are being questioned. Asking someone *how* something happened rather than *why* they did something also encourages that person to discuss his or her motives in context—to create a **vocabulary of motives**. This discussion will provide you with more useful qualitative data than would a short, direct answer that a 'why' question might elicit.

Third, you must acknowledge the various constraints that can intrude in a social setting that might also affect respect for the person. The TCPS notes several such constraints:

> Certain factors may diminish a person's ability to exercise their autonomy, such as inadequate information or understanding for deliberation, or a lack

BOX 10.1 ❋ CORE PRINCIPLES OF ETHICS

RESPECT FOR PERSONS

Respect for persons recognizes the intrinsic value of human beings and the respect and consideration that they are due. It encompasses the treatment of persons involved in research directly as participants and those who are participants because their data . . . are used in research. Respect for persons incorporates the dual moral obligations to respect autonomy and to protect those with developing, impaired, or diminished autonomy.

Autonomy includes the ability to deliberate about a decision and to act based on that deliberation. Respecting autonomy means giving due deference to a person's judgement and ensuring that the person is free to choose without interference. Autonomy is not exercised in isolation but is influenced by a person's various connections to family, to community, and to cultural, social, linguistic, religious, and other groups.

CONCERN FOR HUMAN WELFARE

The welfare of a person is the quality of that person's experience of life in all its aspects. Welfare consists of the impact on individuals of factors such as their physical, mental, and spiritual health, as well as their physical, economic, and social circumstances. Thus, determinants of welfare can include housing, employment, security, family life, community membership, and social participation, among other aspects of life.

JUSTICE

Justice refers to the obligation to treat people fairly and equitably. Fairness entails treating all people with equal respect and concern. Equity requires distributing the benefits and burdens of research participation in such a way that no segment of the population is unduly burdened by the harms of research or denied the benefits of the knowledge generated from it.

Source: CIHR, NSERC, and SSHRC. 2010. *Tri-Council Policy Statement: Ethical Conduct for Research Involving Humans*. Ottawa: CIHR, NSERC, and SSHRC, 8–10.

of freedom to act due to controlling influences or coercion. Such constraints may include the fear of alienating those in positions of authority, such as professional or personal caregivers, researchers, leaders, larger groups, or a community to which one belongs. (CIHR, NSERC, and SSHRC 2010: 9)

In short, you should be mindful of the fears that a research participant has by virtue of his or her precarious personal and social position.

Fourth, use an approach that fits the circumstances of the individual participant, group, community, and/or culture. If you are doing field research, ensure that your level of participation is appropriate to the setting. Also, ensure that your approach shows your respect for your participants' values. Remember that you are a guest in the setting and that you must adapt your behaviour to fit with the social norms of the community.

Fifth, forgo a 'remedial' attitude. Your job is not to find a remedy for a problem or to 'fix' things. Recall that qualitative research is *descriptive* and *analytical* rather than *prescriptive*. Thus, you should focus on observing what you see and assessing it in its own terms. You should also remember this approach when you write up your research. (We will look at *ethical writing*—writing that strives towards accuracy, precision, and clarity and offers a balanced perspective—in more depth later in this chapter.)

Finally, try to form authentic relationships with your participants. You should treat your participants as valued partners in the research process, not as subjects to be studied from a distance. Getting to know your participants as individuals will also help you to dispel your own biases. This goal is essential to conducting ethical research—you must be able to step out of your own immediate cultural and social worlds in order to understand the world of your research participants.

To illustrate the importance of this final point, let's look at the example Timothy Diamond set in his study of nursing homes, which you first encountered in Chapter 3. In his study, Diamond demonstrated high ethical resolve and established authentic relationships with the staff and the residents of nursing homes. As he notes, these genuine relationships permitted him to identify and overcome his own prejudices and stereotypical views of nursing homes. Box 10.2 presents some of Diamond's self-identified assumptions and his reactions to becoming aware of his faulty views. In addition, by abandoning his preconceived ideas and by having an open and observant attitude—in other words, by bursting out of his own bubble—Diamond was able to transform his original question, 'What can we do for them?', into a more productive qualitative research question, 'What is their life like?'

Developing a Research Question

As you have learned, the birth of a research question often begins with a fascination with a topic or a social setting. For example, Herbert J. Gans' classic 1967 study of the 'Levittowners' started when he and his wife mortgaged a home in Levittown, New Jersey, and he began taking notes on the social interactions among neighbours, newcomers, and local, rural residents.[1] Although it is easy to get caught up in the excitement

Box 10.2 ❖ Preconceived Ideas that Stood in the Way of Doing Ethical Research

- Assumption: Minimum wage is a liveable wage:
    Eventually, the very concepts of job and wage versus unemployment and poverty that I had brought with me began to break down. . . . Full-time work meant earning less than the cost of subsistence; it did not alleviate poverty.

- Assumption: Under-paid workers should simply find new jobs:
    Among the many insults that nursing assistants absorb . . . I came to think of none more naive than to enquire why they don't just get another job.

- Assumption: Patients in nursing homes are bedridden:
    . . . I had been under the impression that nearly all people in nursing homes were bedridden. In fact, many were up and dressed, walking around, and free to leave the building during certain hours.

- Assumption: Public aid provides a safety net:
    [P]ossessions were continually being lost and not replaced, having fallen through the large holes in the net. . . . What sometimes initially appeared as crazy behaviour emerged over time as rational, desperate attempts to guard what was slipping away.

- Assumption: Life in nursing homes is better than life on the streets:
    I clung for a while to the notion that residence in a nursing home must at least be better than living on the streets. [Yet an encounter with a homeless woman who said she would rather live in an abandoned building than in a nursing home] had opened even this assumption up for debate.

- Assumption: People who live in nursing homes have been abandoned by their families:
    It is an easy explanation, but . . . it rests on oversimplification. Listening to the residents' everyday conversations about their families did not lead to the inference that they were abandoned.

- Assumption: People who live in nursing homes lead lives of passivity:
    I had thought of residents as on the receiving end of human activity, acted upon rather than acting. . . . Getting to know the residents, however, dissolved that notion.

- Assumption: Nursing homes are silent, lonely places:
    Not only did people in the day room have a lot to say to the nursing staff, but quiet friendships bloomed throughout the room.

Source: Quotations from Timothy Diamond. 1992. *Making Gray Gold: Narratives of Nursing Home Care*. Chicago: University of Chicago Press, 44–5, 46, 63, 68, 69–70, 70, 84–5, 100.

of developing your own ideas in the early stages of your research project, to do ethical research, you must remain open-minded as you take notes and investigate your research questions. Almost invariably, you will make these necessary, early notes long before you have the opportunity or enough detailed knowledge to submit your research ideas to a research ethics board.

One barrier to such an approach is trying too hard to support your early ideas. The advice in Chapter 3, that you should not end the research where you start, is meaningful when it comes to doing ethical research. When we start a research project, we tend to imagine what the answers to our research question(s) might be. Yet, given our limited experience and unfamiliarity with the life-world of the groups and peoples we wish to study, it is unlikely that our imagined answers will reflect the reality of the situation. After all, if you do not belong to a group, how can you know what it is like to be a member? All too often, such imaginings can lead us to start 'defining and inventing' the motives of others (Conn 1971: 78; Becker 1996). The predispositions, stereotypes, and prejudices we bring to the research environment render a disservice to the people we aim to study: these pre-established notions, in effect, pre-empt participants' explanations, experiences, and points of view.

A second barrier to open-mindedness arises when there is a conflict of interest. When the public insists that social research be 'relevant' or 'applied', as is increasingly the case today, researchers may feel pressure to secure funding from organizations that aim to develop social policy. Often, these agencies purport to be interested in 'solving' social problems. At first glance, these might seem like praiseworthy objectives, but there is a downside to associating your research process with outside interests. To begin with, the kinds of questions you might ask under those conditions of funding are likely to represent the interests of funders or administrators rather than those of research participants. Merlinda Weinberg (2002), for example, learned that the administrators of the maternity home she was studying wanted her reports and field notes about how the residents were being cared for; the administrators planned to use these forms to comply with an external funder's requirement. External influences also present you with a more tenacious problem: Should you leave it to those who fund the research to define the social problem to be studied? Such a definition could force you to take an approach that is too narrow. For example, if you were asked by a school board to study the 'problem' of high school dropouts, the organization might insist that you look for factors outside the school environment to explain the phenomenon. Yet, to focus on finding 'answers' that will satisfy the constituents of the supporting organization, you would have to ignore the many school-based factors that could lead students to leave school before they graduate. In the end, your study would not accurately reflect the situation of your participants.

Field Work

Doing field work has a surprising number of unexpected—and unpredictable—ethical dimensions. In general, field work entails a long period of study. As you can see from the list of studies presented in Table 10.1, a qualitative researcher might spend several months or more than eight years making observations in the field.[2] In addition, it can take another two or three years (or even longer) to publish the study. The intensity of time and energy required to complete a field study presents the researcher with an ever-shifting environment in which he or she must consider the ethical dimensions of the study. Still, whether long or short, the time spent doing field work entails gaining access to the research setting, spending time in the community, and finally leaving the field. Each of these aspects demands ethical reflection on the part of the researcher.

Gaining Access to the Field

In most field research, unless you are conducting covert research (discussed later in this chapter), you will need to explain your presence to those whose lives you are planning to study. Generally, you will contact a community leader—a gatekeeper—to get permission to study in a particular setting. While you might find it intimidating to approach a community leader, your efforts will always pay off in the end. When I

TABLE 10.1 **Length of Time in the Field**

Topic of Study	Time Spent in the Field	Researcher and Publication Date
Household Work	8 years	A.R. Hochschild, 1989
Shoplifting	8 years	M.O. Cameron, 1973
Tattoo Shops	7 years	C. Sanders, 1989
Hotel Staff	5 years	R. Prus and S. Irini, 1980
Doomsday Cult	4 years	J. Lofland, 1977
Drug Dealers	4 years	P.A. Adler, 1985
Homeless Women	4 years	E. Liebow, 1993
Unwed Mothers	4 years	P. Rains, 1971
Biker Gangs	3 years	D. Wolf, 1991
TV News Studio	3 years	D.L. Altheide, 1976
Urban Youth	3 years	E. Anderson, 1976
Medical School	2 years	H.S. Becker et al., 1961
Hobos	1 year	N. Anderson, 1923
Magicians	5 months	R.A. Stebbins, 1984

was beginning my first field research project in a remote Icelandic village of 500 inhabitants, I had to approach the highly respected *oddvitinn*, the chairman of the village, to ask for entry into his community. To make the situation more nerve-racking, I was in an unfamiliar country, I had just ridden on a regional bus for two hours, and I'd had no hand in choosing the village. (An Icelandic agricultural economist whom I had befriended and who learned of my wish to study a fishing village put me on the bus and suggested I get off at the end of the ride!) As I stepped off the bus, into rain that swept horizontally across the landscape, the environment seemed utterly forlorn to me. Yet, I made my way to the *oddivtinn* and respectfully expressed my desire to study 'his' village. Fortunately, he agreed, and my time in the village was productive. Being honest with my intentions foreclosed any future problems.

The ethics involved in studying a private organization or a corporation are often more complex. Gaining formal approval from a company's CEO or president might involve the company's legal department. In general, very few corporations grant researchers access to their internal workings. Libels, lawsuits, the inevitable fall of 'whistle-blowers', and the power of multinationals can be a disincentive to any kind of research in a corporate setting. When a corporation does grant access, the company often wants to direct the research, a practice that can result in a conflict of interests. One example is the corporation that invited Arlie R. Hochschild (1997) to study it as a 'family-friendly' company. The organization might even restrict the researcher from using particular words or phrases in the analysis. For example, one researcher wanted to study the ethical aspects of decision making in a company and was given the go-ahead to do the research but was not allowed to use the word *ethics*!

Accessing government agencies can pose similar ethical dilemmas. Elliott Leyton (1978) provides a good example of how a researcher can resist the temptation to align him or herself with the interests of the agency under study. In his ethnographic study of the Workmen's Compensation Board in Newfoundland, 'The Bureaucratization of Anguish' (1978), Leyton clearly aligned his ethical duties with his participants while meeting his moral obligation to accurately and fairly substantiate his findings. In the end, his study critiqued the government agency, revealing how incompatible the actions of the bureaucracy were in relation to ameliorating the suffering of widows whose husbands had died of industrial disease.

More often, researchers are allowed to study government programs only within tight regulations set by the government. One such project, which is currently the subject of considerable ethical controversy, involves the United States Army's Human Terrain System (HTS) program in Iraq and Afghanistan. The program hires social scientists and combines scholarly research with military information-gathering (Institutional Review

Blog 2009). The intent is to gather ethnographic information on local populations as a means of limiting the danger of war on those populations. In the end, however, the interests of the military come first.

Spending Time in the Field

The approach you take while spending time in the field can take on a broad range of tones. Generally, the tone will depend on the character of the community or subculture to be studied and the personality of the researcher. Some researchers present themselves quietly, while others have a more visible profile, either because of their outgoing nature or because their physical appearance—their age, skin colour, gender, and so on—stands out in contrast to the physical characteristics of the other members of the group. Whatever the tone of the participation, you must be aware of the effect your presence has on the community. While members of a group may accept the idea of you taking notes on their environment, they might (silently) object or find it irksome if you are too obvious. Thus, you should always respect the group's boundaries by not ostentatiously taking notes. As you spend time in the setting and get to know the culture of the community, you will learn the least obtrusive ways to publicly take field notes.

The longer you stay in the setting, the more informed you will become of its routines and activities, and the more your participants will become familiar with *your* routines and activities. This familiarity has obvious benefits (for example, participants tend to be more open with individuals they recognize), but it also presents some ethical dilemmas. Sometimes, participants will become aware of your access to many corners of the setting, and they will try to get you to reveal information you have gained from others. You must exercise the utmost constraint in not revealing the sources of your information. Not only must you avoid directly naming the participants you have talked to, you must avoid conveying any details that would inadvertently reveal the source of the information. Your task is to safeguard the dignity of all of your participants. This can be quite challenging if the research setting is a small locale, as almost everyone will know everyone else and whom you have talked with. Thus, anonymity is probably ruled out, but confidentiality remains a viable and important ethical dimension.

Close relationships with participants can provide additional ethical tensions. While many researchers form genuine friendships with their participants, you must be careful to avoid letting such friendships interfere with your ethical obligations to the other participants or to the community as a whole. In particular, initiating an intimate relationship with or even marrying a participant confounds many ethical issues—all of which must be resolved in a manner that fits the situation. Marrying a member of the research setting in advance of doing the research (and perhaps choosing the setting because of such an entree) casts the ethical issues in an entirely different light than starting a relationship once in the field. The ethics of field work that involve intimate relations are very complex and contingent on a large number of factors. Given the almost limitless factors that affect interpersonal relationships, it is not feasible to set rules in advance, yet circumspection, caution, and consideration are watchwords that can apply to almost every field setting (see, for example, Bryant 1999).

Leaving the Field

As you learned in Chapter 4, you should try to leave your setting as a good guest would leave his or her host. If you have established friendships with some participants, exiting the setting can be an intricate and delicate process. You do not want to suggest that the friendships were anything less than authentic, and you do not want anyone to feel betrayed by your departure. You may want to keep in contact with some participants, if only in a casual way. As a follow-up, you may also want to inform interested participants of your findings—passing along such information demonstrates your respect for the group and your appreciation for their participation. In some cases, you may wish to maintain a friendship, transmuting your status as 'researcher' into a position of 'friend'. It is not uncommon for relationships formed in the field to flower into genuine friendships that sometimes last for a lifetime.

Covert Field Research

Covert research is not to be confused with 'deception' in research. Deception involves lying, at least in the initial stages of research; covert research implies the need for protection from danger, both for the individuals under study and for the researcher. Thus, many researchers support covert research as an ethical option in a variety of closed settings. Some researchers, with support from their universities, might feel justified in conducting covert research in authoritarian or dictatorial countries, where the controlling regime would not otherwise allow research to be conducted, on the grounds that a study of the social life in that setting would benefit the wider population. Similar arguments are made by researchers interested in examining social situations of institutionalized individuals. For example, while the administrators of a nursing home might refuse a researcher open access to the environment, perhaps because they are worried that such a study could undermine their routines or reflect negatively on their practices, a study of residents' experiences could lead to reforms that improve these individuals' daily lives. Many people—not just researchers—would argue that the ethics behind such research are sound.

As you can see, the ethics of covert research are closely tied to the intent of the researcher. If the researcher acts to support the welfare of a general population, the covert methods he or she uses become highly justifiable. On the other hand, it is never honourable to use people as a means of pursuing a hidden, self-motivated research agenda. For this reason, many individuals have argued against secretive government-based intrusions into personal life for intelligence, police, or military purposes. Of course, researchers who do covert research on behalf of such agencies would probably argue that they *are* working for the good of the public.

The decision to carry out covert research is not an easy one. If you find yourself in a research situation in which you are considering using covert methods, ask yourself the following questions: Will the study focus on an important issue? Could the study bring to light a hidden injustice or give a voice to an underrepresented group? Do you have a moral duty to conduct the research? Could the study help to improve the situation of a particular group? Has access to the setting been restricted by individuals who do not have a legitimate right to speak for the group? Could you be subject to physical or other harm if you were known as a researcher? If you can answer 'yes' to all or most of these questions, covert research may be an ethically viable option.

Covert research is part of the history of social-science research, and some of this research has achieved notoriety. Among the most famous covert studies are Leon Festinger et al.'s 1956 study of a doomsday cult and Laud Humphreys' 1970 work on homosexual behaviour in public washrooms. Festinger was interested in the social dynamics of a cult whose members believed that the world would come to an end in the very near future. His students posed as 'seekers' collecting information and making covert field notes of their experiences. One student was so convincing that he became one of the leaders! In their published account, the researchers were careful to protect the identities of those involved with the cult, and the resulting study contributed to our understanding of how cults operate. In Humphreys' case, he covertly observed men engaging in sexual acts in public washrooms, jotted down their cars' licence plate numbers, found their addresses in car records, and visited them at home under the pretext of doing another research project. Although he preserved complete anonymity of the men he observed, and although his study contributed to improving the social and political climates towards gay rights, many objected to his methods as unethical because he observed and interacted with the men in his study under a false pretence.

Ultimately, the greatest argument in support of covert research is that it is the only way to achieve total anonymity—the researcher does not reveal his or her name to the group being studied, and the researcher does not reveal the name(s) of the group or its participants in the research (W.C. van den Hoonaard 2003).

Any published report from the research cannot be traced back to members of the researched group.

Interviews and Transcriptions

The ethical considerations involved in interview situations are generally less ambiguous. Whether the interview is spontaneous or planned well in advance, you will always have the time and the opportunity to inform your participants of your research interest and to ask for their permission to be interviewed.

Consent

In private or face-to-face situations, researchers are expected to seek informed consent from participants. In medical and most quantitative studies, researchers use consent forms that participants must sign before the start of the research, and many research ethics boards require researchers to use forms of consent, duly signed by the research participant. Typically, the form explains the purpose and the methodology of the study, informs the participant that he or she can stop the interview at any time without any personal risk, and provides a guarantee of confidentiality and anonymity. The use of signed consent forms, however, is highly contested by qualitative researchers for a number of ethical reasons.

First, there are certain settings in which it would be inappropriate or insensitive to seek individual written consent—for example, in cultures that nurture a sense of collectivity (and where the individual's identity only makes sense insofar as it is part of that collectivity) or in a setting where illiteracy is the norm. Second, some collectives might interpret the researcher's seeking *individual* consent as an affront to the larger group. Third, some participants might want to protect their anonymity by not attaching their name to an 'official' document. This is often the case when the research is focussed on individuals living on the margins of society, those involved in illegal activities, or even those who occupy positions of power and prestige. Finally, some participants might see the need to sign a consent form as a serious betrayal of the trust that has developed over the course of previous interactions with the researcher. With the presentation of a formal consent form, what was initially a friendly soliciting of the perspectives and insights of a participant becomes a hopelessly unnatural relationship.

To overcome these obstacles, many qualitative researchers ask for their participants' verbal consent and provide an information sheet that contains the same information that would be found on a consent form. The information sheet does not require the signature of the participant; more often than not, it is the researcher who signs the information sheet because the sheet entails promises made by the researcher.

Content Analysis

Doing content analysis involves few ethical considerations, but you must be careful to avoid misrepresenting what you find. When studying the content of historical or even recent documents, you should always be mindful of **presentism**, that is, the belief that today's standards are a valid guide to studying older texts and social phenomena. For example, it isn't fair to criticize the lack of knowledge about sterilization in medical practice in the eighteenth century. Neither is it fair to analyze the frequency of the words *man* and *mankind* in pre-contemporary texts as a measure of lack of consideration for the social roles of women.

Similarly, you must not allow your own tastes and opinions to guide your analysis. If you do, you could misjudge the content or even entirely miss the point. For example, if a researcher who is generally uncomfortable with age disparity in sexual relationships were to watch the film *Harold and Maude* (1971) without making efforts to overcome his or her own biases, that researcher might easily misplace the intent of the film. In addition to embodying major social and cultural concerns of its time, the film challenges ageism by depicting a touching, intimate relationship between a 20-year-old man and a 79-year-old woman.

The meanings we attach to words are so deeply imbedded in our own culture and life experience that it is often difficult to step beyond the pale of personal experience. If you suspect that your analysis is too restricted by your own point of view, you might want to call upon a colleague or someone else involved in the research to conduct an independent content analysis. By comparing your own notes to those made by an individual with a different point of view, you may be able to identify and rule out the effects of presentism and bias in your work.

Analyzing Data

If faithfulness is a moral aim, then the ethical concept that will guide you through your analysis is faithfulness to data. Rather than contorting data to fit a theory or theories, you have an obligation to 'listen' carefully to the data, much of which has been generously donated by research participants. William Least Heat-Moon, a Pulitzer Prize–winning author, powerfully describes the struggle between theory and data he faced when he was drawing together his observations for his study of a small Kansas county:

For thirty months, maybe more, I've come and gone here and have found stories to tell, but . . . I had not discovered the way to tell them. My searches and researches, like my days, grew more randomly than otherwise, and every form I tried contorted them, and each time I began to press things into cohesion, I edged not so much toward fiction as toward distortion, when what I wanted was accuracy; even when I got a detail down accurately, I couldn't hook it to the next without concocting theories. . . . I was hunting a fact or image and not a thesis to hold my details together, and so I arrived at this question: should I just gather up items like creek pebbles into a bag and then let them tumble into their own pattern? (Least Heat-Moon 1991: 14–15)

In the end, Least Heat-Moon surrendered to the data, trusting that it would 'yield a landscape with figures' truly representative of the community he wanted to depict.

Writing Up Research

The process of writing up data requires a great deal of ethical reflection. In many ways, your writing reveals your ethical stance. As you are deciding what to include in your write-up, you will have to consider the extent to which you will address ethical aspects of your research methods and findings. Many of these aspects could have the power to raise awareness of issues central to your study. They might also be useful points of consideration for other researchers.

When you are writing up your report, remember that your task is to communicate your findings to your readers, who might include your professor, classmates, other researchers, or members of the general public. As one who has thought a lot about writing, I sum up my goal as 'protecting the dignity of the reader'. You can accomplish this goal in several ways.

Writing with Concision and Clarity

While you learned the importance of clear and concise writing in Chapter 8, a few points bear repeating as you consider the ethics of writing. Following the advice to avoid jargon and use short, straightforward sentences in your write-up will show your reader that you are not trying to confuse the issues, that you have nothing to hide. Using the active voice and the first-person perspective will also help you to accomplish this goal by forcing you to unambiguously state who conducted the research, who led the interviews, who did the coding, and who did the analysis. Recall the ambiguity in the passive sentence 'The interview was conducted'. Upon reading this sentence, the reader has no sense as to who conducted the interview. Why not clear up this confusion and take responsibility for your own actions: 'I conducted the interview'. Similarly, instead of stating 'The research was done in this village', say 'I conducted research in this village'.

Offering a Balanced View

When you are writing up your research, it is critical that you focus on presenting a balanced view of your findings. Having researched a topic extensively, passionately, and with a great deal of sacrifice of resources, time, and effort, you may have developed your own moral or ethical judgments, but you must be careful to avoid overtly supporting or criticizing any side of an issue in your report. You must also avoid assigning blame; there is no room for *adhominum* statements in balanced writing. Offering a balanced view fulfills the principle of fostering human dignity on behalf of both research participants and readers.

By offering a balanced view throughout your written account, you allow the reader to make up his or her mind about your data and your findings. You are obligated to present data and findings in as convincing a manner as possible but also in a way that does not take away the reader's ability to decide, on his or her own terms, what the research means. This approach shows that you respect your reader as an intelligent individual. To illustrate the effect a writer's slant can have on the reader, I refer to my experience of reading a study of the sealers who hunt in the St Lawrence Seaway (see van den Hoonaard 1987).[3]

In 1979, anthropologist Guy Wright decided to accompany a group of sealers on their hunt in order to study their lives. He published his account of this voyage in *Sons and Seals: A Voyage to the Ice* (1984). When I picked up this text, I approached the topic with an open attitude: I sided neither with the sealers nor with the anti-sealers. As the text unfolded, I noted that the study was well done, and the writer was able to pull me into the narrative and offer me a glimpse into the lived reality of the sealers. In his initial narrative, the writer achieved the researcher's goal of offering the reader the dignity of being able to make up his or her own mind. In addition, the writer's powerful writing moved me, and I felt an appreciation for the life of sealers. Then, in the last third of the narrative, the writer changed his approach. In no uncertain terms, he began to write disparagingly of the anti-sealers. This sudden shift had the opposite of the intended effect on me—my interest in the sealers' lives, which the writer had so carefully built up, dissipated, and I began to feel a loyalty towards the anti-sealers. What had happened? The writer had stopped offering a balanced view of the topic. He did not allow me to make up my mind about the seal hunt, and I felt that he had betrayed my dignity as an intelligent reader by trying to make up my mind for me. As a result, I felt disinclined to agree with his strongly opinionated assessment.

Ethics in the Digital Age

There is no question that the digital age has had a profound impact on social relations. It has altered the ways in which we communicate with one another and the ways in which we perceive our place in the social world. As you learned in Chapter 9, it has also brought new possibilities to the ways in which we can conduct qualitative research. Yet it has also called into question some of our basic understandings of ethical research practices. In recent years, many researchers have debated whether core ethical principles are still relevant in light of the widespread acceptance of new communications technologies that are undermining our privacy and, some might say, our dignity. Some, including Heather Kitchin (2002), suggest that the application of ethical principles should vary according to the relative accessibility of individual web pages. This argument generally states that postings on freely available web pages should be treated in the same manner as printed materials in magazines, while a higher threshold of ethical circumspection is needed when dealing with information available from web pages that are accessible only through private membership.

At the centre of this debate are issues of anonymity and informed consent. With the rise of Facebook and other new media that reveal so much private information, one may well wonder whether researchers' commitment to maintaining the anonymity of their participants at all cost is not anachronistic. Similarly, many have questioned why researchers should have to fully inform individuals of their role in a research project when hosts of other agencies, both governmental and private, regularly make incursions into the private lives of citizens.

At this point in time, there are no clear responses to such speculations, and the debate may never be resolved. Yet I would argue that no matter how much technology affects our lives, there will always be the need for us to use a moral compass to foster human dignity, ensure the welfare of the people we study, and promote justice.

Summary

As you have learned in this chapter, conducting qualitative research involves many ethical considerations. Qualitative researchers are well aware that, once the research gets underway, questions of ethics can fluctuate in unpredictable ways. Yet this does not mean that you should abandon ethical principles—far from it! Rather, you must put great efforts into determining the ethical principles that fit the circumstances. Of course, not everyone will agree on what is ethical in any given situation, and ethical contradictions and paradoxes will always persist. For example, does the safeguarding of human welfare mean that anonymity be maintained even if the research participant insists that his or her name be disclosed in research? Although there are no clear answers to these sorts of questions, you would do well to consider the dignity of your participants as your foremost goal when making ethical decisions.

Key Terms

ethics code	research ethics	vocabulary of
presentism	board	motives

Questions for Critical Thought

1. What are the advantages of doing covert research? What are the disadvantages? Are there ethical principles that could sustain the choice of covert research?

2. Is it possible for a researcher to do away with concerns of anonymity and confidentiality and still be ethical in his or her approach? Why or why not?

3. How might research participants interpret ethical dimensions of research differently from the way researchers interpret them? Should such differences affect the way research is carried out?

Exercises

1. Think about a research assignment that you have recently completed or one that you are planning to undertake. Make a list of the ethical issues that could be relevant to your study.

2. Read one Canadian ethnography that predates the first TCPS (that is, one that was published before 1998) and one that is contemporary. Try to select ethnographies that examine the same type of social setting. Are they different in terms of how they address ethical issues?

Suggested Readings

The following five scholarly journals, each of which is available online, deal with ethics in research. Increasingly, qualitative research journals are publishing articles on ethics and research:

Ethics and Information Technology. www.springerlink.com/content/1388-1957

International Journal of Ethics. www.novapublishers.com/catalog/editorial. php?products_id=1676

IRB: Ethics and Human Research. www.thehastingscenter.org/Publications/IRB/

Journal of Academic Ethics. www.springerlink.com/content/111139/

Journal of Empirical Research on Human Research Ethics. www.csueastbay.edu/ JERHRE/

Related Websites

American Anthropological Association Statement on Ethnography and Institutional Review Boards

www.aaanet.org/stmts/irb.htm

This statement pertains to research by American anthropologists.

Institutional Review Blog

www.institutionalreviewblog.com/2009/12/after-human-terrain-will-aaa-debate.html

This site is devoted to discussing the latest developments in ethics in the social sciences.

Panel on Research Ethics

http://pre.ethics.gc.ca/eng

This is the portal to the website of the Interagency Advisory Panel on Research Ethics (PRE). Here, you will find links to the revised *Tri-Council Policy Statement*, a tutorial on the TCPS, and additional information on and publications from PRE.

Canadian Association of Research Ethics Boards

www.careb-accer.org

You may wish to subscribe to the listserv of the Canadian Association of Research Ethics Boards. Although the topics are primarily about biomedical research, there are occasions when sociological issues are raised.

Appendix A

Selected List of Qualitative Research Resources

Studies by Canadian Scholars

Albas, Daniel, and Cheryl Albas. 1989. 'Modern Magic: The Case of Examinations', *The Sociological Quarterly* 30, 4: 603–13.

Aronson, Jane. 2002. 'Elderly People's Accounts of Home Care Rationing: Missing Voices in Long-Term Care Policy Debates', *Ageing and Society* 4, 22: 399–418.

Atkinson, Michael. 2003. *Tattooed: The Sociogenesis of a Body Art.* Toronto: University of Toronto Press.

Bennett, John, and Rowley, Susan. 2004. *Uqalurait: An Oral History of Nunavut.* Montreal: McGill-Queen's University Press.

Botsford Fraser, Marian. 2001. *Solitaire: The Intimate Lives of Single Women.* Toronto: Macfarlane Walter & Ross.

Bridgman, Rae. 2003. *Safe Haven: The Story of a Shelter for Homeless Women.* Toronto: University of Toronto Press.

Briggs, Jean. 1999. *Inuit Morality Play: The Emotional Education of a Three-Year-Old.* New Haven, CN: Yale University Press.

Burman, Patrick. 1988. *Killing Time, Losing Ground: Experiences of Unemployment.* Toronto: Thompson Educational Publication.

Cairns, Kathleen V., and Eliane Leslau Silverman. 2004. *Treasure: The Stories Women Tell about the Things They Keep.* Calgary: University of Calgary Press.

Cavanagh, Sheila L. 2010. *Queering Bathrooms: Gender, Sexuality, and the Hygienic Imagination.* Toronto: University of Toronto Press.

Clarke, Laura Hurd. 2011. *Facing Age: Women Growing Older in Anti-Aging Culture.* Lanham, MD: Rowman & Littlefield Publishers.

Counts, Dorothy Ayres, and David Reese Counts. 2001. *Over the Next Hill: An Ethnography of RV'ing Seniors in North America.* Peterborough, ON: Broadview Press.

De Santis, Solange. 1999. *Life on the Line: One Woman's Tale of Work, Sweat and Survival.* New York: Doubleday.

Desroches, Frederick J. 2005. *The Crime That Pays: Drug Trafficking and Organized Crime in Canada.* Toronto: Canadian Scholars Press.

Dietz, Mary Lorenz. 1983. *Killing for Profit: The Social Organization of Felony Homicide.* Chicago: Nelson-Hall.

Dorais, Louis Jacques. 1997. *Quaqtaq: Modernity and Identity in an Inuit Community.* Toronto: University of Toronto Press.

Dossa, Parin. 2009. *Racialized Bodies, Disabling Worlds: Storied Lives of Immigrant Muslim Women.* Toronto: University of Toronto Press.

Doucet, Andrea. 2007. *Do Men Mother?: Fathering, Care, and Domestic Responsibility.* Toronto: University of Toronto Press.

Draper, Harold. 1998. *Growing Up in Manitoba.* Regina, SK: Canadian Plains Research Center.

Driban, Paul. 1985. *We Are Metis: The Ethnography of a Halfbreed Community in Northern Alberta*. New York: AMS Press.

Folson, Rose Baaba. 2004. *Calculated Kindness: Global Restructuring, Immigration, and Settlement in Canada*. Halifax: Fernwood Publishing.

Fox, Bonnie. 2010. *When Couples Become Parents: The Creation of Gender in the Transition to Parenthood*. Toronto: University of Toronto Press.

George, Glynis. 2000 *The Rock Where We Stand: An Ethnography of Women's Activism in Newfoundland*. Toronto: University of Toronto Press.

Gilead, Lisa. 1990. *The Northern Route: An Ethnography of Refugee Experiences*. St John's, NL: ISER Books.

Haas, Jack. 2004. *Seeking Bliss: A Study of Addiction and Recovery*. Cowichan Bay, BC: Mosaic Publishers.

Haas, Jack, and William Shaffir. 1987. *Becoming Doctors: The Adoption of a Cloak of Competence*. Greenwich, CT: Jai Press.

Handa, Amait. 2001. *Caught between Omissions: Exploring 'Culture Conflict' among Second Generation Asian Women in Canada*. Toronto: Women's Press.

Harmon, Lesley D. 1989. *When a Hostel Becomes a Home: Experiences of Women*. Toronto: Garamond Press.

Harrison, Deborah. 2002. *The First Casualty: Violence against Women in Canadian Military Communities*. Toronto: J. Lorimer

Harrison, Deborah, and Lucille Laliberté. 1994. *No Life Like It: Military Wives in Canada*. Toronto: J. Lorimer.

Hiebert, Carl. 2003. *Us Little People: Mennonite Children*. Erin, ON: Boston Mills Press.

Jeffrey, Leslie Ann, and Gayle MacDonald. 2006. *Sex Workers in the Maritimes Talk Back*. Vancouver: UBC Press.

Karabanow, Jeff. 2004. *Being Young and Homeless: Understanding How Youth Enter and Exit Street Life*. New York: Peter Lang Publishing.

Kelly, Jennifer. 2003. *Borrowed Identities*. New York: Peter Lang Publishing.

Kelly, Katherine, and Mark Douglas Totten. 2002. *When Children Kill: A Social-Psychological Study of Youth Homicide*. Peterborough, ON: Broadview Press.

Low, Jacqueline. 2004. *Using Alternative Therapies: A Qualitative Analysis*. Toronto: Canadian Scholars Press.

Luxton, Meg. 1980. *More than a Labour of Love: Three Generations of Women's Work in the Home*. Toronto: Women's Press.

McLellan, Janet. 2009. *Cambodian Refugees in Ontario: Resettlement, Religion, and Identity*. Toronto: University of Toronto Press.

Makabe, Tomoko. 1998. *The Canadian Sansei*. Toronto: University of Toronto Press.

Malacrida, Claudia. 2003. *Cold Comfort: Mothers, Professionals, and Attention Deficit Disorder*. Toronto: University of Toronto Press.

Malacrida, Claudia. 1998. *Mourning the Dreams: How Parents Create Meaning from Miscarriage, Stillbirths, and Early Infant Death*. Edmonton: Qual Institute Press.

Mandell, Deena. 2002. *Deadbeat Dads: Subjectivity and Social Construction*. Toronto: University of Toronto Press.

March, Karen. 1995. *The Stranger Who Bore Me: Adoptee–Birth Mother Relationships*. Toronto: University of Toronto Press.

Martin, Karen. 1998. *When a Baby Dies of SIDS: The Parents' Grief and Search for Reason.* Edmonton: Qual Institute Press.

Namaste, Viviane. 2000. *Invisible Lives: The Erasure of Transsexual and Transgendered People.* Chicago: University of Chicago Press.

Noivo, Edite. 1997. *Inside Ethnic Families: Three Generations of Portugese-Canadians.* Montreal: McGill-Queen's University Press.

Okihio, Norman. 1997. *Mounties, Moose, and Moonshine: The Patterns and Context of Outport Crime.* Toronto: University of Toronto Press.

O'Reilly-Fleming, Thomas. 1993. *Down and Out in Canada: Homeless Canadians.* Toronto: Canadian Scholars Press.

Pawluch, Dorothy. 1996. *The New Pediatrics: A Profession in Transition.* New York: Aldine de Gruyter.

Pawluch, Dorothy, William Shaffir, and Charlene Miall. 2005. *Doing Ethnography: Studying Everyday Life.* Toronto: Canadian Scholars' Press.

Preston, Richard. 2002. *Cree Narrative: Expressing the Personal Meaning of Events.* Montreal: McGill-Queen's University Press.

Prus, Robert. 1989. *Pursuing Customers: An Ethnography of Marketing Activities.* Newbury Park, CA: Sage.

Prus, Robert. 1989. *Making Sales: Influence as Interpersonal Accomplishment.* Newbury Park, CA: Sage.

Prus, Robert, and Lorne Dawson. 1991. 'Shop 'til You Drop: Shopping as Recreational and Laborious Activity', *Canadian Journal of Sociology* 16, 2: 145–64.

Prus, Robert, and Styllianoss Irini. [1980] 1988. *Hookers, Rounders, and Desk Clerks: The Social Organization of the Hotel Community.* Salem, WI: Sheffield Publishing.

Prus, Robert, and C.R.D. Sharper. 1991. *Road Hustler: Hustlers, Magic, and the Thief Subculture.* New York: Kaufman & Greenberg.

Pryce, Paula. 1999. *Keeping the Lakes' Way: Reburial and Re-Creation of a Moral World among an Invisible People.* Toronto: University of Toronto Press.

Rains, Pru. [1971] 2007. *Becoming an Unwed Mother.* Piscataway, NJ: Transaction Press.

Rankin, Janet M., and Marie Campbell. 2006. *Managing to Nurse: Inside Canada's Health Care Reform.* Toronto: University of Toronto Press.

Ranson, Gillian. 2010. *Against the Grain: Couples, Gender, and the Reframing of Parenting.* Toronto: University of Toronto Press.

Ranson, Gillian. 2001. '"Men at Work" Change–or No Change?–in the Era of the New Father', *Men and Masculinities* 4, 1: 3–26.

Reiter, Ester. [1991] 2000. *Making Fast Food.* Montreal: McGill-Queen's University Press.

Scott, Susan. 2007. *All Our Sisters: Stories of Homeless Women in Canada.* Toronto: University of Toronto Press.

Shaffir, William. 1974. *Life in a Religious Community: The Lubavitcher Chassidim in Montreal.* Toronto: Holt, Rinehart, and Winston of Canada.

Skelton, Tracey, and Gill Valentine, eds. 1997. *Places of Cool: Geographies of Youth Culture.* New York: Routledge.

Stebbins, Robert A. 1998. *After Work: The Search for an Optimal Leisure Lifestyle.* Calgary: Detselig Enterprises.

Stebbins, Robert A. 1996. *The Barbershop Singer: Inside the Social World of a Musical Hobby.* Toronto: University of Toronto Press.

Stebbins, Robert A. 1991. *Amateurs: On the Margin between Work and Leisure.* Beverly Hills, CA: Sage.

Stebbins, Robert A. 1990. *The Laugh-Makers: Stand-Up Comedy as Art, Business, and Life-Style.* Kingston, ON: McGill-Queen's University Press.

Stebbins, Robert A. 1987. *Canadian Football: The View from the Helmet.* London, ON: University of Western Ontario Press.

Stebbins, Robert A. 1984. *The Magician: Career, Culture and Social Psychology in a Variety Art.* Toronto: C. Irwin.

Theberge, Nancy. 2000. *Higher Goals: Women's Ice Hockey and the Politics of Gender.* Albany, NY: State University of New York Press.

Thiessen, Ilka. 2006. *Waiting for Macedonia: Identity in a Changing World.* Toronto: University of Toronto Press.

van den Hoonaard, Deborah K. 2010. *By Himself: The Older Man's Experience of Widowhood.* Toronto: University of Toronto Press.

van den Hoonaard, Deborah K. 2001. *The Widowed Self: The Older Woman's Journey through Widowhood.* Waterloo, ON: Wilfrid Laurier University Press.

van den Hoonaard, Deborah K., and Will C. van den Hoonaard. 2006. *The Equality of Women and Men: The Experience of the Baha'i Community of Canada.* Douglas, NB: Deborah K. and Will C. van den Hoonaard

van den Hoonaard, Will C. 2011. *The Seduction of Ethics: The Transformation of the Social Sciences.* Toronto: University of Toronto Press.

van den Hoonaard, Will C. 1991. *Silent Ethnicity: The Dutch of New Brunswick.* Fredericton, NB: New Ireland Press.

Wolf, Daniel R. 1991. *The Rebels: A Brotherhood of Outlaw Bikers.* Toronto: University of Toronto Press.

Zine, J. 2008. *Canadian Islamic Schools: Unraveling the Politics of Faith, Gender, Knowledge, and Identity.* Toronto: University of Toronto Press.

Qualitative Research Journals

Forum: Qualitative Social Research
International Journal of Qualitative Methods
Journal of Contemporary Ethnography
Qualitative Health Research
Qualitative Inquiry
Qualitative Report
Qualitative Sociology
Qualitative Sociology Review
Symbolic Interaction

Note: These are only a few of the journals that publish qualitative work. As you progress through your studies, you will find that various disciplines also have journals that spotlight qualitative research—for example, *Family Relations* in family studies or the *Journal of Aging Studies* in gerontology.

APPENDIX B

Sample Field Notes

I wrote these field notes at the end of a three-month trip to South Florida in 2002. The wetlands are part of a water reclamation project. They include a half-mile boardwalk loop, islands, trees, and many different kinds of birds. Alligators are always an attraction and a topic of conversation. In the notes, I have given people whom I recognized nicknames to keep them straight. I can, thus, follow them through all of my field notes. At the time of day I recorded these notes, around sunrise, I observed two types of people: birders and joggers. I already knew, when I wrote these notes, that the two groups do not always get along. The birders put their cameras and tripods 'in the way' of joggers, and the joggers make enough noise to startle the birds. I, like many of the joggers, walked around the loop several times each morning, but I also slowed down for the birders. Hence, I had a friendly relationship with members of both groups.

Wetlands, South Florida

14 March 2002, 7:00 am

Well, this morning the woman who's been coming for 3 years said to me, 'I see you're becoming a regular'. She didn't stop moving, so I couldn't tell her that I would be leaving soon. The second time I saw her she told me that there was a 'huge gator at 8'. Remember the numbers on the fence? Anyway, by the time I got to 8, the gator was gone.

The big excitement is the great blue heron. She's drawing 3–5 tripod people each day . . . 2 new people come every day. Today there was another young woman with a tripod—she mentioned to someone that she 'does this' for a living. She also tried to look, by invitation, in another man's camera, but the eye piece was too high. While I was there, we got to see the mother feed her two babies. For the first time, a man lent me a pair of binoculars (unasked) and a woman I see all the time told me I should look through a scope set up on a tripod that was aimed beautifully to see the babies. Everybody there seemed to be very cheerful and enjoying the event. There were, of course, walkers who did not slow down at all to join the party.

Also the black woman—always there—said hello as always. This then combines with what's going on with the birders. At one point when we crossed paths where the birders are taking pictures of the great blue heron and her babies (2)—she said to me, that the babies were born and she did not know how many there are. She was visibly excited by this. Then she asked one of the birders and he said 2 and she said that next time she would bring her binoculars. Also, I heard one tripod man complain to another about the joggers—I didn't see anyone jogging.

Saw a young woman (!) with a tripod—but so different. She was very young—20s I'd say—and she was wearing a Nike T-shirt and no shoes—really bare feet. When she was set up near the great blue heron, she looked towards me as I passed, but I was invisible to her; her face was completely impassive.

Wetlands, South Florida

16 March 2002, 6:50 am

I discovered today that the weekend begins on Friday—I arrived at 6:50—10 minutes earlier than usual. The parking lot was already packed. There were several people there walking who I didn't know but who seemed to be quite familiar with the place. The woman who's been walking for 3 years was alone at first but then joined another woman and even changed direction.

The young Nike woman with bare feet was back—this time with shoes. Also another young woman with a tripod. When they saw each other they hugged and one asked the other where have you been. Then Nike woman and tripod man introduced themselves. Turns out that they have been corresponding via email. I also heard one man tell another (both tripods) that people have heard of him.

I think if I were staying, I'd get a pair of binoculars and start hanging out with the birders a little. Right now my whole view of the place is based on my experience as a walker.

The weather is quite warm now—in the 70s and humid when I get there—really almost too warm for a brisk walk. No alligators today.

I did see a few more single women today—almost all with Walkmans—actually almost everyone who walks alone is wearing a Walkman.

I've been seeing a new bird the last few days. First I thought it was the moorhen with the red beak but it seemed to have green and purple feathers. I thought it might be some mating plumage or something, because I heard someone point out that some birds' colourful wings were a mating thing. Anyway, as I was leaving I noticed on that bulletin board right at the start of the walk—the one with the pamphlets on it—that someone had stapled a page from one of those calendars like the trivia calendar we used to get, but this was from the National Audubon Society and it was describing this new bird, which is a purple something.

As I left I noticed licence plates from FL, NJ, and VT. The friendly security guard was there but stayed in his car. I noticed a security camera in the parking lot yesterday.

APPENDIX C

Checklist for Writing Research Reports

☐ I have devised a title that accurately reflects the contents of my report.

☐ I have included a clear overview of my report in the introduction.

☐ I have kept my topic in view throughout my report (there are no paragraphs that are not directly related to my topic).

☐ I have used bridging terms and phrases to link all my ideas in a smooth and flowing fashion.

☐ I have organized the content of each section in a clear and logical manner.

☐ I have grammatically integrated all quotations into my own writing.

☐ I have written a final paragraph that is conclusive without being repetitive.

☐ I have used the active voice wherever possible.

☐ I have properly cited my sources and included all cited works in a references section at the end of my report.

☐ I have not left an extra space between paragraphs.

☐ I have used an appropriate font size (generally, 12 points for running text).

☐ I have used standard margins (generally, between 1 and 1.25 inches, or between 2.5 and 3 centimetres).

☐ I have numbered the pages using the automatic function within the computer program.

☐ I have carefully proofread my work to ensure there are no errors in spelling, punctuation, or grammar.

Notes

Chapter 1

1. 'Sarah' is a pseudonym. It is common in qualitative research to hide the identities of research participants to ensure confidentiality. It is also quite common for researchers to quote interview transcripts verbatim in their reports to capture the power of their participants' own words. Chapter 8, 'Writing Up Qualitative Research', discusses more about the use of pseudonyms in reporting on qualitative research.

Chapter 2

1. Although I have developed this analogy further, I first came across it in Rubin and Rubin (1995), in which the authors compare designing a qualitative interview study to planning a vacation.

2. As Brenda H. Vrkljan explains, 'older drivers use the term *copilot* to describe their close working relationship with passengers' (2009: 373).

3. One indication that a term has a negative connotation is the use of changing terminology or euphemisms to escape a connotation that results from prejudice. Until the connotation changes, the new term will eventually attract negative associations, a new term will appear, and the cycle will continue.

Chapter 4

1. Before the field of sociology gained prominence in Canada, early interest in field research was rooted in developments in anthropology. Early anthropological studies tied to the Victoria Memorial Museum in Ottawa, with an anthropological division headed by the famous American linguist and anthropologist Edward Sapir, led to detailed and influential ethnographic studies of First Nations peoples. In addition, the Royal Ontario Museum in Toronto took a deep interest in cultural diversity throughout the world (Darnell 1997).

2. A rough outline of the institutional spread of interactionist-type sociology in Canada during the twentieth century has been put together by Fatima Camara and Rick Helmes-Hayes (2003) and Emily Milne and Rick Helmes-Hayes (2010).

3. See Appendix A for a list of recent qualitative studies by Canadian researchers and Jean (2006) for a history of the development of field research in Quebec.

4. The Red Hat Society is a '"disorganization" of women who are gathering together in small clusters, large crowds . . . to share one another's lives and to make our own fun' (Cooper 2004: xi). It takes its inspiration from a poem by Jenny Joseph, 'Warning', which begins with the following lines: 'When I am an old woman, I shall wear purple, with a red hat which doesn't go, and doesn't suit me' (cited in Cooper 2004: xiii). There are chapters all over North America.

5. Diamond did mention to other workers that he was working on a book if they asked him what he, a white male, was doing working as a nursing assistant.

6. In one of the highest ethical stances recorded in the literature, Wolf (1991: 18–9) was prepared to abandon his project and destroy his field notes if the Rebels refused him permission to write up the study. Fortunately, they agreed to let him publish his results.

7. The most celebrated sponsor in the annals of ethnography is 'Doc', the individual who helped William Foot Whyte (1955) in his study of 'corner boys' (Hammersley and Atkinson 1983: 58). Doc has become so famous in the history of ethnography that many researchers talk about finding their Doc as an important early step in their field work.

Chapter 5

1. As long ago as 1956, Mark Benney and Everett C. Hughes noted, 'There is an enormous amount of preparatory socialization in the respondent role—in schools and jobs, through the mass media—more and more of the potential respondents of the Western world are readied for the rap of the clipboard on the door' (1956: 139).

2. For this reason, qualitative researchers often use the term *participant* instead of *interviewee*. After all, we participate together to accomplish an in-depth interview.

Chapter 6

1. This shift has resulted in the explosion of the market for self-help books. See Kaminer 1992 for a critical discussion of the self-help movement.

2. To understand the influence a 'frame' can have on a topic, think about news reports you have heard, seen, or read that discuss elderly drivers. You will likely notice that such stories usually have a biomedical frame. That is, these articles usually focus on the physical decline that comes with aging. The stories often discuss whether doctors can or cannot determine who should not be allowed to drive or focus on the need to require driving tests for 'seniors' to ascertain whether or not they are still capable of driving safely. These stories almost never discuss societal issues that may affect older drivers. For example, perhaps in recognition of demographic changes, we should not be designing roads, street signs, and speed limits with young drivers in mind. The absence of these discussions in the news media is largely a result of the biomedical framing of the issue.

3. As you think about these findings, keep in mind that this study was done before 2001. We can guess that, since 9/11, there has likely been a more intense focus on fear as the awareness of terrorism has become more prominent.

4. Clarke named her study 'The Case of the Missing Person' to underline her finding that the articles contained no profiles of individuals with Alzheimer's from their own perspective.

5. We studied nine films made between 1942 and 1990. You can see these stages during the airport scenes in a more recent film, *Love Actually* (2003). Towards the end of this film, a widowed stepfather and his young stepson, Sam, who has recently lost his mother, race to the airport so that Sam can say goodbye to a girl in his class. When the two get to the airport, liminality takes over as Sam undertakes a traditional activity in the transition stage in movies, the tunnel run. Sam runs at breakneck speed through the airport and even security to get to the gate before the girl disappears into the plane. Norms mean nothing as Sam manages to see his 'love' off. In the end, both father and son are reincorporated as men who have what it takes to take a chance on love.

Chapter 7

1. Box 8.1 illustrates a memo I wrote while doing focussed coding.

2. Those who do narrative analysis focus on the structure of the story as much as its content (see Chapter 9 for a discussion). For our purposes here, we will focus on the content of the story to provide material for analysis.

3. Often, people use civil inattention to avoid embarrassing someone else. Will C. van den Hoonaard (2010) notes a good example of this use of civil inattention that comes from a trip he took to Oslo, Norway. He reports that he was reading his morning newspaper in a restaurant when the paper suddenly caught fire! He dropped the newspaper onto the table and banged on it to put out the flames. His silverware was bouncing around and making a great deal of noise. When he looked up, he saw that all the other people in the restaurant were 'looking into their cups as if they'd never seen coffee before'. Through their civil inattention, the people were preserving his dignity and avoiding embarrassment.

Chapter 8

1. You will recall that earlier, in Chapter 3, we suggested that it is a good idea to start your project from where you are, but that the project should not end there. Wolcott is making the same point. If you find that you feel so strongly about a topic or research question that data are unlikely to change your opinion, the topic is not for you. Early writing may help you discover this situation.

2. This analogy was inspired by a conversation with a colleague, Christine Cornell, some years ago.

3. When I was interviewed on CBC Radio about *The Widowed Self*, the interviewer told me that she had cried through the first chapter.

4. This exercise is loosely based on Richardson (1994: 525).

Chapter 9

1. Maines (2001) illustrated this point when he analyzed data from his research on diabetes self-help groups using a narrative approach and discovered that the narratives functioned to establish group boundaries and hierarchy within the groups.

2. Matzoh is the unleavened bread that Jews eat during Passover to remind them that they did not have time to let their bread rise when they were escaping from Egypt.

3. Thompson has created a website for her film, http://coveredthemovie.com, on which she has posted various resources, including excerpts from her film and a short video about the making of *Covered*. In the videos, you can see how effective and meaningful the images of the women are.

4. Researchers have found that men are often reluctant to talk about emotional events or situations when they are in an interview situation in which they feel they are not in control (see, for example, Schwalbe and Wolkomir 2001).

5. This exercise is based on an example from Howard S. Becker (1986b: 232).

Chapter 10

1. Immediately after World War II, the Levitt brothers came up with the idea of expanding cities into suburbs with affordable homes using one of four or five blueprints (which made the homes inexpensive). This architect-accountant pair built three 'Levittowns': one on Long Island (New York), one in New Jersey, and another in Pennsylvania. The street plan, street names, and house numbers are similar in all three suburbs.

2. Traditionally, some would argue that a minimum of 2 years is required to understand a new (sub)culture, although others would say that 3 or 4 months are sufficient in some cases. Vicki Smith (2002: 228) looked at the field work behind 50 research

monographs and discovered that it took 8.14 years on average after the start of field work to see its appearance as a book. Arlie R. Hochschild's study *The Second Shift* (1989), which is about how couples share housework, took 13 years of field work and an additional 6 years of writing and preparation before it was published. Daniel R. Wolf took 3 years to do field research among outlaw bikers, and it took 15 years before his book, *The Rebels* (1991), appeared in print. Studying student culture took Cheryl and Daniel Albas (see, for example, 2009) more than 25 years of detailed observation and recording.

3. As you probably know, seal hunting was (and still is) quite controversial in Canada. A quick Internet search will provide you with a great deal of information on the current state of the debate. In particular, you might be interested in viewing the following news clip, which is related to some people's virulent opposition to Sara Green, former Miss Newfoundland and Labrador, wearing a seal coat: www.youtube.com/watch?v=zvooeJY7S_c.

Glossary

action research See **participatory action research**.

active interview An approach to conducting an interview in which the researcher analyzes not only *what* is said but *how* it is said. It focusses on the interactive process as a source of data that the researcher can analyze to understand the social world of participants.

active voice A style of writing in which the subject of the sentence is the *doer* of the action.

autoethnography An approach to qualitative research in which the researcher analyzes his or her own experiences.

bargain In relation to accessing a setting for field research, a bargain is an agreement a researcher makes with a gatekeeper in exchange for permission to access a social setting. It often entails a promise of confidentiality.

breaching experiment An experiment using the ethnomethodological perspective in which the researcher breaks one of the unspoken laws of interaction.

causal knowledge Knowledge that assumes the world is made up of causes and effects that are external to the individual, observable, and measurable.

civil inattention The wilful lack of attention strangers pay one another in a social setting, often with the motive of remaining inconspicuous, maintaining civility, and/or avoiding embarrassment.

Chicago School of Sociology In the early twentieth century, this group produced the first qualitative studies that relied on an ethnographic style of field work.

closed-ended (or forced-choice) question A question that limits the possible responses to options provided by the researcher. Closed-ended questions are characteristic of quantitative surveys.

codes Names for the topics, activities, events, and people that come up in an interview transcript or field notes.

coding Systematically going through data, finding terms or phrases to categorize chunks of data, and organizing the data into a form the researcher can work with.

community-based research A collaborative approach to research that includes community members in the design, implementation, and analysis of a study. The researcher shares control of the study with the community group involved.

complete observer A field researcher's role in which he or she does not interact with the participants in a social setting and might not inform them that he or she is doing a study.

complete participant A field researcher's role in which he or she attempts to become a full-fledged member of the group he or she is studying, concealing his or her intent from the group.

cultural studies The study of popular culture and its representations. Often, researchers who engage in cultural studies analyze images in the media to identify cultural ideals.

deductive reasoning A process of reasoning in which a researcher 1) puts forth a theory, 2) develops hypotheses based on the theory, 3) collects data based on the hypotheses, and 4) performs an analysis that tests the hypotheses.

definition of the situation A basic concept of symbolic interactionism that states that, in any given situation, an individual's behaviour is influenced more by his or her understanding of the situation than by any objective aspects of the situation itself. Social groups or cultures often share definitions of the situation.

discourse analysis An interpretive approach to research, influenced by the writing of Michel Foucault, that sees language as a social practice and therefore constitutive of social life.

double-barrelled question A question that includes two or more sub-questions in a single question.

emergent design A characteristic of qualitative research. Research strategies change during the course of the research as the researcher becomes familiar with the research setting or social group.

ethics code A code that defines the character of a system (for example, a professional research system) in which morals—an individual's sense of what is 'right' or 'proper' in relation to his or her personal character—are applied.

ethnocentrism The tendency to believe that one's own ethnic group or society is superior to others and, therefore, to use this group as the standard when evaluating other groups.

ethnodramas Plays written by ethnographers that illustrate their research findings.

ethnography In-depth study of a group, culture, or society that usually entails field work.

ethnomethodology An approach in which researchers study people to discover how unwritten or invisible rules allow them to go about everyday life. See also **breaching experiment**.

field notes The detailed records of what researchers see, hear, feel, and do during an observational study.

focussed coding Coding in which the researcher further refines the codes used in the first stage of coding, open coding.

frame An approach to a topic or issue in which certain aspects are emphasized while other aspects are subjugated. When used in the mass media, frames have the power to influence public perceptions of an issue.

gatekeepers Individuals who have the power to deny or grant the researcher access to a social setting, often, but not always, in an official capacity.

generic social processes Aspects of interaction that transcend individual situations (for example, acquiring perspectives, achieving identity, doing activity, developing relationships, experiencing emotionality, and achieving linguistic fluency).

grounded theory A research approach that begins with collecting data about a particular phenomenon and constructs a theory to explain the phenomenon that is grounded in the data.

hierarchy of credibility The common situation in which those in superordinate positions and so-called 'experts' are seen as more credible than those in subordinate or marginal social positions.

ideal types Max Weber's term for abstract concepts that refer to phenomena in general but are not meant to capture the attributes of any particular case.

identity foreclosure In relation to a widow's sense of identity, the process through which a widow loses her sense of identity after her husband dies, even when she attempts to hang on to her identity as a wife. Identity foreclosure takes place on three levels: the subjective level, the interpersonal level, and the institutional level (van den Hoonaard 1997).

impression management Developed by Erving Goffman (1959), this concept explains how people work to control the impression of themselves that they communicate to others through demeanour, expression, dress, and so on.

incorporation The process through which members of a research setting define the researcher's role or social place in the setting.

in-depth interview   A directed conversation in which an interviewer encourages a participant or participants to describe their social world in their own terms.

indicators   Concrete measures that researchers develop to study abstract concepts.

institutional ethnography (IE)   A research method developed by Dorothy Smith (1987) that emphasizes the importance of social, particularly institutional, factors in influencing individuals' daily experiences. A major component of IE is a recognition that texts, or documents, can 'produce and sustain standardized practices' and, through them, 'relations of ruling'.

interactionists   See **symbolic interactionism**.

interview guide   A list of questions and/or topics that a qualitative interviewer plans to include in an interview. In the interview, the interviewer may rearrange the order of the questions, decide not to ask certain questions, and ask additional questions as probes or follow-up questions.

jargon   Technical or specialized terminology used by a specific group. Some writers use jargon in an attempt to sound more intellectual or to limit understanding to a particular group of readers, but you should avoid using jargon when you are writing an academic report.

jottings   Phrases, quotes, keywords, and other short notes that researchers write down in the field and use to develop full field notes.

latent content   Subtle or implicit meanings that require interpretation. Qualitative researchers focus on latent content when they do content analysis.

looking-glass self   The idea that we see ourselves as we believe others see us.

manifest content   Obvious, surface-level meanings that are immediately evident.

memos   Records of ideas or concepts that researchers get while conducting their studies.

mixed-methods research   A recent approach that combines qualitative methods with quantitative methods. Some argue that this approach can result in research findings that are more complete than could be arrived at by either method on its own.

moral entrepreneurs   Individuals or groups who campaign to establish certain social behaviours as deviant or normative.

narrative analysis   An approach to qualitative research that recognizes the centrality of stories in the way people understand and talk about their own lives. It often focusses on the structure of a story as much as its content.

observer as participant   A role in which a field researcher makes his or her presence known to participants but interacts with the group in only limited ways.

open coding   Coding in which the researcher identifies and labels the major themes in transcripts or field notes.

open-ended question   An interview question that allows the participant to supply his or her own answer to a question and to elaborate on that answer. Open-ended questions are characteristic of qualitative interviews.

operationalization   The process of putting a theory into operation by developing hypotheses that are based on the theory.

participant as observer   A role in which a field researcher makes his or her presence known to participants and participates in at least some of the group's activities.

participants   See **research participants**.

participatory action research (PAR)   A form of community-based research that often aims to identify the needs and priorities of the group and to translate findings into a form that can influence social policy or effect interventions to improve the situation of the group.

passive voice   A style of writing in which the subject of the sentence is the *recipient* of the action.

photo elicitation   The use of photographs in interviews to facilitate discussion. Sometimes researchers take the photographs themselves and sometimes they ask research participants to take the photos.

plagiarism   The act of taking someone else's ideas and passing them off as your own. Citing sources as you write up your paper will help you avoid plagiarism.

positivism   The belief that we can use the methods of science to uncover the 'laws' of human behaviour. It implies the ability to predict and, therefore, control human behaviour.

prescriptive   Approaches that dictate right or wrong behaviour. Qualitative research is analytical and descriptive rather than prescriptive.

presentism   The belief that we can use today's standards to evaluate older texts and social phenomena.

prewriting   The early writing that researchers do before they have begun to collect data. Prewriting helps researchers realize what they already know or think they know.

primary group   A group of people with whom an individual has close and long-lasting relationships. Members of a primary group usually include parents, siblings, and close friends.

probes   In in-depth interviews, probes are follow-up questions that ask the participant to elaborate, explain, or provide a story about what he or she has said.

problematize   Questioning commonly held assumptions and looking for underlying meanings.

pseudonyms   Names that researchers use in written reports to refer to individual research participants to ensure participants' anonymity.

random sampling   A method of selecting individuals to take part in a study in which every member of the target group has an equal chance of being chosen to participate.

realist perspective   A view that assumes that reality is out there waiting to be discovered rather than socially constructed.

REB   See **research ethics board**.

reflexivity   The process through which qualitative researchers examine and explain how they have influenced a research project through their social status, situation (gender, age, etc.), and the experiences they bring to the project.

research ethics board (REB)   A body that assesses the ethical implications of research studies and has the power to approve or reject a research proposal. All Canadian researchers who conduct research involving humans must submit their plans to a research ethics board for approval before carrying out their study.

research participants   People who voluntarily take part in a research project, either by allowing the researcher to interview them or by welcoming the researcher into their social setting.

rite of passage   A process of going from one social status to another that includes three stages: separation from a former status and role, transition between the former status and the new status, and incorporation into the new status.

sensitizing concepts   Sociological concepts based on expressions used by research participants that allow the researcher to understand the empirical world of the research participants.

serendipity   In general, a lucky coincidence. Researchers often experience an unexpected, spontaneous moment of inspiration that leads them to discover a social setting, research area, or theoretical insight while not actively looking for one.

snowball sampling   A method of selecting individuals to take part in a study in which the researcher identifies initial participants and then asks them to introduce the researcher to others who fit the sample criteria.

social disorganization   A concept developed by Thomas and Znaniecki (1918) to describe how rapid social change can lead to the loss of norms and values within an established culture.

sociological imagination   The capacity to connect the patterns of individuals with those of society. It distinguishes between private troubles and public issues and is used to understand the connection between biography and history. C.W. Mills (1959) called it the 'promise of sociology'.

sponsors   Individuals who provide access to certain settings and populations in informal ways. They are often central members of their group and lend legitimacy to the researcher by vouching for him or her.

standardized interviews   Thoroughly scripted interviews that aim to collect quantitative data by asking interviewees to choose from a list of predetermined responses. They are most useful when the researcher wants to collect simple, straightforward answers.

stories   Narratives that participants use to make a point or to explain their opinion or action.

symbolic interactionism   A theoretical perspective that assumes that research participants understand their everyday lives and seeks to discover how meanings are shared and created through social interaction.

theoretical saturation   A stage that occurs when the researcher is no longer learning anything new in collecting data. At this point, the researcher stops collecting data.

trust the process   Researchers use this phrase to remind themselves to have faith that there are important themes in their data and that they will have the insight and skill to find these themes.

unobtrusive measures   Research methods that do not involve interaction between the researcher and the participants; the researcher amasses data by collecting and analyzing materials that already exist.

validity   The extent to which the research means what the researcher thinks it means. This standard is most useful in evaluating quantitative research.

verstehen   German for 'sympathetic understanding'. Max Weber (1949) used the word to indicate that researchers should strive to see the world from their research participants' perspective.

virtual ethnography   In-depth study of an online group or culture in which researchers use online communities as research settings.

visual sociology   A research approach in which the researcher uses images as data.

vocabulary of motives   The ways in which people describe and explain their reasons for doing things. These 'vocabularies' are always tied to a particular social context; as such, they are subject to change and interpretation as one's social circumstances change.

References

Adler, P.A. 1985. *Wheeling and Dealing: An Ethnography of an Upper-Level Drug Dealing and Smuggling Community*. New York: Columbia University Press.

—— and P. Adler. 1998. *Peer Power: Preadolescent Culture and Identity*. New Brunswick, NJ: Rutgers University Press.

—— and ——. 1987. *Membership Roles in the Field*. Thousand Oaks, CA: Sage.

Albas, D., and C. Albas. 2009. 'Behind the Conceptual Scene of Student Life and Exams', in A. J. Puddlephatt, W. Shaffir, and S.W. Kleinknecht, eds, *Ethnographies Revisited: Constructing Theory in the Field*, 105–20. New York: Routledge.

—— and ——. 1994. 'Studying Students Studying: Perspective, Identities, and Activities', in M.L. Dietz, R. Prus, and W. Shaffir, eds, *Doing Everyday Life: Ethnography as Human Lived Experience*, 273–89. Mississauga, ON: Copp Clark Longman. Reprinted with permission from Kendall Hunt Publishing Company.

—— and ——. 1988. 'Aces and Bombers: The Post-Exam Impression Management Strategies of Students', *Symbolic Interaction* 11, 2: 289–302.

Allen, R. 1971. *The Social Passion*. Toronto: University of Toronto Press.

Altheide, D.L. 1976. *Creating Reality: How TV News Distorts Events*. Beverley Hills, CA: Sage.

—— and R.S. Michalowski. 1999. 'Fear in the News: A Discourse of Control', *The Sociological Quarterly* 40, 3: 475–503.

Ames, H.B. [1897] 1972. *The City Below the Hill*. Toronto: University of Toronto Press.

Anderson, E. 1976. *A Place on the Corner*. Chicago: University of Chicago Press.

Anderson, N. 1923. *The Hobo*. Chicago: University of Chicago Press.

Atkinson, M. 2003. *Tattooed: The Sociogenesis of a Body Art*. Toronto: University of Toronto Press, at http://site.ebrary.com/lib/unblib/Doc?id=01218915&pp=9-10.

Atkinson, P., and A. Coffey. 1997. 'Analyzing Documentary Realities', in D. Silverman, ed., *Qualitative Research: Theory, Method, and Practice*, 45–62. Thousand Oaks, CA: Sage.

Ayres, L. 2008. 'Semi-Structured Interview', in L. Given, ed., *The Sage Encyclopedia of Qualitative Research Methods*, 810–11. Los Angeles: Sage.

Bayley, C.M. 1939. 'The Social Structure of the Italian and Ukrainian Immigrant Communities: Montreal, 1935–1937', MA Thesis, McGill University.

Baym, N.K. 2000. *Tune In, Log On: Soaps, Fandom, and Online Community*. Thousand Oaks, CA: Sage.

Becker, G. 1997. *Disrupted Lives: How People Create Meaning in a Chaotic World*. Berkeley: University of California Press.

Becker, H.S. 1998. *Tricks of the Trade: How to Think about Your Research while You're Doing It*. Chicago: University of Chicago Press.

——. 1996. 'The Epistemology of Qualitative Research', in R. Jessor, A. Colby, and R. A. Schweder, eds, *Ethnography and Human Development: Context and Meaning in Social Inquiry*, 53–71. Chicago: University of Chicago Press.

——. 1993. 'How I Learned What a Crock Was', *Journal of Contemporary Ethnography* 22, 1: 28–35.

——. 1986a. *Writing for Social Scientists*. Chicago: University of Chicago Press.

——. 1986b. *Doing Things Together: Selected Papers*. Evanston, IL: Northwestern University Press.

——. 1967. 'Whose Side Are We On?', *Social Problems* 14, 3: 239–47.

——. 1963. *Outsiders: Studies in the Sociology of Deviance*. Glencoe, IL: Free Press.

——, B. Geer, and E.C. Hughes. 1968. *Making the Grade*. New York: John Wiley.

——, ——, ——, and A.L. Strauss. [1961] 2009. *Boys in White: Student Culture in Medical School*. Chicago: University of Chicago Press.

Bella, L. 1992. *The Christmas Imperative: Leisure, Family and Women's Work*. Halifax: Fernwood Publishing.

Benney, M., and E.C. Hughes. 1956. 'Of Sociology and the Interview: Editorial Preface', *The American Journal of Sociology* LXII, 2: 137–42.

Berg, B.L. 2009. *Qualitative Research Methods for the Social Sciences*, 7th edn. Boston: Allyn and Bacon.

Booth, C. 1902-3. *Life and Labour of the People in London*. 17 vols. London: Macmillan.

Bouma, G.D., R. Ling, and L. Wilkinson. 2009. *The Research Process: Canadian Edition*. Don Mills, ON: Oxford University Press.

Brody, E. 2010. 'On Being Very, Very Old: An Insider's Perspective', *The Gerontologist* 50, 1: 2–10.

Brown, W.H. 1927. 'The Slovakian Community in Montreal', MA Thesis, McGill University.

Burnet, J. 1951. *Next-Year Country*. Toronto: University of Toronto Press.

Bryant, C.D. 1999. 'Gratuitous Sex in Field Research: "Carnal Lagniappe" or "Inappropriate Behavior"', *Deviant Behavior: An Interdisciplinary Journal* 20: 325–9.

Caissie, L. 2006. *The Raging Grannies: Understanding the Role of Activism in the Lives of Older Women*. PhD Dissertation, University of Waterloo, Waterloo, ON. Retrieved from Dissertations & Theses: Full Text (Publication No. AAT NR23509).

——— and D.K. van den Hoonaard. 2009. Invented Identity and New Social Meanings of Aging: The Zoomers Are Coming! The Zoomers Are Coming! Paper presented to *Symbolic Interaction and Ethnographic Research*, University of Waterloo, ON, 30 April–3 May.

Calasanti, T., and N. King. 2007. '"Beware of the Estrogen Assault": Ideals of Old Manhood in Anti-Aging Advertisements', *Journal of Aging Studies* 21: 357–68.

Camara, F., and R. Helmes-Hayes. 2003. Tracing the Historical Development of Symbolic Interactionism in Canada. Paper presented to the *Twentieth Qualitative Analysis Conference*, Carleton University, Ottawa.

Cameron, M.O. 1973. *The Booster and the Snitch: Department Store Shoplifting*. Toronto: Collier-Macmillan.

Cannell, C.F., G. Fisher, and K.H. Marquis. 1968. *The Influence of Interviewer and Respondent Psychological and Behavioural Variables on the Reporting in Household Interviews*. Washington, DC: Government Printing Office.

Chapoulie, J.-M. 1996. 'Everett Hughes and the Chicago Tradition', *Sociological Theory* 14: 3–29.

———. 1987. 'Everett C. Hughes and the Development of Fieldwork in Sociology', *Urban Life* 15: 259–98.

Charmaz, K. 2009. 'Recollecting Good and Bad Days', in A.J. Puddlephatt, W. Shaffir, and S.W. Kleinknecht, eds, *Ethnographies Revisited: Constructing Theory in the Field*, 48–62. New York: Routledge.

———. 2006. *Constructing Grounded Theory: A Practical Guide through Qualitative Analysis*. Thousand Oaks, CA: Sage.

———. 2001. 'Qualitative Interviewing and Grounded Theory Analysis', in J.F. Gubrium and J.A. Holstein, eds, *Handbook of Interview Research: Context and Method*, 671–94. Thousand Oaks, CA: Sage.

———. 1991a. *Good Days, Bad Days: The Self in Chronic Illness and Time*. New Brunswick, NJ: Rutgers University Press.

———. 1991b. 'Translating Graduate Qualitative Methods into Undergraduate Teaching: Intensive Interviewing as a Case Example', *Teaching Sociology* 19: 384–95.

Christ, T.W. 2007. 'A Recursive Approach to Mixed Methods Research in a Longitudinal Study of Postsecondary Education Disability Support Services', *Journal of Mixed Methods Research* 1, 3: 226–41.

CIHR, NSERC, and SSHRC (Canadian Institutes of Health Research, Natural Sciences and Engineering Research Council of Canada, and Social Sciences and Humanities Research Council of Canada). 2010. *Tri-Council Policy Statement: Ethical Conduct for Research Involving Humans*. Ottawa: CIHR, NSERC, and SSHRC.

———, ———, and ———. 1998. *Tri-Council Policy Statement: Ethical Conduct for Research Involving Humans*. Ottawa: CIHR, NSERC, and SSHRC.

Clarke, D. 2010. *A Sociological Study of Scholarly Writing and Publishing: How Academics Produce and Share Their Research*. Lewiston, NY: Edwin Mellen Press.

Clarke, J.N. 2006. 'The Case of the Missing Person: Alzheimer's Disease in Mass Print Magazines, 1991–2001', *Health Communication* 19, 3: 269–76.

——— and J. Binns. 2006. 'The Portrayal of Heart Disease in Mass Print Magazines, 1991–2001', *Health Communication* 19, 1: 39–48.

Clark-Ibáñez, M. 2004. 'Framing the Social World with Photo-Elicitation Interviews', *American Behavioral Scientist* 47, 12: 1507–27.

Conn, P.J. 1971. 'Roderick Hudson: The Role of the Observer', *Nineteenth-Century Fiction* 26, 1: 65–82.

Cooley, C.H. 1902. *Human Nature and the Social Order*. New York: Scribner's and Sons.

Cooper, S.E. 2004. *The Red Hat Society: Fun and Friendship after Fifty*. New York: Warner Books.

Creme, P., and M.R. Lea. 2008. *Writing at University: A Guide for Students*, 3rd edn. Berkshire, UK: Open University Press.

Cressey, P.G. 1932. *The Taxi-Dance Hall*. Chicago: University of Chicago Press.

Creswell, J.W. and V.L. Plano Clark. 2007. *Designing and Conducting Mixed Methods Research*. Thousand Oaks, CA: Sage.

Curry, T. 1986. 'A Brief History of the IVSA', *Visual Sociology Review* 1, 1: 3–5.

Darnell, R. 1997. 'Changing Patterns of Ethnography in Canadian Anthropology:

A Comparison of Themes', *The Canadian Review of Sociology and Anthropology* 34, 3: 269–96.

Davidman, L. 1999. 'The Personal, the Sociological, and the Intersection of the Two', in B. Glassner and R. Hertz, eds, *Qualitative Sociology as Everyday Life*, 79–88. Thousand Oaks, CA: Sage.

———. 1991. *Tradition in a Rootless World: Women Turn to Orthodox Judaism*. Berkeley: University of California Press.

Davidson, K. 1999. *Gender, Age and Widowhood: How Older Widows and Widowers Differently Realign Their Lives*. PhD Thesis, Department of Sociology, University of Surrey, Guildford, Surrey, UK.

Davidson, M.H. 1933. 'The Social Adjustment of British Immigrant Families in Verdun and Point St Charles', MA Thesis, McGill University.

Dawson, C.A. 1936. *Group Settlement*. Toronto: Macmillan.

——— (with R.W. Murchie). 1934. *The Settlement of the Peace River Country*. Toronto: Macmillan.

——— and W.E. Gettys. [1929, 1935] 1948. *An Introduction to Sociology*. New York: Ronald.

——— and E. Younge. 1940. *Pioneering on the Prairie Provinces*. Toronto: Macmillan.

Denzin, N.K. 2009. 'Researching Alcoholics and Alcoholism in American Society', in A.J. Puddlephatt, W. Shaffir, and S.W. Kleinknecht, eds, *Ethnographies Revisited: Constructing Theory in the Field*, 152–68. New York: Routledge.

———. 1987. *The Alcoholic Self*. Newbury Park, CA: Sage.

DeVault, M. 1999. *Liberating Method: Feminism and Social Research*. Philadelphia: Temple University Press.

Diamond, T. 1992. *Making Gray Gold: Narratives of Nursing Home Care*. Chicago: University of Chicago Press.

Dickson, G. 2000. 'Aboriginal Grandmothers' Experience with Health Promotion and Participatory Action Research', *Qualitative Health Research* 10, 2: 188–213.

Dietz, M.L. 1994. 'On Your Toes: Dancing Your Way into the Ballet World', in M.L. Dietz, R. Prus, and W. Shaffir, eds, *Doing Everyday Life: Ethnography as Human Lived Experience*, 66–84. Mississauga, ON: Copp Clark Longman.

Dohaney, M.T. 1989. *When Things Get Back to Normal*. Porters Lake, NS: Pottersfield Press.

Doucet, A. 2007. *Do Men Mother?: Fathering, Care, and Domestic Responsibility*. Toronto: University of Toronto Press.

Dowling, M. 2008. 'Reflexivity', in L. Given, ed., *The Sage Encyclopedia of Qualitative Research Methods*, 747–8. Los Angeles: Sage.

Duneier, M. 1999. *Sidewalk*. New York: Farrar, Strauss, and Giroux.

———. 1992. *Slim's Table Race, Respectability, and Masculinity*. Chicago: University of Chicago Press.

Dunn, J.L. 2009. 'The Path Taken: Opportunity, Flexibility, and Reflexivity in the Field', in A.J. Puddlephatt, W. Shaffir, and S.W. Kleinknecht, eds, *Ethnographies Revisited: Constructing Theory in the Field*, 277–88. New York: Routledge.

Durkheim, E. [1897] 1951. *Suicide*. Glencoe, IL: Free Press.

Ebaugh, H.R. 1988. *Becoming an Ex: The Process of Role Exit*. Chicago: University of Chicago Press.

Ellis, C.S. 2008. 'Autoethnography', in L. Given, ed., *The Sage Encyclopedia of Qualitative Research Methods*, 48–51. Los Angeles: Sage.

———. 1993. '"There Are Survivors": Telling a Story of Sudden Death', *The Sociological Quarterly* 34, 4: 711–30, at http://www.jstor.org/stable/4121376.

Emerson, R.M., R.I. Fretz, and L.L. Shaw. 1995. *Writing Ethnographic Fieldnotes*. Chicago: University of Chicago Press.

Esterberg, K. 2002. *Qualitative Methods in Social Research*. Boston: McGraw Hill.

Falardeau, J.-C., ed. 1953. *Essais sur le Québec contemporain*. Québec: Les Presses Universitaires Laval.

Fals-Borda, O. 1987. 'The Application of Participatory Action Research in Latin America'. *International Sociology* 2, 4: 329–47.

Faris, R.E. 1967. *Chicago Sociology: 1920–1932*. Chicago: University of Chicago Press.

Ferrell, J. 2006. *Empire of Scrounge: Inside the Urban Underground of Dumpster Diving, Trash Picking, and Street Scavenging*. New York: New York University Press.

Ferris, K.O. 2004. 'Seeing and Being Seen: The Moral Order of Celebrity Sightings', *Journal of Contemporary Ethnography* 33, 3: 236–64.

Festinger, L., H.W. Riecken, and S. Schachter. 1956. *When Prophecy Fails*. New York: Harper and Row.

Fine, G.A. 1996. *Kitchens: The Culture of Restaurant Work*. Berkeley: University of California Press.

Firestone, M.M. 1967. *Brothers and Rivals: Patrilocality in Savage Cove*. St John's, NL: Institute of Social and Economic Research, Memorial University of Newfoundland.

Firmin, M.W. 2008. 'Unstructured Interview', in L. Given, ed., *The Sage Encyclopedia of Qualitative Research Methods*, 907. Los Angeles: Sage.

Fontana, A., and A.H. Prokos. 2007. *The Interview: From Formal to Postmodern*. Walnut Creek, CA: Left Coast Press.

Furman, F.K. 1997. *Facing the Mirror: Older Women and Beauty Shop Culture*. New York: Routledge.

Gans, H. 1967. *The Levittowners: Ways of Life and Politics in a New Suburban Community*. New York: Random House.

Garfinkel, H. 1967. *Studies in Ethno-methodology*. Englewood Cliffs, NJ: Prentice-Hall.

Giddings, L.S. 2006. 'Mixed-Methods Research: Positivism in Drag?', *Journal of Nursing Research* 11, 3: 195–203.

Given, L., ed. 2008. *The Sage Encyclopedia of Qualitative Research Methods*. Los Angeles: Sage.

Glaser, B. 1978. *Theoretical Sensitivity: Advances in the Methodology of Grounded Theory*. Mill Valley, CA: Sociology Press.

——— and A. Strauss. 1965. *Awareness of Dying*. Chicago: Aldine.

——— and A. Strauss. 1967. *The Discovery of Grounded Theory*. Chicago: Aldine.

Glassner, B., and R. Hertz, eds. 1999. *Qualitative Sociology as Everyday Life*. Thousand Oaks, CA: Sage.

Goffman, E. [1974] 2004. 'On Fieldwork', Transcribed and Ed. by L.H. Lofland in D. Weinberg, ed., *Qualitative Research Methods*, 147–53. Malden, MA: Blackwell.

———. 1963. *Behavior in Public Places*. Glencoe, IL: Free Press.

———. 1961. *Asylums*. Garden City, NY: Anchor Books.

———. 1959. *The Presentation of Self in Everyday Life*. New York: Anchor Books.

Gold, R.L. 1958. 'Roles in Sociological Field Observations', *Social Forces* 36: 217–33.

Gubrium, J.F. 2009. 'How Murray Manor Became an Ethnography', in A.J. Puddlephatt, W. Shaffir, and S.W. Kleinknecht, eds, *Ethnographies Revisited: Constructing Theory in the Field*, 121–34. New York: Routledge.

———. 1986. *Oldtimers and Alzheimer's: The Descriptive Organization of Senility*. Greenwich, CT: JAI Press.

——— and J.A. Holstein. 2009. *Analyzing Narrative Reality*. Los Angeles: Sage.

——— and ———. 2001. 'From Individual Interview to Interview Society', in J.F. Gubrium and J.A. Holstein, eds, *Handbook of Interview Research: Context and Method*, 3–32. Thousand Oaks, CA: Sage.

Haas, J., and W. Shaffir. [1987] 2009. *Becoming Doctors: The Adoption of a Cloak of Competence*. Greenwich, CT: JAI Press.

——— and ———. 1994. 'The Development of a Professional Self in Medical Students', in M.L. Deitz, R. Prus, and W. Shaffir, eds, *Doing Everyday Life: Ethnography as Human Lived Experience*, 188–202. Mississauga, ON: Copp Clark Longman.

Hammersley, M., and P. Atkinson. 1983. *Ethnography: Principles in Practice*. London: Tavistock Publications.

Harman, Lesley D. 1989. *When a Hostel Becomes a Home: Experiences of Women*. Toronto: Garamond Press.

Hay, G. 2010. 'Biography of John Howard'. Kingston, ON: The John Howard Society, at http://www.johnhoward.ca/bio.htm.

Helmes-Hayes, R. 2010. 'Studying "Going Concerns": Everett C. Hughes on Method', *Sociologica* 2: 1–26.

———. 1994. 'C.A. Dawson and W.E. Gettys' *An Introduction to Sociology* (1929): Canadian Sociology's First Textbook', *Canadian Journal of Sociology* 19, 4: 461–97.

——— and M. Santoro. 2010. 'Introduction', in 'The Marginal Master: Return to Everett C. Hughes', *Sociologica* 2.

Heilman, S. 2009. 'The Ethnography behind Defenders of the Faith', in A.J. Puddlephatt, W. Shaffir, and S.W. Kleinknecht, eds, *Ethnographies Revisited: Constructing Theory in the Field*, 197–211. New York: Routledge.

Hine, C.M. 2008. 'Virtual Ethnography', in L. Given, ed., *The Sage Encyclopedia of Qualitative Research Method*, 921–4. Los Angeles: Sage.

Hochschild, A.R. 1997. *The Time Bind: When Work Becomes Home and Home Becomes Work*. New York: Henry Holt.

———. 1989. *The Second Shift: Working Parents and the Revolution at Home*. New York: Avon.

———. 1979. 'Emotion Work, Feeling Rules, and Social Structure', *American Journal of Sociology* 85, 3: 551–75.

Holder, T.J.M. 2010. 'Gender Ads: The Goffman Take', at http://www.intcul .tohoku.ac.jp/˜holden/Presentations/ IAMCR-genderPres/Goffman.html.

Holstein, J.A., and J.F. Gubrium. 1995. *The Active Interview*. Thousand Oaks, CA: Sage.

Holt, N.L. 2003. 'Representation, Legitimation, and Autoethnography: An Autoethno-graphic Writing Story', *International Journal of Qualitative Methods* 2, 1: 18–28.

Hughes, E.C. [1960] 2002. 'The Place of Field Work in Social Science', in D. Weinberg, ed., *Qualitative Research Methods*, 139–47. Malden, MA: Blackwell.

———. [1971] 1984. *The Sociological Eye*. New Brunswick, NJ: Transaction.

———. 1943. *French Canada in Transition*. Chicago: University of Chicago Press.

———, B. Junker, R. Gold, and D. Kittel, eds. 1952. *Cases in Fieldwork*. Chicago: University of Chicago.

Humphreys, L. 1970. *Tearoom Trade: Impersonal Sex in Public Places*. Chicago: Aldine Publishing Co.

Institutional Review Blog. 2009. 'After Human Terrain, Will AAA Debate IRBs?', at http://www.institutionalreviewblog.com/2009/12/after-human-terrain-will-aaa-debate.html.

ISER (Institute for Social and Economic Research). 2010. 'About Us', at http://www.mun.ca/iser/about/.

IVSA (International Visual Sociology Association). 2010. 'About IVSA', at http://www.visualsociology.org/about.html.

Jean, B. 2006. 'The Study of Rural Communities in Quebec: From the "Folk Society" Monographic Approach to the Recent Revival of Community as Place-Based Rural Development', *Journal of Rural and Community Development* 1: 56–68.

Jordan, S. 2008. 'Participatory Action Research', in L. Given, ed., *The Sage Encyclopedia of Qualitative Research Methods*, 601–3. Los Angeles: Sage.

Junker, B. 1960. *Fieldwork*. Chicago: University of Chicago Press.

Kamali, A. 1991. 'Writing a Sociological Student Term Paper: Steps and Scheduling', *Teaching Sociology* 19, 4: 506–9.

Kaminer, W. 1992. *I'm Dysfunctional, You're Dysfunctional: The Recovery Movement and Other Self-Help Fashions*. Reading, MA: Addison-Wesley.

Kaufman, S. 1986. *The Ageless Self: Sources of Meaning in Late Life*. Madison: University of Wisconsin Press.

Keegan, S. 2008. 'Photographs in Qualitative Research', in L. Given, ed., *The Sage Encyclopedia of Qualitative Research Methods*, 619–22. Los Angeles: Sage.

Kenyon, G.M., and W.L. Randall. 1999. 'Introduction: Narrative Gerontology', *Journal of Aging Studies* 13, 1: 1–5.

——— and ———. 1997. *Restorying Our Lives: Personal Growth through Autobiographical Reflection*. Westport, CN: Praeger.

King, S. 1998. *Bag of Bones*. New York: Scribner.

Kirby, S.L., L. Greaves, and C. Reid. 2006. *Experience Research Social Change: Methods Beyond the Mainstream*, 2nd edn. Peterborough, ON: Broadview Press.

Kitchin, H. 2002. 'The Tri-Council on Cyberspace: Insights, Oversights, and Extrapolations', in Will C. van den Hoonaard, ed., *Walking the Tightrope: Ethical Issues for Qualitative Researchers*. Toronto: University of Toronto Press.

Klinker, J.F., and R.H. Todd. 2007. 'Two Autoethnographies: A Search for Understanding of Gender and Age', *The Qualitative Report* 12, 2: 166–8.

Kontos, P.C., and G. Naglie. 2006. 'Expressions of Personhood in Alzheimer's: Moving from Ethnographic Text to Performing Ethnography'. *Qualitative Research* 6, 3: 301–17.

Kosher4Passover. 2010. 'The Four Questions', at http://kosher4passover.com/4questions.htm.

Kuhn, T. [1962] 1970. *The Structure of Scientific Revolutions*, 2nd edn. Chicago: University of Chicago Press.

Lafrance, M.N. 2009. *Women and Depression: Recovery and Resistance*. London: Routledge.

Lateiner, D. 2004. 'Introduction', in G.C. Macaulay, trans., *Herodotus, the Histories*. New York: Barnes and Noble Classics.

Least Heat-Moon, William. 1991. *Prairy Erth (A Deep Map): An Epic History of the Tallgrass Prairie Country*. Boston: Houghton Mifflin.

Lee, B., B. Kim, and S. Han. 2006. 'The Portrayal of Older People in Television Advertisements: A Cross-Cultural Content Analysis of the United States and South Korea', *International Journal of Aging and Human Development* 63, 4: 279–97.

Leyton, E. 1978. 'The Bureaucratization of Anguish: The Workmen's Compensation Board in Industrial Disaster', in D. Handelman and E. Leyton, eds, *Bureaucracy and World View: Studies in the Logic of Official Interpretation*, 71–134. St John's, NL: Institute of Social and Economic Research, Memorial University of Newfoundland.

Liebow, E. 1993. *Tell Them Who I Am: The Lives of Homeless Women*. New York: Free Press.

———. 1967. *Talley's Corner*. Boston: Little, Brown.

Lofland, J. 1977. *Doomsday Cult: A Study of Conversion, Proselytizing, and Maintenance of Faith*. Englewood Cliffs, NJ: Prentice-Hall.

—— and L.H. Lofland. 1995. *Analyzing Social Settings: A Guide to Qualitative Observation and Analysis*. Belmont, CA: Wadsworth Publishing Company.

Loseke, D.R. 2009. 'Solving the Mysteries of Shelter Work for Battered Women', in A.J. Puddlephatt, W. Shaffir, and S.W. Kleinknecht, eds, *Ethnographies Revisited: Constructing Theory in the Field*, 263–76. New York: Routledge.

Low, J. 2004. *Using Alternative Therapies: A Qualitative Analysis*. Toronto: Canadian Scholars' Press.

Luxton, M. 1980. *More than a Labour of Love: Three Generations of Women's Work in the Home*. Toronto: The Women's Press.

McCloskey, R. 2008. *An Institutional Ethnographic Explorations of the Transitional Experience of Nursing Home Residents to and from a Hospital Emergency Room*. PhD Dissertation, Interdisciplinary Studies, University of New Brunswick, Fredericton, NB.

McIntyre, A. 2008. *Participatory Action Research*. Los Angeles: Sage.

Maines, D.R. 2001. *The Faultlines of Consciousness: A View of Interactionism in Sociology*. New York: Aldine de Gruyter.

———. 1993. 'Narrative's Moment and Sociology's Phenomena: Toward a Narrative Sociology', *The Sociological Quarterly* 34, 1: 17–38.

Malacrida, C. 1998. *Mourning the Dreams: How Parents Create Meaning from Miscarriage, Stillbirth and Early Infant Death*. Edmonton: Qual Institute Press.

Mandell, D. 2002. *Deadbeat Dads: Subjectivity and Social Construction*. Toronto: University of Toronto Press, at http://site.ebrary.com/lib/unblib/Doc?id=10219353&ppg=14.

Manning, P.K., and B. Cullum-Swan. 1994. 'Narrative, Content, and Semiotic Analysis', in N.K. Denzin and Y.S. Lincoln, eds, *Handbook of Qualitative Research*, 463–77. Thousand Oaks, CA: Sage.

March, K. 1995. *The Stranger Who Bore Me: Adoptee–Birth Mother Relationships*. Toronto: University of Toronto Press.

Marshall, C., and G.B. Rossman. 2006. *Designing Qualitative Research*, 4th edn. Thousand Oaks, CA: Sage.

Martin-Matthews, A. 1991. *Widowhood in Later Life*. Toronto: Butterworths.

Mason, J. 2002. *Qualitative Researching*, 2nd edn. Thousand Oaks, CA: Sage.

Maxwell, J,A. 2005. *Qualitative Research Design: An Interactive Approach*, 2nd edn. Thousand Oaks, CA: Sage.

Mayan, M. 2009. *Essentials of Qualitative Inquiry*. Walnut Creek, CA: Left Coast Press.

Mills, C.W. [1959] 1976. *The Sociological Imagination*. New York: Oxford University Press.

Milne, E., and R. Helmes-Hayes. 2010. 'The Rise [and Fall?] of McMaster University as the Centre of Symbolic Interactionism in Canada, 1967–2010', Paper presented to the *Annual Meeting of the Society for the Study of Symbolic Interactionism*, Atlanta, GA.

Mishler, E.G. 1986. *Research Interviewing, Context and Narrative*. Cambridge, MA: Harvard University Press.

Mitchell, R.G., and K. Charmaz. 1996. 'Telling Tales, Writing Stories: Postmodernist Visions and Realist Images in Ethnographic Writing', *Journal of Contemporary Ethnography* 25, 1: 144–66.

Oakley, A. 1981. 'Interviewing Women: A Contradiction in Terms', in H. Roberts, ed., *Doing Feminist Research*, 30–61. London: Routledge and Kegan Paul.

Oliffe, J.L., and J.L. Bottorff. 2009. 'Further than the Eye Can See?: Photo Elicitation and Research with Men', *Qualitative Health Research* 17, 6: 850–8.

Parmelee, J.H., S.C. Perkins, and J.J. Sayre. 2007. '"What about People Our Age?"': Applying Qualitative and Quantitative Methods to Uncover How Political Ads Alienate College Students', *Journal of Mixed Methods Research* 1, 2: 183–99.

Pawluch, D. 2009. 'Conceptualizing a Profession in Process: The New Pediatrics Revisited', in A. J. Puddlephatt, W. Shaffir, and S.W. Kleinknecht, eds, *Ethnographies Revisited: Constructing Theory in the Field*, 318–30. New York: Routledge.

———. 1996. *The New Pediatrics: A Profession in Transition*. New York: Aldine de Gruyter.

Philbrook, T. 1966. *Fisherman, Logger, Merchant, Miner: Social Change and Industrialism in Three Newfoundland Communities*. St John's, NL: Institute of Social and Economic Research, Memorial University of Newfoundland.

Prus, R. 2009. 'Hookers, Rounders, and Desk Clerks: Encountering the Reality of the Hotel Community', in A.J. Puddlephatt, W. Shaffir, and S.W. Kleinknecht, eds, *Ethnographies Revisited: Constructing Theory in the Field*, 238–50. New York: Routledge.

———. 2005. 'Studying Human Knowing and Acting: The Interactional Quest for Authenticity', in D. Pawluch, W. Shaffir, and C. Miall, eds, *Doing Ethnography: Studying Everyday Life*, 7–23. Toronto: Canadian Scholars' Press.

———. 1993. The Ethnographic Research Tradition: Studying Human Lived Experience. Paper presented to *Symbolic Interaction and Ethnographic Research*, Waterloo, ON, 19–22 May.

———. 1987. 'Generic Social Processes: Maximizing Conceptual Development in Ethnographic Research', *Journal of Contemporary Ethnography* 16, 3: 250–93, at http://jce.sagepub.com/cgi/content/refs/15/3/250.

——— and S. Irini. [1980] 1988. *Hookers, Rounders, and Desk Clerks: The Social Organization of the Hotel Community*. Salem, WI: Sheffield Publishing Company.

Puddlephatt, A.J. 2003. 'Chess Playing as Strategic Activity', *Symbolic Interaction* 26, 2: 263–84.

———, W. Shaffir, and S.W. Kleinknecht, eds. 2009. *Ethnographies Revisited: Constructing Theory in the Field*. New York: Routledge.

Rabinow, P., ed. 1984. *The Foucault Reader*. New York: Pantheon Books.

Rains, P. 1971. *Becoming an Unwed Mother*. Chicago: Aldine.

Reinharz, S. 1999. 'Enough Already!: The Pervasiveness of Warnings in Everyday Life', in B. Glassner and R. Hertz, eds, *Qualitative Sociology as Everyday Life*, 31–40. Thousand Oaks, CA: Sage.

———. 1992. *Feminist Methods in Social Research*. New York: Oxford University Press.

Richardson, L. 2007. *Last Writes: A Daybook for a Dying Friend*. Walnut Creek, CA: Left Coast Press.

———. 1994. 'Writing: A Method of Inquiry', in N.K. Denzin and Y.S. Lincoln, eds, *Handbook of Qualitative Research*, 516–29. Thousand Oaks, CA: Sage.

———. 1990. *Writing Strategies: Reaching Diverse Audiences*. Newbury Park, CA: Sage.

Riesman, D. 1983. 'The Legacy of Everett Hughes', *Contemporary Sociology* 12, 5: 477–81.

——— and H.S. Becker. 1984. 'Introduction to the Transaction Edition', in E.C. Hughes, *The Sociological Eye*, v–xiv. New Brunswick, NJ: Transaction.

Riessman, C.K. 2001. 'Analysis of Personal Narratives', in J.F. Gubrium and J.A. Holstein, eds, *Handbook of Interview Research: Context and Method*, 695–710. Thousand Oaks, CA: Sage.

Rose, D. 2004. 'Analysis of Moving Images', in S.N. Hess-Biber and P. Leavy, eds, *Approaches to Qualitative Research: A Reader in Theory and Practice*, 350–66. New York: Oxford University Press.

———. 1998. 'Television, Madness and Community Care', *Journal of Community & Applied Social Psychology* 8: 213–28.

Ross, A.D. 1954. 'Philanthropic Activity and the Business Career', *Social Forces* 32: 274–80.

———. 1953. 'The Social Control of Philanthropy', *American Journal of Sociology* 58, 5: 451–60.

———. 1952. 'Organized Philanthropy in an Urban Community', *Canadian Journal of Economics and Political Science* 18, 4: 474–86.

Rossman, G.B., and S.F. Rallis. 1998. *Learning in the Field: An Introduction to Qualitative Research*. Thousand Oaks, CA: Sage.

Rothe, J.P. 1990. *The Safety of Elderly Drivers: Yesterday's Young in Today's Traffic*. New Brunswick, NJ: Transaction.

Rubin, H.J., and I.S. Rubin. 1995. *Qualitative Interviewing: The Art of Hearing Data*. Thousand Oaks, CA: Sage.

Saldaña, J. 2008. 'Ethnodrama', in L. Given, ed., *The Sage Encyclopedia of Qualitative Research Methods*, 283–5. Los Angeles: Sage.

Sanders, C. 2009. 'Colorful Writing: Conducting and Living with a Tattoo Ethnography', in A.J. Puddlephatt, W. Shaffir, and S.W. Kleinknecht, eds, *Ethnographies Revisited: Constructing Theory in the Field*, 63–76. New York: Routledge.

———. 1999. 'Earn as You Learn: Connections between Doing Qualitative Work and Everyday Life', in B. Glassner and R. Hertz, eds, *Qualitative Sociology as Everyday Life*, 41–8. Thousand Oaks, CA: Sage.

———. 1994. 'Tattoo You: Tattoos as Self-Extensions and Identity Markers', in M.L. Dietz, R. Prus, and W. Shaffir, eds, *Doing Everyday Life: Ethnography as Human Lived Experience*, 203–12. Mississauga, ON: Copp Clark Longman.

———. 1991. 'The Armadillos in Dracula's Foyer: Conventions and Innovation in Horror Cinema', in P. Loukides and L. Fuller, eds, *Beyond the Stars: Studies in American Popular Film Vol. 2*, 143–59. Bowling Green, OH: Popular Press.

———. 1989. *Customizing the Body: The Art and Culture of Tattooing*. Philadelphia: Temple University Press.

Schatzman, L., and A. Strauss. 1972. *Field Research Strategies for a Natural Sociology.* Englewood Cliffs: NJ: Prentice Hall.

Schwalbe, M.L., and M. Wolkomir. 2001. 'Interviewing Men', in J.F. Gubrium and J.A. Holstein, eds, *Handbook of Interview Research,* 203–19. Thousand Oaks, CA: Sage Publications, Inc.

Schwartz, H., and J. Jacobs. 1979. *Qualitative Sociology: A Method to the Madness.* New York: The Free Press.

Scott, M., and S. Lyman. 1981. 'Accounts', in G. Stone and H. Faberman, eds, *Social Psychology through Interaction,* 343–61. New York: Wiley.

Shaffir, W. 2009. 'On Piecing the Puzzle: Researching Hassidic Jews', in A.J. Puddlephatt, W. Shaffir, and S.W. Kleinknecht, eds, *Ethnographies Revisited: Constructing Theory in the Field,* 212–24. New York: Routledge.

———, M.L. Dietz, and R. Stebbins. 1994. 'Field Research as Social Experience: Learning to Do Ethnography', in M.L. Dietz, R. Prus, and W. Shaffir, eds, *Doing Everyday Life: Ethnography as Human Lived Experience,* 30–54. Mississauga, ON: Copp Clark Longman.

———, R.A. Stebbins, and A. Turowetz. 1980. *Fieldwork Experience: Qualitative Approaches to Social Research.* New York: St Martin's Press.

Shaw, C. 1930. *The Jack-Roller: A Delinquent Boy's Own Story.* Chicago: University of Chicago Press.

Silk Road Foundation. 2000. 'Marco Polo and His Travels', at http://www.silk-road.com/artl/marcopolo.shtml.

Silverman, D. 1997. 'Towards an Aesthetics of Research', in D. Silverman, ed., *Qualitative Research: Theory, Method, and Practice,* 239–53. London: Sage.

———. 1993. *Interpreting Qualitative Data: Methods for Analyzing Talk, Text, and Interaction.* London: Sage.

Smith, D. 1987. *The Everyday World as Problematic: A Feminist Sociology.* Toronto: University of Toronto Press.

Smith, V. 2002. 'Ethnographies of Work and the Work of Ethnographers', in P. Atkinson, A. Coffey, S. Delamont, J. Lofland, and L. Lofland, eds, *Handbook of Ethnography,* 220–33. London: Sage.

Statistics Canada. 2006. 'Census Form 2006', at http://www.statcan.gc.ca/imdb-bmdi/instrument/3901_Q2_V3-eng.pdf.

Stebbins, R.A. 2008. 'Serendipity', in L. Given, ed., *The Sage Encyclopedia of Qualitative Research Methods,* 814–15. Los Angeles: Sage.

———. 1984. *The Magician: Career, Culture and Social Psychology in a Variety Art.* Toronto: Irwin.

Stoddart, K. 1991. 'Writing Sociologically: A Note on Teaching the Construction of a Qualitative Report', *Teaching Sociology* 19, 2: 243–8, at http.www.jstor.org/stable/1317857.

Sudnow, D. 1967. *Passing On: The Social Organization of Dying.* Englewood Cliffs, NJ: Prentice-Hall.

Thomas, W.I. 1937. *Primitive Behavior.* New York: McGraw-Hill.

Thomas, W.I., and F. Znaniecki. 1918. *The Polish Peasant in Europe and America.* Boston: Gorham Press.

Thompson, B.Y. 2010. 'Director's Statement', at http://coveredthemovie.com/.

Thorne, S. 2008. *Interpretive Description.* Walnut Creek, CA: Left Coast Press.

US Census Bureau. 2010. 'United States Census 2010', at http://2010.census.gov/2010census/pdf/2010_Questionnaire_Info.pdf.

van den Hoonaard, D.K. 2010. *By Himself: The Older Man's Experience of Widowhood.* Toronto: University of Toronto Press.

———. 2009. 'Widowers' Strategies of Self-Representation during Research Interviews: A Sociological Analysis', *Ageing and Society* 29, 2: 257–76.

———. 2005. '"Am I Doing It Right?": Older Widows as Interview Participants in Qualitative Research', *Journal of Aging Studies* 19, 3: 393–406.

———. 2003. 'Expectations and Experiences of Widowhood', in J.F. Gubrim and J.A. Holstein, eds, *Ways of Aging,* 182–200. Malden, MA: Blackwell Publishing.

———. 2002. 'Life on the Margins of a Florida Retirement Community', *Research on Aging (Special Issue on Retirement Communities)* 24, 1: 50–66.

———. 2001. *The Widowed Self: The Older Woman's Journey through Widowhood.* Waterloo, ON: Wilfrid Laurier University Press.

———. 1999. 'No Regrets: Widows' Stories about the Last Days of their Husbands' Lives', *Journal of Aging Studies* 13, 1: 59–72.

———. 1997. 'Identity Foreclosure: Women's Experiences of Widowhood as Expressed in Autobiographical Accounts', *Ageing and Society* 17: 533–51.

———. 1994. 'Paradise Lost: Widowhood in a Florida Retirement Community', *Journal of Aging Studies* 8, 2: 121–32.

———. 1992. *The Aging of a Florida Retirement Community.* PhD Dissertation, Department of Sociology and Anthropology, Loyola University of Chicago, Chicago, IL.

van den Hoonaard, W.C. 2011. *The Seduction of Ethics: The Transformation of the Social Sciences.* Toronto: University of Toronto Press.

———. 2010. Personal communication.

———. 2009a. 'On Developing and Using Concepts in an Icelandic Field-Research Setting', in Puddlephatt, A.J., W. Shaffir, and S.W. Kleinknecht, eds, *Ethnographies Revisited: Constructing Theory in the Field,* 92–104. New York: Routledge.

———. 2009b. Personal communication.

———. 2003. 'Is Anonymity an Artifact in Ethnographic Research?', *Journal of Academic Ethics* 1, 2: 141–51.

———. 2000. 'Getting There without Aiming at It: Women's Experiences in Becoming Cartographers', *Cartographica* 37, 3: 47–60.

———, ed. 2002. *Walking the Tightrope: Ethical Issues for Qualitative Researchers.* Toronto: University of Toronto Press.

———. 1997. *Working with Sensitizing Concepts: Analytical Field Research.* Thousand Oaks, CA: Sage.

———. 1991. *Silent Ethnicity: The Dutch of New Brunswick.* Fredericton, NB: New Ireland Press.

———. 1987. 'Guy D. Wright, *Sons and Seals*', *Anthropologica* 29, 2: 214–16.

——— and A. Connolly. 2006. 'Anthropological Research in Light of Research-Ethics Review: Canadian Master's Theses, 1995–2004', *Journal of Empirical Research on Human Research Ethics* 1, 2: 59–70.

——— and D.K. van den Hoonaard. 1991. Airports as Caricature: Exploring Film and Children's Books. Paper presented to the *Fifth Annual Qualitative Research Conference*, Ottawa, 14–17 May.

van den Scott, L.-J. 2009. 'Cancelled, Aborted, Late, Mechanical: The Vagaries of Air Travel in Arviat, Nunavut, Canada', in P. Vannini, ed., *The Cultures of Alternative Mobilities: Routes Less Travelled,* 211–26. Surrey, UK: Ashate.

van Gennep, A. [1909] 1960. *The Rites of Passage.* London: Routlege.

Van Manaan, J. 1988. *Tales of the Field: On Writing Ethnography.* Chicago: University of Chicago Press.

Vera, H. 1989. 'On Dutch Windows', *Qualitative Sociology* 12, 2: 215–34.

Vrkljan, B.H. 2009. 'Constructing a Mixed Methods Design to Explore the Older Driver-Copilot Relationship', *Journal of Mixed Methods Research* 3, 4: 371–85.

Wadel, C. 1969. *Marginal Adaptations and Modernization in Newfoundland: A Study of Strategies and Implications of Resettlement and Redevelopment of Outport Fishing Communities.* St John's, NL: Institute of Social and Economic Research, Memorial University of Newfoundland.

Warren, C.A.B., and T.X. Karner. 2010. *Discovering Qualitative Methods: Field Research, Interviews, and Analysis,* 2nd edn. New York: Oxford University Press.

Waterfield, R., trans. 1998. *Herodotus, the Histories.* Oxford: Oxford University Press.

Webb, E.J., Campbell, D.T., Schwart, R.D., and Sechrest, L. 1966. *Unobtrusive Measures: Nonreactive Research in the Social Sciences,* Chicago: Rand McNally.

Weber, M. 1949. *The Methodology of the Social Sciences.* Trans. E.A. Shils and H.A. Finch. Glencoe, IL: Free Press.

Weinberg, M. 2002. 'Biting the Hand that Feeds You and Other Feminist Dilemmas in Fieldwork', in W.C. van den Hoonaard, ed., *Walking the Tightrope: Ethical Issues for Qualitative Researchers,* 79–94. Toronto: University of Toronto Press.

West, C. 1999. 'Not Even a Day in the Life', in B. Glassner and R. Hertz, eds, *Qualitative Sociology as Everyday Life,* 3–12. Thousand Oaks, CA: Sage.

——— and D.H. Zimmerman. 1987. 'Doing Gender', *Gender and Society* 7, 2: 280–91.

Whyte, W.F. 1955. *Street Corner Society.* Chicago: University of Chicago Press.

Wilcox-Magill, D. 1983. 'Paradigms and Social Science in English Canada', in J. Paul Grayson, ed., *Introduction to Sociology,* 1–34. Toronto: Gage.

Wilson, R.A. 1966. *Feminine Forever.* New York: Evans.

Wood, L.A., and R.O. Kroger. 2000. *Doing Discourse Analysis: Methods for Studying Action in Talk and Text.* Thousand Oaks, CA: Sage.

Wolcott, H.F. 1995. *The Art of Fieldwork.* Walnut Creek, CA: AltaMira Press.

———. 1990. *Writing Up Qualitative Research.* Newbury Park, CA: Sage.

Wolf, D.R. 1991. *The Rebels: A Brotherhood of Outlaw Bikers.* Toronto: University of Toronto Press.

Wright, G. 1984. *Sons and Seals: A Voyage to the Ice.* St John's: Institute of Social and Economic Research, Memorial University of Newfoundland.

Index